Herbert C. Sigman

A HISTORY OF CANADIAN WEALTH

A History of Canadian Wealth

By Gustavus Myers
Vol. I

First Canadian Edition
With an Introduction by Stanley Ryerson

Toronto
James Lewis & Samuel, Publishers
1972

CONTENTS

WRITINGS BY
GUSTAVUS MYERS

History of Public Franchises in New York City. New York, 1900.

The History of Tammany Hall. New York, 1901; with additions, 1917.

History of the Great American Fortunes. 3 vols., Chicago, 1909-1910; 1 vol., New York, 1936; in German, *Geschichte der grossen Vermogen in Amerika.* 2 vols., Berlin, 1923.

Beyond the Borderline of Life. Boston, 1910. A summing up of results of investigation of psychic phenomena.

History of The Supreme Court of the United States. Chicago, 1912. A volume of 823 pages.

History of Canadian Wealth. 1914.

"A Study of the Causes of Industrial Accidents," in *Journal of the American Statistical Association* 14 (Sept. 1915): 672-694.

The German Myth. New York, 1918.

Ye Olden Blue Laws. New York, 1921. An article on "blue laws" in the *Encyclopedia of Social Sciences* is by Myers.

The History of American Idealism. New York, 1925.

America Strikes Back. New York, 1935.

The Ending of Hereditary American Fortunes. New York, 1939.

History of Bigotry in the United States. New York, 1943. Initiated in 1925, resumed and completed just before the author's death and published posthumously.

INTRODUCTION

Ever since the 1920s and 30s, Gustavus Myers's *History of Canadian Wealth* has held a very special place in the affections of progressives and the Left in Canada. As the one and only available interpretation of this country's history in terms of a radical social criticism, it helped shape the thinking of more than one generation of young activists and trade unionists. For those who already had some knowledge of socialist theory, it performed the invaluable service of offering a "translation" of that theoretical approach into vivid and familiar Canadian terms. For those whose first encounter with Socialist thought was in reading these pages, there was the exciting experience of having "dull Canadian history" come alive. It came alive because it became *understandable*. And in those years, as since, such understanding was a weapon of criticism in a world of conflict.

Such a pioneering work of radical social history could not but be viewed dimly by those with a stake in the corporate business society whose origins and dynamic Myers had set about dissecting. What Marx called the academic "hired prize-fighters" of private enterprise[1] are not an unknown species for us. A loud silence or a lordly condescension were their chosen weapons. They use them yet. Thus a learned article on "the concept of social class in Canadian history" blandly informs us that no significant work has been written using class analysis.[2] The blind spot, surely, is class conditioned! Myers did exist. His book still does. Or again, there are those who react to a mention of the work with something like: "Oh, you mean that SCANDALOUS book about the interconnections of business and politics." But is it the *book* or the *interconnections* that merit the epithet? Similarly, for Pierre Berton, Myers is a "muckraking business historian."[3]

Even Harold Innis in 1929 airily dismissed Myers's work with the remark: "It is scarcely necessary to dwell on the work of Gustavus Myers, *History of Canadian Wealth* (Chicago, 1914), who has treated Canadian history as an evolution of the predatory culture." Curiously, just a few pages earlier Innis was lamenting the lack of "a philosophy of economic history or an economic theory suited to Canadian needs." Anything resembling a Marxian approach was ruled out, presumably as being part of "the attempt to fit the phenomena of new countries to the economic theories of old countries; or to give it a slant or bias toward this or that school of political science or history."[4] Many years later, Innis's tone had changed somewhat. "There is much to be said for the Marxian approach to Canadian history," he wrote, "but not sufficient to support absolute certainty. Intellectual honesty and curiosity demand fresh interpretations and not the same interpretation."[5]

Republication of the *History of Canadian Wealth* in our present context of social and political ferment seems to me to be an act of public service. Insights into the dynamic of today's corporate business empires and of the countermovements they impel to action are needed urgently. For a work published on the eve of World War I to shed such light as this does on the historic roots of our contemporary crisis of society, bears witness to the enduring power of Socialist thought. That Myers's book should be sought after as it is today, testifies to a growing interest in Marxian theory, of which this *History* was a remarkable — if uncompleted — pioneering expression.

The book's interest, then, is one of *actuality*, and this in a double sense: first, as a pioneering, eminently readable "live" history of the roots and growth of a capitalist society in Canada; and second, as a stimulus to much-needed further work. Which is not to say that there is no problem of situating Myers and his contribution historically, in their relation to radical movements and Marxian thought. A word on this aspect, then, before touching on the content of the *History*.

II

Gustavus Myers was born March 20, 1872, in Trenton, New Jersey.[6] His parents were Julia (Hillman) and Abram Myers, the latter being of Dutch descent, the son of a major who had served in Napoleon's Old Guard at Waterloo, emigrated to England and then (in 1817) to Norfolk, Virginia. Abram Myers had gone to California in the 1849 gold rush, returning thereafter to Philadelphia. Here Gustavus attended private school, worked first as a reporter (1890) on the *Philadelphia Record*, then as a feature writer in New York, contributing to a wide range of newspapers, magazines and, on occasion, learned publications.

His first book has been described as "a sensational indictment of franchise practices": it was published in 1900 under the title, *A History of Public Franchises in New York City*. In the following year Myers's *History of Tammany Hall* appeared (reprinted in 1917); publishers had refused to accept it, and the book finally had to be issued on a subscription basis.[7]

These were the years when a group of young American liberals, social critics and literary men, embarking on a wide-ranging exposure of big (and ever bigger) business, earned from Theodore Roosevelt the contemptuous sobriquet of "muckrakers."[8] (The term comes from John Bunyan's *Pilgrim's Progress*.) In the words of the preface to volume three of Vernon Parrington's *Main Currents in American Thought*, "A set of intellectuals turned critical began to scrutinize the economic, political and social institutions of America." The counterpart, in the field of social criticism, of the Progressive and early Socialist movements, the muckrakers "attacked the plutocracy where its joints creaked ... [they] made the liberals conscious of what was going on behind the closed doors of the directors' meetings." Their writings were the response to a challenge: the coming of the era when, in Parrington's words, "The rule of the captains of industry had come ... henceforth the destiny of the country lay in the hands of its business men."[9] Among these literary snipers and iconoclasts, who represented a trend although they never constituted an organized group, were Lincoln Steffens, Ida Tarbell, George E. Russell, Upton Sinclair and — somewhat a case apart — Gustavus Myers. Of Myers's development from journalism to research in depth, he was to write:

> In the course of research upon my *The History of Tammany Hall* I had come across some documentary facts which severely shattered the inculcated conception that, with an exception here and there, the great private fortunes were unquestionably the result of thrift and sagacious ability. When *The History of Tammany Hall* was finished in 1900, I decided to devote further years to exploratory research upon the actual genesis and development of great American fortunes, and proceeded in the work.[10]

His researches carried him beyond the sensational

individual case-instances with which he and others had started on the work of exposure. "While the other muck-rakers captured popular attention with articles on trusts, insurance, labor trouble; impure food, and other national scandals," Myers began a systematic study of "the true history of capitalism in America. He turned up "staggering amounts of material on the great financiers of America," embodied in his *History of the Great American Fortunes*.[11] He found no publisher for it, until finally the Socialist co-operative, Charles H. Kerr & Co. of Chicago (publishers, in 1906, of the first American edition of Marx's *Capital*), agreed to issue it. The book first appeared in a three-volume edition in 1909-10; it was re-issued, in the Modern Library edition, in 1936.

At the time when Myers started doing research on the origins of the great Canadian fortunes, there existed as yet "no economic work tracing the sources of these accumulations of private wealth in Canada."[12] One has but to examine the footnotes in the *History of Canadian Wealth* to verify the truth of Myers's assertion that "the author of these present volumes has had to dig laboriously into the Canadian archives, and tediously explore great numbers of official documents." A continuing interest is shown many years later in his citing (in *The Ending of Hereditary American Fortunes*, published in 1939) testimony given at the hearings of the 1934 Canadian royal commission on price spreads.

When Myers first embarked on his researches, he wrote, "I was in no sense a radical. My state of mind was that of a political reformer, and some years were to elapse before I grasped the significance of economic considerations and changes."[13] Starting out from an intensive probing of what Lincoln Steffens called "the practise of low politics," Myers evolved from a left-liberal to a broadly Marxian Socialist outlook. But the *History of Canadian Wealth* (1914) was to mark the limit of his political and intellectual advance. His radicalism faded in the face of the imperial onslaught of the world war years. After 1914 he appears to have shrunk not only from any further deepening of his theoretical conceptions, but even from the position he had reached. World War I thus led to a basic reversal of direction, including a break with the Socialist party. Most of the muckrakers, as Lewis Filler observes, "fell short of completing their work. They retreated in the face of organized business's attacks, and they broke down completely in their first experience of international affairs." It was "the debacle."[14] Myers, who served on government information and shipping boards in the war years, was to produce, in his 1925 *History of American Idealism*, what amounts to an unabashed apologia for US imperialism: the Spanish-American war, Panama, the Philippines are dealt with in a chapter entitled "Liberty for Other Lands"! Further on one reads: "In the proclamation of the Monroe Doctrine and in the Spanish-American War the world saw two great examples of America's transcending localities and boundaries and unselfishly acting for the well-being and interest of other peoples. In the World War this concern for humanity was extended to cover every continent."[15] Myers's later works, on hereditary fortunes and on bigotry, are those of a cautious liberal reformer. He died in New York City on December 7, 1942.*

*A note on the "mystery" of volume two
The title page reads: *History of Canadian Wealth* Vol. I. A second volume (which would have continued the account from 1890 or so onwards) never appeared. In the 1930s it used to be said that the CPR had engineered its suppression. Apocryphal? Perhaps. The

III

In his preface of 1909 to the *History of the Great American Fortunes*, Myers had dissociated himself both from those who glamourized "the possessors of towering fortunes," and from those who offered mere sensationalized denunciations of the "monsters of political and commercial crime." His objection was that "these superficial effusions and tirades" were "based upon a lack of

story was not inconsistent with the kind of efforts that had been deployed by business interests to stifle his earlier exposures of profiteering and legalized plunder of the public. According to the late Professor J.C. Hemmeon of McGill, who knew Myers, the latter himself had decided not to go on with the book.[16] A suggestion that he may have feared a possible libel action from the wounded corporation is unconvincing, to say the least, considering that so scrupulous was his researching of the facts that throughout his long career of probing the raw nerves of the rich, he never had to face a suit for libel. Pending further research, a tentative explanation might seek the answer elsewhere — in the *date* of this book's appearance: 1914. The world war stopped Myers's theoretical development towards Marxism in its tracks. The liberalism that had been his initial starting point, that he never wholly abandoned, now reasserted itself. He was not the only Socialist for whom, in those years, advance became retreat. Such — for the time being at least — is my hypothesis.

**Since the above was written, I have learned from Mr. D. Drache of Atkinson College, Toronto, that in the course of earlier research in connection with this book, he had been in communication with the author's widow, Mrs. Genevieve Whitney Myers, now living in Arkansas, about her husband's work in Canada. She informed him that Myers's Canadian research was interrupted when they moved to Washington shortly after the outbreak of World War I; he never resumed that research, and the planned second volume was never written.

understanding of the propelling forces of society . . . They give no explanation of the fundamental laws and movements of the present system, which have resulted in these vast fortunes; nor is there the least glimmering of a scientific interpretation of a succession of states and tendencies from which these men of great wealth have emerged . . . the natural, logical outcome of a system based upon factors the inevitable result of which is the utter despoilment of the many for the benefit of a few."[17]

Herein, precisely, lay the great merit of the *History of Canadian Wealth.* It provided for the first time — despite its limitations — a popular introduction to socio-economic history in terms of a dynamic of class structure. Capitalism as a social system, with ruthless exploitation as its impelling motive, emerges from these pages. There unfolds a succession of patterns of piracy, extending from the "primitive accumulation" of the merchant adventurers to the rise of the railway barons: eras that were to overlap and interweave in the transactions of the Hudson's Bay Company and the Grand Trunk.

Of New France Myers writes:

Thus, the dominating class was the fur traders; of this class the merchants were a substantial part, pursuing their search for wealth with the most unscrupulous eagerness.

Accompanying the sway of the merchant class was that of the seigneurs or feudal lords, vested with the ownership of immense stretches of territory and with the powers, rights and privileges of a transplanted feudalism which, it was sanguinely hoped, could be established artificially, by decree, in the new country.[18]

With the coming of the nineteenth century, "The dominant class ... were the mercantile and shipping merchants ... " — precursors of the "trading and sundry other men of capital" who set about obtaining (from governments largely made up of themselves) railway charters that conferred vast and elastic "privileges and powers, immunities and rights."[19] In Myers's narrative, *corruption* is the keynote. Corruption and the suborning of the state for the private enrichment of élites has been the constant corollary of "free enterprise" since its inception. In the bourgeois-democratic state (whether republic or constitutional monarchy), as Engels remarked, "wealth exercises its power indirectly, but all the more surely. On the one hand, in the form of the direct corruption of officials, of which America provides the classical example; on the other hand, in the form of an alliance between government and Stock Exchange, which becomes the easier to achieve the more the public debt increases and the more joint-stock companies concentrate in their hands not only transport but also production itself ... "[20] Herewith is laid the basis for the state monopoly capitalism that was to emerge in the present century.

Myers's handling of the workings of this process is marked by both the enthralling "detective-story" quality of the exposures — and a theoretical weakness. Capitalism is not corruption alone; Myers understood this, else he could not have set his story in the broadly Marxiantype framework that he did. A key to this element in his approach is his affirmation that " ... they who control the means by which a dependent class must live, control the livelihood and conditions of that class ... "[21] Yet so all-pervading is the emphasis on the role of what Myers had designated earlier as the "designing men and corporations that by the adroit use of corrupt politics vested in themselves huge corporate privileges and powers and enormous wealth,"[22] that the role of *production*, of productive labour as the well-spring of wealth, is overshadowed. All the feverish abandon of the landowner-capitalist élites in their scramble for pelf and power, for public monies and resources, all their legalized public theft and illicit bribery and political corruption, depended in the last resort on the extraction of surplus values from living labour. Without the productive labour of working people in town and countryside (starting with Indian trappers, later embracing pioneer settlers and "mechanics," workers in the factories and mines of the metropolis and the railway-building and growing manufactures of the colonies), there could not have taken place the initial accumulation of capital and its subsequent self-expansion through re-invested profits. Myers indicates something of this. Yet in certain passages, the exploitation of labour by capital tends to appear to be simply the result of *sub*-standard wages,* as in such "special cases" as that of the underpaid Chinese workers imported by the thousands as railroad construction labour — as though "normal" wages were not perfectly compatible with the extraction of capitalist profit!

Involved here is a crucial limitation in Myers's theoretical position. He had perhaps never wholly settled accounts with an early predilection that later was to become dominant: a kind of positivist "fetishism of facts" and a corresponding disinterest in matters of

*On the connection between workers' wages and company profits, Myers cited, in his last book but one, the instance (in 1938) of Canadian F.W. Woolworth's employees paid seven dollars a week while the employers, in their US and Canadian operations, took in some twenty-eight millions in profit.[23]

theory. Thus, in the preface to his *History of American Idealism* (1925), he writes: "Restricting itself as this book does to essential facts, all theory and every byway of theory are avoided."[24] The preface to the 1936 edition of his *History of the Great American Fortunes* states: "My business is purely that of a historian, relating what has been done, and not venturing into theoretical or speculative fields as to the adoption of this or that system."[25] Assuredly, without the solid framework of fact, no hypothesis, generalization or theory is possible; and it is Myers's great achievement to have compiled a staggering quantity of facts, and moreover to have *interpreted* them, in this book at least, in the light of a Marxian approach. His limitation — and it is common to both an early Marxism in America and a much later, dogmatic congealing of the theory — lies in an element of *economism* that leaves out or underestimates entire areas of reality.*

It is these areas of theoretical underdevelopment that have long awaited further cultivation. Such beginnings as have been made should not be overlooked (a fate they

*In his article on social class, S.R. Mealing writes that, as compared with other branches of the discipline, "Social history . . . has probably had a stronger tendency than any other . . . to content itself with the original positivist program in history: to describe the facts without analysis, explanation, synthesis, or the intrusion of ideas of any kind."[26] Such "social history" must refer to that of certain old school-texts in which the one lonely chapter on the Industrial Revolution simply listed technical inventions, wholly severed from the wars and reigns amid which it was sandwiched. It is not the social history of, for instance, E.H. Hobsbawm's *Industry and Empire* and *Age of Revolution*. In Myers's thinking the positivist strain was at odds with a genuine striving for theoretical depth; a measure of success in achieving the latter did not outlive the turning point of 1914, the former at last becoming paramount.

have largely shared with Myers: the academic world nestles in a society of the corporate élites), but the main thing is to go much further. There are hopeful signs that this is perhaps starting to happen. The areas of focus, I would suggest, include all of these:

1. Political structures and the State. The nearest Myers comes to mentioning Confederation is a fleeting reference in the course of a discussion of railway policies ("After the formation of the Dominion of Canada in 1867 . . ." p. 245). The Red River episode of 1849 (pp. 138 ff.) and the uprising of 1869-70 (pp. 146 ff.) are dealt with briefly, but not the uprising of 1885; the name of Riel appears once.

The treatment of the 1837-38 insurrections in terms of the bourgeois revolution (chapter seven, "Revolt against Feudalism"), on the other hand, remains a landmark in historiography. Colonialism, land monopoly and the market for "domestic manufactures" comprise the basic socio-political and economic framework. "Intrinsically," Myers writes, the revolt was one "of upspringing capitalist forces, but superficially its character was composite, blending a variety of factors and elements." Starting in the first decade of the 1800s, the popular movement "arose from the definite and well-understood material interests of a considerable body of settlers who, seeing the abundant natural resources about them, wanted a free hand in developing the fur, hemp, flour and lumber trade and a command of resources with which to engage in manufacturing." Mackenzie's demand for freedom of trade was "the very quintessence of rising capitalism" . . . "One of the main pleas of the insurrectionists was that capital should have a free hand . . ." [27] It got it, of course, only after the long-drawn, tortuous emergence of a state formed by a bourgeois "revolution from above": a process that Myers does not examine.

2. The national question. Myers gives a vivid account of the exploitation, oppression and decimation of the Indians — "the real producers of the huge wealth from the fur trade, estimated on competent authority at £20,000,000, which had already gone to England" . . . "It has been estimated that at least one half of the revenues of the Hudson's Bay Company have come back to Canada for investment."[28] Of the 1857 hearings of the Parliamentary committee on the company's operations, and the public reactions to it, he emphasizes the colonial context and class character of the issue. The hearings produced "the deepest kind of a public sensation . . ."

> By "public sensation" is meant merely among that part of the people having no direct pecuniary interest in trade and commerce. The trading class, with all its aristocratic auxiliaries, sought to minimize the horrors, and to justify the "exigencies of trade" on the score of their "adding to the wealth of England." While one branch of the English trading class was benefiting from the exploitation in Canada, other branches were pocketing profits from that in India and elsewhere, from the opium traffic in China and from the horrors of the factory system in England itself.[29]

The national question of French and English Canada, however, simply isn't in the picture. The Conquest is mentioned as fleetingly as is Confederation: "Following the battle of Quebec and the British conquest of Canada, the English became absolute masters of the fur trade."[30] And that's all: except for a reference to the "superficially composite" character of 1837 in which, together with the anti-colonial and bourgeois-market issues, were "interwoven . . . a diversity of other factors which, although extraneously religious or sentimental, were in reality largely of a distinct economic nature."[31] (Mentioned among the "other factors" are ecclesiastical power, inequitable class taxation, problems of professionals — but not the internal national question in the Canadas.) It was not that simple, surely.*

3. **Capitalist industrialization.** Sir Hugh Allan, "an aggressive type of capitalist," was president of fifteen corporations and vice-president of six others. These comprised "telegraph, navigation, coal and iron, tobacco, cotton manufacturing, sewing machine, cattle, rolling mills, paper, car, elevator, coal and other companies."[32] His Allan Line of steamships had made him rich through "squeezing of laborers" (their conditions were cited in connection with the 1887 royal commission inquiry into capital and labour). But the actual process of implanting and growth of industrial capitalist production, of which proprietary wealth and the exploitation of wage-labour are the fundament, is not examined. Even today, there is no adequate published study of the historical stages in the industrial revolution and the productive process in Canada. The most important work — H. Claire Pentland's "Labour and the Development of Industrial Capital in Canada" (U. of T. PhD thesis, 1960) — has yet to be published.** For the 20th century, L.C. and F.W. Park, in

*As argued in my *Unequal Union: Roots of Conflict in the Canadas* (Toronto: Progress Books, 1968). A certain element of mechanistic thinking underlies the "economic determinism" that is so often and so erroneously equated with Marxism. Myers was by no means free of it.

**Part of Pentland's argument is contained in an article in the *Canadian Journal of Economics and Political Science*. See also (in connection with point four, following) his paper on the Lachine strike of 1843, in *Canadian Historical Review* 29, no. 3 (Sept. 1948): 255-277.

The Anatomy of Big Business (1958), analyze the movement of concentration and centralization of capital and
the emergence of the contemporary finance oligarchy:
phenomena whose prelude is to be found in the "compact centralization" of banks and industry referred to in
Myers's preface.

4. **Working-class conditions and struggles.** Myers's pages
from time to time give some intimation of the appalling
conditions endured by working people in the immigrant
ships, the repressive character of the "law and order"
imposed by the capitalist class, and some facets of the
exploitation on which the "self-expansion" of capital
rests. Yet there is a curiously marginal quality to many
of the cases that Myers cites. In the royal commission
findings of 1887-88, it is the insurance deduction
exacted from its workers by the Allen Line that is
highlighted. Similar secondary aspects have been referred
to above, as receiving the major emphasis: an approach
that is of a piece with Myers's neglect of the capital/
wage-labour relationship at the "point of production"
that is the real core of the process. There is little, also,
on the actual struggles conducted by workers all through
the nineteenth century. For this, Myers can scarcely be
blamed: the data for a history of these struggles is only
now beginning to be systematically researched and
studied.*

---

*Among the instances of this new production: H.C. Pentland's
work on the Lachine strikes of the 1840s; C. Lipton's *Trade
Union Movement of Canada* (1966); the articles by Catharine
Vance in the *Marxist Quarterly* and, by the same: *Not by gods but
by people: the story of Bella Hall Gauld* (1968); R. Desrosiers and
D. Héroux' *Le travailleur québécois et le Syndicalisme*; J. Hamelin,
P. Laroque and J. Rouillard, *Répertoire des Grèves dans la
Province de Québec au 19e siècle* (1970); F. Harvey's study on
"Les Travailleurs québécois et la Commission du Travail,

INTRODUCTION

The "fifty big shots" — the dominant tycoons of
industry, finance and trade in the 1930s — were the
target of those in the labour and farm movements who
saw in monopoly the main, concentrated profiteering
enemy of social progress and democracy in this country.
Who Owns Canada? published by CCF researchers, listed
them and detailed their vast holdings. The 1938 submission of the Communist party to the Rowell-Sirois
Commission on Dominion-Provincial Relations probed
the relationships of monopoly, state power and fiscal
policy, corporate profit and social poverty. It is startling
to read in the opening lines of Myers's preface to this
book that by 1914, such has been the concentration of
wealth that

Already, it is estimated, less than fifty men control
$4,000,000,000, or more than one third of Canada's
material wealth as expressed in railways, banks, factories, mines, land and other properties and resources.

As for the aspect that has come to occupy so large a
place in our present preoccupations — the United States
takeover of Canada, a side effect of the massive shift in
the centre of gravity of the world-capitalist empires — it
is interesting to note Myers's reference to the relative
strengths of British and US capital in Canada at that
time: somewhat over $2 billions British, and $500
millions US ; $180 millions of the latter were "in 300
factories which, to a great extent, [were] branches of
the American Trusts."[33]

Myers was clearly a trailblazer, in that he both ex-
plored the historical roots and pointed to the basic
contemporary trend of capitalist society in Canada:

1886-1889" (Laval thesis, 1971); and Evelyn Dumas: *Dans le
Sommeil de nos Os: quelques grèves au Québec de 1934 à 1944*
(1971).

xxii

towards the domination of the economy by corporate monopoly, within the context of what has been referred to as "The single most influential, deciding factor in Canadian life . . . the presence of an imperial power in Canada's national affairs."[34] The framework of historical change whose "Law of motion" Marx had laid bare in *Capital* enabled Myers to explain Canadian development in a way that was entirely new. This American Socialist was, in fact, our first social historian.

<h2 style="text-align:center">IV</h2>

Social history in Canada has been slow in getting weaned from ancient orthodoxies. An academic boycott — one aspect of it expressed in the smug silence or "clever" sneers about this book — only now is beginning to be overcome, in response to an impact derived rather from the outer world than from within the discipline itself. In an article on social class, a rarity in a half-century of publication of the *Canadian Historical Review*, S.R. Mealing observed: "Canadian historians have written very little lower-class history . . . *They have undertaken no systematic analysis of the structure of Canadian society.*[35] (Emphasis mine.) Why should they, since that is supposedly a matter for sociology or economics to see to? History, meanwhile, basks in Olympian complacency:

> For history is the oldest, the most solidly established of all Canadian studies. It is the most articulate, the most productive of the social sciences.[36]

It is also given to ignoring the phenomenon of social class. When confronted with inescapable indications of that reality, acute allergy sets in. Thus, in a significant contribution to the debate over the existence (or non-existence) of a bourgeoisie in New France, Cameron Nish can take every step but the last one. He can tell us that

such factors as possession of money, close ties of inter-
marriage and "domination of the political society by a
group owning vast economic interests" all add up to "a
closed group, synonymous with a class"; that this group
"by its economic, political and social activities met the
requirements of a bourgeois class"; further, that "to this
class belonged Cugnet, the Vaudreuils, de la Gorgendière,
Rainbault, the Bouchers, Taschereaus . . . the *bourgeois-
gentilshommes* of New France."

All of which Nish himself torpedoes with the staggering assertion that since the term of social classification,
"habitant," was used loosely as referring to great and
small alike, "the question of class structure in New
France simply did not pose a problem." There were
merely questions of "prerogatives" and "differences of
social status." If one "cannot conclude with certainty as
to the existence of a bourgeois class . . . The reason is
quite simple: the concept of class originates in a much
later period than the one under study."[37]

This, of course, is nonsense. Does Nish think that
social classes came into existence only after social philos-
ophers invented the word?

S.R. Mealing's admonition regarding the persistent
failure of Canadian historians to take social class and
social structure into account seems to have fallen on deaf
ears. "Confederation . . . was apparently the one major
nineteenth century instance of constitution-making in
which class played "no significant role . . ."[38] Whoever
wrote *that* must surely, none the less, have heard of the
Grand Trunk crowd and the Bank of Montreal. And
(since the writer was none other than Professor Mealing,
in the self-same article) he might even have had an
inkling of a bloc of class forces comprising the Toronto
and Montreal commercial-industrial bourgeoisie and the

Quebec Church. Unless the role class forces did play is considered significant and analyzed as such, Confederation is either just plain inexplicable, or an embodiment of the Hegelian Idea (the "idea of unity," in D.G. Creighton's "explanation"[39]) or an act of immaculate conception.

Could it be that those whose response to the concept of social class ranges from a discreet shrinking to a panic flight are in fact unwilling to face the social reality it designates. How much easier to take is the idyllic vision of society as nothing else but individuals, their inter-actions and their attitudes — as against one of class structure and struggle, rooted in relationships of *exploitation*, and founded on *property* in land, slaves or capital and wage-labour! Easier and, for corporate business society, advantageous. Not for nothing are successive contingents of students stuffed with the gospel of "possessive individualism": whether via Ayn Rand, or Hayek or, on a loftier level, Sir Karl Popper, intoning his denial of "the empirical existence of social wholes or collectives" — thereby endowing with an aura of philosophy a Chamber of Commerce platitude of social irresponsibility.[40]

Myers's treatment of social class may lack some of the refinements so dear to our latter-day sociological sophisticates. His rough-and-ready groupings are none the less grounded in a reality that the more "acceptable," subjective-idealist interpretations regularly camouflage or conceal. A structure of social class in terms of ownership of the means of production, wage-labour and assorted small producers, the whole constituting a dynamic, evolving social-economic formation: if this representation of a capitalist society that emerged from feudalism makes history intelligible, it is perhaps because it is *true*.

It has been said more than once that Canadian history is "dull" because so much of it has focused on constitutional-political development, at the expense of the individual. No, counters Myers, the trouble has rather been that histories "have been absurdly and erroneously made to revolve around personalities instead of social and economic forces."[41] The fact that in his treatment of capitalist accumulation and the rise of the bourgeoisie to power he leaves out much, or that his approach might suffer at times from a sort of mechanist economic determinism, is understandable in the pioneering stage his work represents. As an early Marxian first answer to what he called "conventional, so-called history," it was the prelude to today's belated emergence of social history in what has been described as a "counterbody of historical writings on Canada."[42] Myers's achievement stands as a landmark in Canadian historiography.

V

In the preface to a curious novel, *Kings of Capital and Knights of Labor* (1885), the Reverend John M. Leavitt, president of Lehigh University, enumerated "Dangers from three sources [that] imperil our American Institutions . . . POLITICAL CORRUPTION . . . SOCIAL DANGERS . . . Capital and Labour are in open war. If their difficulties are not adjusted, our country will be shaken as by earthquakes. And to the perils of these struggles must be added evils from the enormous fortunes in the hands of the few to the injury of the many, and of the Republic itself."

A similar expression of upper-class anxiety made itself heard in an august Anglo-Canadian publication, in the year that the *History of Canadian Wealth* appeared. Whereas Dr. Leavitt had prescribed "Bible Christianity" as the remedy for social ills, this diagnostician, writing on "The Higher National Life" in Canada, called merely for "sane leadership":

> We share . . . with our neighbours the danger of a great class-embitterment . . . We know nothing, it is true, of the ferocity with which the struggle of capital and labour is being waged across the border. But we do know the danger of class-division.[43]

So in the Canadian instance as in the American, it is *class reality* that asserts its presence.

Such was the social background of Gustavus Myers's crusade in the early 1900s against entrenched corruption and corporate greed, in behalf of the cause of labour in North America. The Canadian working people of hand and brain who strive today for an alternative to a society founded on private corporation profit, are greatly in his debt.

Stanley Bréhaut Ryerson
Département d'histoire
Université du Québec à Montréal

REFERENCE NOTES

1. *Capital*, preface to the second edition (Chicago: Charles H. Kerr, 1906), vol. 1, p. 19. "The class-struggle . . . sounded the knell of scientific bourgeois economy. It was thenceforth no longer a question whether this theorem or that was true, but whether it was useful to capital or harmful, expedient or inexpedient, politically dangerous or not. In place of disinterested enquirers, there were hired prize-fighters; in place of genuine scientific research, the bad conscience and the evil intent of apologetic."

INTRODUCTION

2. S.R. Mealing, "The Concept of Social Class and the Interpretation of Canadian History," *Canadian Historical Review* 46, no. 3 (Sept. 1965): 212. "No important attempt has been made to base an analysis of our history on class, nor is there any weight of research to suggest that such an analysis is possible."

3. *The National Dream* (Toronto: McClelland and Stewart, 1970), p. 313. Berton cites the *Great American Fortunes* but not the *History of Canadian Wealth.*

4. H.A. Innis, "The Teaching of Economic History in Canada," *Essays in Canadian Economic History* (1929), pp. 12, 10.

5. Quoted in Donald Creighton, *Harold Innis: Portrait of a Scholar* (Toronto: U. of T. Press, 1957), p. 93.

6. Detailed data on Myers's biography are hard to come by. Sources utilized here include *Who Was Who in America* (1950, vol. 2, p. 391) and *The National Cyclopaedia of American Biography* (vol. 19, pp. 443-44); references for which I am indebted to Mlle Juliette Bourque of the Public Archives of Canada, Mrs. Phyllis Clarke of Toronto, and the librarians of the Department of Labour, Ottawa; and to Professor Stephen Scheinberg, Sir George Williams University, for the references to Myers in Lewis Filler, *Crusaders of the American Dream.* *The Encyclopedia Americana* (Vol. 19, p. 663) contains the following additional item on Gustavus Myers: "Brother of the painter Jerome Myers, he was brought up in poverty, and with little formal education, but succeeded in gaining a foothold as a newspaper man in his early twenties." The brother, Jerome, was a painter and illustrator of everyday life in the streets of New York. His credo — "The song of my work is a song of the poor, far from the annals of the rich" — is set forth in the prologue to his autobiography, *Artist in Manhattan* (1940). Curiously, this work makes no mention whatever of Gustavus, five years his junior.

7. Writes Myers: "Not a single publisher in New York or elsewhere would publish it." *History of the Great American Fortunes*, preface to the second edition (New York: Modern Library, 1936), p. 20.

8. *The Autobiography of Lincoln Steffens* (1931), p. 357. "I did not intend to be a muckraker; I did not know that I was one till President Roosevelt picked the name out of Bunyan's *Pilgrim's Progress* and pinned it on us; and even then he said that it did not mean me. Those were innocent days . . ."

9. E.H. Eby, "Vernon Louis Parrington," in a foreword to Parrington's *Main Currents in American Thought* (1927), vol. 3, p. xiii; Parrington, *Main Currents in American Thought*, vol. 3, pp. 404-412.

10. *Great American Fortunes*, p. 19.

11. Filler, *Crusaders of the American Dream*, p. 119.

12. Preface to *History of Canadian Wealth*, p. xxxiv.

13. *Great American Fortunes*, p. 19.

14. Filler, *Crusaders of the American Dream*, pp. 394, 413.

15. *The History of American Idealism* (1925), p. 325. Cf. also pp. 222, 235-36, 255.

16. I am indebted to Senator Eugene Forsey, who studied under J.C. Hemmeon at McGill, for this item of information.

17. *Great American Fortunes*, p. 25.

18. *History of Canadian Wealth*, pp. 11, 15.

19. Ibid., p. 69.

20. F. Engels, *Origin of the Family, Private Property and the State*, ch. 9.

21. Preface to *History of Canadian Wealth*, p. xxxiv.

22. *The History of Tammany Hall* (1901, 1917), p. 403.

23. *The Ending of Hereditary American Fortunes* (1939), p. 329.

24. *American Idealism*, p. viii.

25. *Great American Fortunes*, p. 23.

26. Mealing, "Social Class and Canadian History," p. 202. Cf. n. 2.

27. *History of Canadian Wealth*, pp. 97, 71, 98, 99.

28. Ibid., pp. 135-137.

29. Ibid., p. 142.

30. Ibid., p. 53.

31. Ibid., p. 100.

32. Ibid., p. 224.

33. Ibid., p. xxxiii. See also Kari Levitt, *Silent Surrender* (Toronto: Macmillan, 1970), for a remarkable analysis of subsequent developments.

34. D. Drache, "Rediscovering Canadian History," in *Canadian Journal of History and Social Science* 6, no. 3 (Apr.-Mar. 1971): 34.

35. Mealing, "Social Class and Canadian History," p. 212.

36. D.G. Creighton, in the Canadian Historical Association presidential address, 1957.

37. C. Nish, *Les Bourgeois-Gentilshommes de la Nouvelle-France* (Montreal: Fides, 1968), pp. 184, 183. I have argued this point more fully in a review of the book, in the *Revue du Centre d'Etude du Québec*, no. 3 (mai 1969): 74-77.

38. Mealing, "Social Class and Canadian History," p. 209.

39. Creighton writes, on the Act of Union of 1841, that it "was simply another variant of that idea of unity and expansion which had moved New France in the days of Frontenac and La Salle, and was to inspire the Dominion of Canada in the time of Sir John Macdonald and the Canadian Pacific Railway." *Dominion of the North* (Toronto: Macmillan, 1944), p. 247.

40. F. Hayek, in *Capitalism and the Historians* (Chicago: U. of Chicago Press, 1954); K. Popper, "Prediction and Prophecy," in *Theories of History*, ed. P. Gardiner (New York: Free Press, 1959), p. 281: as against "naive collectivism," Popper insists on an analysis "in terms of individuals and their actions and relations."

41. Preface to *History of Canadian Wealth*, p. xxxv.

42. Drache, "Rediscovering Canadian History," p. 33.

43. W.S. Milner, "The Higher National Life," in *Canada and Its Provinces* (1914), vol. 12, p. 406.

PREFACE

The rapid concentration of wealth in Canada is no mere fancy. Already, it is estimated, less than fifty men control $4,000,000,000, or more than one-third of Canada's material wealth as expressed in railways, banks, factories, mines, land and other properties and resources.

To say that this small group of individuals control so vast a wealth and the agencies of its production does not imply that they own it all. Between ownership and control there is a difference, yet the reverse of that commonly supposed. By means of their control of financial markets and distributive systems, a small number of men may effectively control sources of wealth which still may remain under individual ownership, as witness the case of the farms, of which control farmers throughout Canada are bitterly complaining. Also it is not necessary for magnates to own all of the stock of railroads, banks, factories and mines; much of that ownership may be distributed among small shareholders, yet by their predominantly large holdings of stock, and through their power of directorship, those magnates can and do control those diversified, and often financially interconnected, sources of wealth.

The process of centralization of wealth has been steadily going on for nearly thirty-five years. The removal of unrestricted competition was first evidenced in the case of the railways of Canada. Beginning in about the year 1879, a considerable number of smaller and formerly independent railways (some of which had already amalgamated) were absorbed by the large systems such as the Grand Trunk

Railway, and later by the Canadian Pacific Railway, and other railways. Of more than 140 separate and privately owned railways chartered and constructed at different times, a large number are now integral parts, either by purchase or by lease, of the main and great railway systems in Canada.

The highly centralized character of the Canadian banks is well known; the branches of the important banks extend over an immense territory; twenty-six of these institutions have 2,888 branches; the Royal Bank alone has 338 branches, and the Bank of Commerce 367.

Perhaps nowhere in the world can be found so intensive a degree of close organization as among the bank interests in Canada. In the United States there are no less than 18,000 banking institutions, of which about 6,000 are under Federal charters, the remainder under State Laws. While a small group of financial industrial magnates exercise a preponderating control over the large banks, and in turn practically sway many of the small banks in the United States, and thereby concentrate in themselves the powers of a financial Trust, still the control there is nothing like, in compact centralization, that existing in Canada. The immense capacity of this concentration in controlling the finances and every sphere of activity dependent upon finance, is so obvious that it requires no explanation. To these ramifications of power is added another huge power possessed by the Canadian banks. This is their privilege, allowed by law, of putting out enormous quantities of their privately-issued money, or, in other words, bank notes — a power far exceeding even the great power held by banks in other countries.

Of the rapidity of concentration of industrial concerns in Canada much less is generally known. From January, 1909, to January, 1913, there were 56 industrial mergers or amalgamations which absorbed 248 individual companies. The total capitalization of 206 of these individual companies was about

$167,000,000; this amount was increased with the amalgamating process. The authorized capitalization, including bonds, of these 56 industrial mergers was almost $457,000,000, or to be precise, $456,938,266. Many of the large individual companies thus absorbed were themselves the outgrowth of previous combinations.

Aside from the consideration of native Canadian capital, the amount of British capital put in Canada has been stupendous. In 1911, Sir George Paish, one of the editors of the London *Statist,* estimated that £372,541,000 of British capital had gone to Canada, chiefly in the form of investments; of that sum £223,740,000 was represented by investments in Canadian railways. Since 1911, at least £120,000,000 more of British capital has been placed in Canada. The total of British capital in Canada is, therefore, more than $2,000,000,-000. Capital in Canada from various Continental countries of Europe is computed at about $140,000,000. Of the $500,000,-000 of United States capital active in Canada, $180,000,000 is represented in 300 factories which, to a great extent, are branches of the American Trusts.

This process of centralization is, it is needless to say, still continuing and has by no means reached its culmination. Economic forces are more powerful than statute laws, particularly so seeing that what is called the machinery of Government is administered at all times either directly by the beneficiaries or by the representatives of those ruling forces, no matter by what political name they may be pleased to call themselves.

In such an era, with fundamental economic questions — that is to say, problems of existence itself — pressing harder and harder upon the attention of those that produce the wealth, such a work as this is essential as a means of diffusing information. Since the control of so vast an aggregation of wealth is centered in so few hands, the questions of whence came these overawingly great private fortunes and of the evolution of this centralized wealth become of paramount interest. What was the origin of much of these mighty masses of capital? What their particular sources? By what means was this immense material wealth extracted, by what methods possessed?

To give a vital survey of these developments is the purpose of this work. Necessarily, the investigation takes us back to remote times, for the aggregations of wealth that we see today are not in essence a sudden appearance, but are the result of cumulative methods, processes and transactions extending through centuries.

It will be seen that from the earliest searchings for wealth in Canada to the present time there has been a vital, definite connection, the developments of each successive period bearing a close relevancy to those preceding. From primitive powers conferred, and from fortunes amassed in fur trading, land and commerce, came the wealth often invested later in mercantile establishments, land companies, banks, railway projects, mines and factories; and all of these pyramidically reproduced still other accumulations of wealth progressively invested and reinvested. Did we not trace this wealth to its primary sources, and give a continuous depiction of its development, the narrative would be headless, unfinished and disconnected, and leave some of the most important facts enshrouded in mystery.

Although long ago it was recognized that they who control the means by which a dependent class must live, control the livelihood and conditions of that class, yet it is not inordinately astonishing that thus far no economic work tracing the sources of these accumulations of private wealth in Canada has preceded these present volumes.

The reasons for this deficiency are not obscure. One reason is that the general attention has hitherto been focussed on other subjects and issues, ignoring the economic factors, the all-important significance of which was not adequately understood. With the growth of general intelligence and the accompanying great pressure of economic considerations, this understanding has been intensified, and is becoming still more so.

Another reason has been that the sources of information, such as histories, upon which the general public has had to depend for knowledge, have been absurdly and erroneously made to revolve around personalities instead of social and economic forces. Various arid volumes have come bulkily from the presses, but they either give no account of the currents of these successive economic forces, or they but incidentally mention only a few, vague, isolated facts. In the mistaken aim to present personalities as the determiners of events, these writers have far subordinated or ignored the realities, unconscious of the fact that such personalities are but the creatures of distinct and often sharply contesting economic forces.

Hence it is that to get the underlying, authentic facts — as much as possible, at least, from the available original sources — the author of these present volumes has had to dig laboriously into the Canadian archives, and tediously explore great numbers of official documents. Great as is the mass of facts here related, it can be well understood that the entire range of facts covering all the multitude of transactions of centuries can never be given in full. Many of them never found their way into official documents, and in other cases important governmental papers and returns, embodying certain definite valuable facts and connecting links, were never published.

Nevertheless a myriad of documents have been accessible to anyone animated by an aim to make a sincere quest for the facts. That many, if not most of them, have never heretofore been consulted is a striking commentary upon the character of conventional, so-called history. Studiously or misinformingly avoiding the basic facts, and interpreting human progress and activities by the light of such superficialities, these products (whatever their motive), had the result of conserving outworn traditions and perpetuating fallacious conceptions.

Expanding intelligence, however, is not content with narratives obsolete in treatment, misleading in substance and spiritless in character. No longer is the diverting, obscuring or glozing of the facts accepted; actualities, not appearances, are demanded. Having a knowledge of the fundamental facts we can be prepared to reject old standards and forms and unsatisfactory systems. We can then also rightly comprehend the nature of the processes that have resulted in conditions as we know them, and can directly apply that knowledge toward the obliteration of all that stands in the way of the full, unshackled social, industrial and intellectual development of mankind.

GUSTAVUS MYERS.

HISTORY OF CANADIAN WEALTH

CHAPTER I

THE QUEST OF TRADE AND NEW SOURCES OF WEALTH

When the Spanish explorers first saw the mouth of the St. Lawrence River, "lined with high mountains and covered with snow," they spontaneously named the unappealing country "Acanada," signifying, "Here is nothing." [1]

The first sources of wealth were the waters of the ocean yielding their primitive supplies of cod, walrus and whale. Thither came vessels from Spain, England, France and Holland to load themselves with this abundant spoil from the Newfoundland Banks. The great demand in Roman Catholic countries for fish assured certain and large profits, and the prolific supplies of oil from the whale presented tempting opportunities to the roving mariners; from a single whale as many as four hundred barrels of oil were frequently taken. There was the vast wealth of the sea, but the annoying problem to these fishing traders and colonizers was how to get the necessary contingent of maritime laborers.

[1] De Meulles to the King of France, 1684, *Report on Canadian Archives*, 1899 Vol., p. 43. The volumes of these archives are not numbered but bear the date of the year in which they were issued by the Archives Bureau of the Dominion Government.

Convicts Impressed as Colonists

A distant, supposedly barren land to which it required a hundred days or more of tedious sailing to get, did not allure European workers. Cartier showed, in 1541, how it was possible to make up the deficiency in manning his armed expedition when he impressed the convicts from the jails for maritime service.[2] These unfortunates were not convicts in the modern sense; at a time when the slightest theft was punishable by hanging, and begging was a crime, the term convict covered conviction for even the pettiest and most inconsequential offenses. When, in 1598, La Roche was planning an expedition to Newfoundland he secured official permission to take " criminals " from the jails of Brittany and Normandy; he picked out " two hundred sturdy beggars, male and female," but took only sixty of them along, and of these forty-eight died during the rigors of the winter on Sable Island, and one was hanged for theft.[3]

In 1578 there were thirty to fifty English fishing sail on the Newfoundland Banks, and perhaps two hundred vessels from Spain. Twenty vessels from Biscay were engaged in whale hunting. Seven years later the fishing fleet numbered three hundred Spanish, French, English and Dutch vessels, the crews of which were armed for possible fighting service. A quarter of a century later the French fishing fleet alone comprised six hundred vessels, or nearly that number.

From these fishing expeditions developed an auxiliary traffic which subsequently became the principal trade, producing colossal profits, engendering conflicts and wars, and directly and indirectly causing a great and continuous sacrifice of human life. This was the fur trade, the main and long-continued source of primitive accumulation of wealth in Canada,

---

[2] Biggar's *Early Trading Companies of New France*, p. 15.
[3] *Ibid.*, pp. 41–42.

of which wealth the great bulk went, during centuries, to European capitalists to be invested successively in land, trade, factories, banks, transportation systems and other channels both in Europe and in Canada and in other countries.

The Fur Trade and the Trading Companies

Going ashore to dry fish, fishing merchants soon learned from the Indians of the prevalence of fur-bearing animals. In the hunting of these the Indians were adepts. Innocent of the mercantile value of either their furs or fabricated commodities, the aborigines were easily persuaded into exchanging furs for trivial trinkets. In those days, a beaver skin could be bought with a needle, a harness bell or a tin mirror.[4] The arts of persuasion were assisted by gratuities of liquor. When the fishing fleets, loaded with furs, returned to Europe, the news excited the cupidity of some of the more enterprising of the sea-port town merchants who began to estimate rightly the great wealth-producing possibilities of the fur trade.

The first fur-trading company organized was the Company of Canada, promoted by David Kirke and Associates. Chartered by King Charles I, it was vested with the right to exploit the fur trade of the St. Lawrence, but its operations came to a sudden end when, in 1632, England restored Canada to France.

In the interval, Champlain's Company, that of Rouen and St. Malo, had been established in 1614; its shares were apportioned among the merchants of those two towns. The charter of this Company was given upon the express condition of certain colonizing performances, but the obligation was not taken seriously by the company, which confined itself

---

[4] So, in his Memoirs concerning Canada, wrote De la Chesnaye, who had come to Canada to represent the interests of the Company of Rouen.— *Report on Canadian Archives,* 1899 Supplement, p. 39.

to sending to Canada one solitary family. Its monopoly was abolished in 1620. The next year a charter was granted, on the customary terms and requirements of introducing settlers and missionaries, to the Company of De Caen, organized by William De Caen and his nephew, merchants of Rouen. This Company absorbed Champlain's, and the united corporations carried on their trade until 1633, although not in its later years without competition from a rival trading company.

Enormous Powers of Monopolies

This competitor was the Company of New France, established in 1627 by Cardinal Richelieu.

Unlike the previous companies, the Company of New France was not owned by merchants of the smaller towns; its principal stockholders were Parisians, who, seeing the richness and extent of the fur trade, aimed at concentrating the monopoly in themselves. They received a full monopoly for 15 years with full ownership of the entire valley of the St. Lawrence. For these exclusive grants they were required to introduce three hundred colonists every year up to 1643 — an obligation which was only nominally carried out, yet the Company continued to hold its monopoly until 1663.

Following the cancellation of the charter of the Company of New France, came the Company of the West Indies, chartered by Louis XIV in 1664. Its alleged object was the conversion to Christianity of the Indian tribes, but its privileges were enormous, covering trade in the West Coast of Africa, the East Coast of South America, Canada, Acadia and Newfoundland. The stock of this Company seems to have been used largely for stock-jobbing purposes; in spite of its vast powers and privileges, the Company did not flourish, and its charter was revoked in 1675. Various other companies came into existence, the most important of which was the French

East India Company. This corporation had the sole privilege of exporting beaver from Canada.

Necessarily all of these companies had to depend to a considerable extent for their supplies of furs upon individual or itinerant traders who roamed afar among the Indian tribes, and brought back their bales of furs. But as no one could trade with the Indians without an annual license, and these licenses were annulled at will by the French officials or distributed among favorites, the state of the fur trade was one of uncertainty. Having only a transient permission, the French traders followed no system and made no permanent establishments of any importance, but went whither they could easily and most quickly enrich themselves. This was even more so with respect to the illicit traders who, denied licenses, carried on the trade clandestinely.

Debauching the Indians with Brandy

The principal means used in trading with the Indians was in debauching them with brandy, and then swindling them of their furs. This abuse became so notorious that on April 17, 1664, the Sovereign Council issued a decree prohibiting bartering or giving intoxicating drinks to the Indians.[5] This decree was called forth by the consequences of debauching an innocent race, hitherto immune from the knowledge of liquor, and the demoralization, atrocities and conflicts following in its wake. The traders ranging the woods, however, were far away from the reach of enforcing officials, and continued their debauching process.

On November 10, 1668, pleading as an excuse that the freedom of sale of strong drink would cause less demoralization than a restraint impossible to enforce, although admitting the pernicious influence of drink upon the Indians, the Sovereign

[5] *Report on Canadian Archives*, 1899 Vol., p. 54.

Council gave permission to all Frenchmen inhabiting Canada
to sell and deliver strong drinks to the Indians.[6] A proclamation the next year forbade the lying in wait for the Indians in
the woods or going to meet them, and prohibited drunkenness
among the Indians.[7]

Immorality, Theft and Murder

"What does the most harm here," wrote Mother Mary of
the Incarnation, Quebec, in 1669, "is the traffic in wine and
brandy. We preach against those who give these liquors
to the savages; and yet many reconcile their consciences to
the permission of this thing. They go into the woods and
carry drinks to the savages in order to get their furs for
nothing when they are drunk. Immorality, theft, and murder ensue. . . . We had not yet seen the French commit such
crimes, and we can only attribute the cause of them to the
pernicious traffic in brandy." [8]

Writing on November 2, 1672, to Colbert, Minister of
Finance under Louis XIV, Governor Frontenac outlined the
measures he had taken to keep in check the "ever-active ambition of the Jesuits" and he continued, "But whatever pre-
tense they manifest, they will not extend that language
[French], and to speak frankly to you, they think as much
about the conversion of Beaver as of souls; for the majority
of their missions are pure mockeries . . ." [9] In another letter
to Colbert, in 1674, Frontenac told of his difficulties with the
Jesuits whom he had spoken to in vain regarding the state of
the missions, "they having declared to me that they were here
only to endeavor to instruct the Indians, or rather *to get*

[6] *Ibid.*, p. 55.
[7] *Ibid.*, p. 56.
[8] De Brumath's *Bishop Laval*, p. 113.
[9] Paris Documents, *Documents Relating to the Colonial History of
the State of New York*, Vol. IX, p. 68.

Beavers, and not to be parish priests to the French." [10] But the Governor was himself accused by Duchesenau,— appointed on May 30, 1675, Intendant of Police, Justice and Finance in Canada,— of being interested in the Indian trade illicitly; that he had intermediaries to extort and receive presents and bribes of packages of beaver of large value which his henchmen disposed of for him.[11]

Trading Interests Supreme

We are told that in 1677 when Bishop Laval complained to King Louis XIV of the widespread debauchery, Colbert ordered an inquiry to be made by twenty competent persons in the colony. "Unfortunately," says De Brumath, "the persons chosen for this enquiry were engaged in trade with the savages; their conclusions must necessarily be prejudiced." Describing how their report minimized the extent of the traffic in strong drink, De Brumath goes on: "We cannot help being surprised at such a judgment when we read over the memoirs of the time, which all agree in deploring the sad results of this traffic. The most crying injustice, the most revolting immorality, settlements devastated by drunkenness, agriculture abandoned, the robust portion of the population ruining its health in profitless expeditions; such were some of the most horrible fruits of alcohol. And what do we find as a compensation for so many evils? A few dozen rascals enriched, returning to squander in France a fortune shamefully acquired. . . ." [12]

[10] *Ibid.,* p. 120.
[11] Duchesenau to De Seignelay, Nov. 10, 1679, *Ibid.,* p. 135.
[12] *Bishop Laval,* p. 173. The "Twenty Principal Inhabitants" reported that the prohibition of the trade in spirits "would ruin trade, without any equivalent and without remedying the evils . . . because the English and Dutch sell it freely to the Indians, and will attract to themselves both the Indians and the trade in furs."— See *Report on Canadian Archives,* 1900 Vol., p. 71.

Laval's emissary to Colbert was Dudouyt, a priest, who has transmitted to us a long account of the interview, ". . . On this point," he wrote to Laval, " I told him that the inclination of the Indians for becoming intoxicated is much stronger than that of the people of Europe; that they have much greater weakness in resisting it; that it is universal, and that the disorders committed by the Indians are more aggravated, and this I proved to him, my Lord, in this way: If, in a bourgade, there be liquor freely accessible to the Indians they usually all become intoxicated, old, young, great, small, women and children, so that there is hardly one left unintoxicated; that if there be liquor for two days, drunkenness will continue for two days; if there is enough for a week, it will last a week; if for a month, it will last a month; that we do not see in Europe. . . . It means, my Lord, persons who wish to have beavers from the Indians by means of liquor without respect to the risk of disorders they cause by that means, and without regard to their own salvation or that of the Indians." Dudouyt told Colbert that Intendant Talon had caused the removal of all of the penalties and ordinances against the excessive use of liquors, and that moderation was necessary.[13]

Commenting upon this protest, Charlevoix later wrote that the secret had been discovered by the fur traders of how to persuade the King's Council that the trade was absolutely necessary to attach the natives to the French interests, and of how to represent successfully that the abuses were greatly exaggerated.[14]

Official Participation in the Fur Frauds

Duchesenau wrote from Quebec, November 10, 1679, that he had done his best to prevent the interdicted Indian trade

[13] *Report on Canadian Archives,* 1885 Vol., p. ci.
[14] *Ibid.,* p. x.

from being carried on by illicit traders, but, "All that has been in vain, inasmuch as several of the most considerable families in this country are interested therein, so that the Governor lets them go on, and even shares in their profits." [15]

In the next year Duchesenau informed the French Government that there were great complaints against Governor Perrot of Montreal, who had occupied that post since 1670.

The complaints against Perrot were "as well on account of his violent conduct as for his open trading. He is accused of having excited a sedition at Montreal with a view to obtain the repeal of the King's Ordinance forbidding subordinate Governors imprisoning people. This sedition I allayed." Duchesenau went on to remark that Monsieur Dollier, Superior of the Montreal Seminary, "while an honest man," was not altogether a stranger to illicit enterprises in fur trading.[16] Perrot was accused of pocketing 40,000 livres in a single year for his fur-trading operations, but denied that the amount was that large.[17]

Between Frontenac, Governor and Lieutenant-General of Canada, and Intendant Duchesenau an embroilment existed as to the respective rights and priority of each. It was in the course of this dispute that Duchesenau reported the prevailing abuses. He described the traffic of carrying brandy to the Indians, and intoxicating them.

"The Missions," he drily wrote on November 13, 1680, "cannot be too much encouraged and too much countenance be given to the gentlemen of St. Sulpice and the Jesuit Fathers among the Indians, inasmuch as they not only place the coun-

[15] Paris Documents, *Documents Relating to the Colonial History of the State of New York,* Vol. IX, p. 131.
[16] *Ibid.,* p. 142.
[17] Perrot was later required to face charges. Arrested and convicted, he was imprisoned nearly a year in Quebec, and later sent to the Bastile in Paris. A favorite at court where he had powerful friends, he was soon released, and later appointed to the Governorship of Acadia.

try in security and bring peltries hither, but greatly glorify God, and the King, as eldest son of the Church, by reason of the large number of good Christians formed there." [18] He added that " the desire of making money everywhere has led the Governor, Sieurs Perrot, Boisseau, and De Lut, and Patron, his uncle, to send canoes, loaded with peltries, to the English." The report, he said, was notorious that 60,000 livres worth of peltries had been sent thither; that the officials violated their own edicts by selling beaver to the English who paid them double what they received from the French in Quebec.[19]

Violence Supports Fraud

" Violence, upheld by authority, decides everything," reported Duchesenau in his Memoir. The Governor did as he pleased, and knew how to take measures to prevent complaints from reaching the Government. " The authority with which the Governor is invested is an easy means of success herein, because, in the administration of justice and in what regards trade, he does only what he pleases, and in one or the other favors only those whose business has relation to his speculations, or who are interested with him. The force he has at hand sustains his interests, and he employs it only to intimidate the people, so as to prevent them from complaining, or to glaze over his violences by exacting from individuals false statements, [by] which he can weaken what may be said against him, and to turn whatever he does to his own advantage." [20]

[18] Paris Docs., *Documents Relating to the Colonial History of the State of New York,* Vol. IX, p. 150. Duchesenau's Memoir. In 1691 the Religieuses Hospitalieres of Montreal applied for and obtained trading licenses on the ground that they needed funds " to assist them in the re-establishment of their house."— *Rep. on Canadian Archives,* 1899 Vol., p. 292.
[19] *Ibid.,* p. 160.
[20] *Ibid.,* p. 157.

Dealing with the quarrels of the head officials, Edouard
Richard says that these and many other disputes " often originated in commercial rivalry. The profits to be derived by
the privileged ones from the beaver trade were apparently the
most seductive, for notwithstanding the reiterated prohibitions
and threats of the minister, we find governors and intendants
mutually accusing one another of participating in the trade in
an underhand manner." [21] Precisely what measure of weight
can be put to all of these charges and countercharges it is now
impossible to say, but so far as Perrot was concerned he
carried on the trade with flagrant openness.

So great was the general scramble on the part of all classes
to participate in the profits of the fur trade that farmers
abandoned their farms to go long distances hunting or trading, against which practice the King ordered Frontenac, in
1672, to issue the most stringent injunctions.[22] Agriculture
and manufacturing were considered far subordinate by the
settlers in their avidity to have a hand in the fur spoils, although the King of France sought repeatedly to encourage the
establishment of both.

The Fur Traders Dominate

Thus, the dominating trading class was the fur traders;
of this class the merchants were a substantial part, pursuing
their search for wealth with the most unscrupulous eagerness.

The King had put in practice the endowing with commodities of soldiers and young women who married, and the
granting of certain articles to new immigrant families. Talon
wrote from Quebec to Colbert in November, 1670, that this
practice " is not agreeable to the merchants, who would like
everything to be got from themselves, good or bad, at so high

---

[21] *Report on Canadian Archives,* 1899 Supplement, p. 12.
[22] *Ibid.,* 1899 Vol., p. 58.

a rate that it would require double the expense were people reduced to what they would wish." [23]

Constantly committing frauds in their fur dealings with the fur companies,[24] the merchants, at the same time, demanded and received the greatest consideration, and filled high official posts. Whatever abuses they committed, whatever their frauds, the King's Cabinet usually sustained them; the expansion of trade was not to be interfered with.

A Royal letter informed Governor Frontenac in 1674 that " He must treat Sieur de Villeray with great consideration, for . . . he is the man who has devoted himself most thoroughly to trade, having vessels in trade with the Western Islands." Frontenac was ordered to restore him to the office of first councilor.[25] Bitterly complaining, as the merchants did, when any measure or law threatened to obstruct or lessen their profits, there was no barrier to their greed and avarice, and no effective restraint upon the facility with which they profited from the debauching and swindling of the Indian tribes. " It will be well," read a communication from the King's Minister to De Costebelle, in 1699, " for the people to do something in the way of cultivating the soil, so as not to be at the mercy of the merchants." [26]

Effects of Debauching the Indians

While the fur traders and merchants were reaping their profits, and the King's Government in France was finding ready justifications for the indiscriminate use of brandy

[23] Paris Docs., *Documents Relating to the Colonial History of the State of New York,* Vol. IX, p. 68. But when it was urged from Canada that a fixed price be placed upon the beaver, royal instructions came from Paris, March 11, 1671, that this would not be permitted : —" Such a restriction would disgust the merchants." *Report on Canadian Archives,* 1900 Vol., p. 252.
[24] *Report on Can. Archives,* 1899 Vol., p. 58.
[25] *Ibid.,* p. 61.
[26] *Ibid.,* p. 337.

among the Indians,[27] Marquis de Demonville was writing, in January, 1690, to the Marquis de Seignelay, King's Minister at Versailles: ". . . I have witnessed the evils caused by that liquor [brandy] among the Indians. It is the horror of horrors. There is no crime that they do not perpetrate in their excesses. A mother throws her child in the fire; noses are bitten off; this is a frequent occurrence. It is another Hell among them during these orgies, which must be seen to be credited. . . . Remedies are impossible so long as everyone is permitted to sell and traffic in ardent spirits. However little each at a time may give, the Indians will always get drunk. There is no artifice that they will not have recourse to, to obtain the means of intoxication. Besides, every house is a groggery.

"Those who allege that the Indians will remove to the English, if Brandy be not furnished them, do not state the truth; for it is a fact that they do not care about drinking as long as they do not see Brandy; and the most reasonable would wish there never had been any such thing, for they set their entrails on fire and beggar themselves by giving their peltries and clothes for drink. . . ."[28]

Beaver "A Mine of Gold"

Beaver was the accepted medium of exchange of the country; there was very little actual money in circulation, and

[27] From Versailles came Royal instructions, in 1691, to the Bishop of Quebec in reply to remonstrances from merchants respecting the opposition of the clergy to the trade in spirits. The Bishop was advised that he must keep watch on the clergy, "and prevent them from disturbing consciences"; that the brandy traffic gave France an advantage over Holland and England, and that the "use of brandy is in itself very wholesome."—*Ibid.*, pp. 290-291.

[28] Paris Docs., *Documents Relating to the Colonial History of the State of New York*, Vol. IX, pp. 441-442. In fact, several Indian tribes and a number of chiefs had earnestly and pathetically implored the French officials not to allow liquors among them.

generally such coin as was current was avariciously hoarded
by the officials and merchants. The deficiency of currency
was at times made up by a fiat issue called "card money."
"Beaver," wrote Randot in his Memorial to Versailles, July
16, 1708, "have always been looked upon here as a mine of
gold of which everyone wanted to take his share. The settlers
spent their time hunting in the woods, preferring a life of
adventure in the woods, which brought them large profits with
little toil, to the cultivation of the land, which requires assidu-
ous labor." [29]

Such official complaints, though frequent, produced little
or no immediate change in conditions.

The vast quantities of beaver gathered — in 1696 there were
4,000,000 livres worth of them — resulted in a considerable
lowering of prices of that commodity, which the Government
sought to prevent by reducing the number of licenses and by
other measures.[30] Randot wrote that the trade of the country was carried on with the sum of 650,000 livres, which sum
was very small, he said, for a population of from 18,000 to
20,000 souls. The prices of merchandise were very high, "and
nevertheless the people will work only for high wages, saying
that they wear out more clothes when working than they can
earn by their labor." The remedy for this state of things, he
concluded, was to induce the people to take to the production
of wheat, cattle, timber, fish, oil and ship building, by finding
them a market for these products. He further pointed out
the great possibilities in developing the fish and oil trade, and
the coal, feldspar, gypsum and timber resources of Cape
Breton.[31]

---

[29] *Report on Canadian Archives,* 1899 Supplement, p. 227. "Memorial
on Affairs in Canada at the Present Time and the Settlement of Cape
Breton."
[30] A Royal proclamation of May 21, 1696, to this effect repealed
trading licenses and condemned offenders to the galleys.
[31] *Report on Canadian Archives,* 1899 Vol., p. 227.

The All-Absorbing Fur Traffic

To a small extent, the utilization of the rich timber resources had already begun in 1686 when the Quebec merchants built a ship to carry boards to La Rochelle, France,[32] and cattle-raising and wheat cultivation were carried on to some slight degree. But the prime and all-absorbing traffic was the fur trade dominated and dictated by the merchants in collusion with royal officials, who, in order to monopolize it, frequently incited the Indians to war with its inevitable train of scalpings, butcheries and other atrocities.[33]

Accompanying the sway of the merchant class was that of the seigneurs or feudal lords, vested with the ownership of immense stretches of territory and with the powers, rights and privileges of a transplanted feudalism which, it was sanguinely hoped, could be established artificially, by decree, in the new country.

[32] *Ibid.,* p. 278.

[33] De Meulles complained to the King in 1684 that Gov. Perrot, in the course of his partnership with De Lut and some Quebec merchants to monopolize all the trade of the West, incited the war with the Iroquois.—*Ibid.,* p. 43. But it appears that De Meulles himself, in 1683, advised war with the Iroquois "who must be humbled or annihilated in the interests of trade."—*Ibid.,* p. 42.

CHAPTER II

THE ECCLESIASTICAL AND FEUDAL LORDS

Aiming to reproduce in Canada the feudal conditions prevailing in France, the Company of New France and successive governors lavishly bestowed on favorites or Roman Catholic orders vast tracts of territory, creating seigneuries and ecclesiastical endowments. Many large grants of land " fit for a kingdom " were made by the Company of New France, but some were annulled later for non-compliance with settlement conditions. The ecclesiastical grants, however, remained intact.

A Gift of Two Million Acres to the Church

The total area granted to the Roman Catholic Church prior to 1763, and mostly in the seventeenth century, was 2,096,754 acres.

Clearly understanding that a strong economic basis provided security and wealth, all of the ecclesiastical orders vied with one another in pleading and scheming for generous grants of land. At a stroke, as it were, many of the Roman Catholic orders were converted into powerful landlords, with immense and positive economic resources guaranteeing them temporal overlordship and progressively increasing wealth for generations. True, much of the land was wilderness, but it was rich in fur-bearing animals, timber, for which the demand in Europe was constantly increasing, and prolific in some other potential resources. The wilderness of that time was certain to be the agricultural domain then and of the future. The land grants to the Roman Catholic Church were:

	Acres.
Quebec Ursulines	164,615
Three River Ursulines	38,909
Recollets	945
Bishop and Seminary of Quebec	693,324
Jesuits	891,845
St. Sulpicians	250,191
General Hospital, Quebec	73
General Hospital, Montreal	404
Hotel Dieu, Quebec	14,112
Soeurs Grises	42,336
Total	2,096,754 [1]

The importance of these great land holdings became more evident as settlement increased, and the wealth derived either from their forced sale, under subsequent Government pressure, or their retention, had a most pertinent and close connection with the later development of modern capitalism. Excepting the Jesuits, whose estates were later appropriated, the time came when the Roman Catholic clergy or orders were able by their ability in commanding money in rents, tithes, or by borrowing from their communicants at absurdly low rates of interest, to invest largely, as we shall see, in railroad and steamship lines and industrial stocks and bonds. The Seminary of St. Sulpice, the landed estate of which in Montreal is of enormous present value, reaching tens of millions of dollars, is now one of the largest holders of stocks and bonds in Canada. Possessing vast wealth, its income is admittedly

[1] Report of Lieut.-Gov. Milnes to the Duke of Portland, Nov. 1, 1800. *Canadian Archives,*— Series Q, Vol. 85, p. 228.

great, yet no one not in the inner circles can state the precise amount; the Sulpicians never, so far as can be learned, have made a public accounting.

Seminary of St. Sulpice's Estate

According to Lindsay's fanciful story, the Seminary of Montreal or St. Sulpice obtained a grant of the Island of Montreal (on which a city of 500,000 population now stands), thus:

The Island had been granted to Jean de Lauson, Intendant of Dauphine, on condition that he should plant a colony upon it, which condition he neglected. The Jesuit Dauversiĕre, assuring Lauson that he "had a command from Heaven" to establish an hospital on the Island, tried to get a cession, but Lauson had not received a duplicate of this heavenly command and demurred at giving away such a finely situated property for nothing. A second time Dauversiĕre, accompanied by de Faucamp and P. Charles Lallemont, the director of the Jesuits, interviewed Lauson, described how the apparition of the Holy Family had appeared to Dauversiĕre in the Church of Notre Dame, and how Jesus had put a ring upon his finger on which were engraved the names of Jesus, Mary, Joseph.

However, whatever the actual considerations, Lauson was induced to cede his grant to the "Associates for the Conversion of the Savages of New France" who conveyed it by deed of gift to the Seminary of St. Sulpice of Paris, in 1663. A year after the British conquest, the Seminary of St. Sulpice of Paris, in 1764, to escape probable confiscation, assigned the property to the Seminary of St. Sulpice, in Montreal.[2] Of the subsequent agitation against this ecclesiastical holding —

[2] Lindsay's *Rome in Canada* (Edit. of 1877), pp. 351–352, citing Faillon's *Vie de Mlle. Mance, et Histoire d'l Hotel Dieu de Ville-Marie dans l'ile de Montreal, en Canada.*

how official reports declared against the validity of the title, and how, nevertheless, the Sulpicians were empowered to retain it — these facts will be narrated in their appropriate place later in this work.

Monks Get the Right of "High Justice"

Once vested with the right of ownership of the Island of Montreal, the Seminary of St. Sulpice claimed the full feudal property right of administering "high and low justice" on their domain. When in March, 1693, an edict from the King appeared, accepting the surrender of this right, but granting the Seminary the right of high justice within the Seminary's enclosure and the farm of St. Gabriel,[3] and also the privilege of nominating the first Royal judge, the Seminary ecclesiastics remonstrated that they did not intend to surrender that right and prayed that their holding of such rights be expressly recognized.[4] Pronson, Superior of the Seminary of St. Sulpice at Paris, promptly proceeded to nominate De Braussoc to be Royal judge on the Island of Montreal.

The domain of the Seminary of St. Sulpice was enlarged, on August 29, 1679, by a grant of islands in the vicinity of Montreal, and later by a grant of the seignory of the Lake of the Two Mountains, near Montreal — a property now of huge value and the title of which has been attacked in the Quebec courts. The conditions on which the Sulpicians were given this property were that at their own expense they should build a church and a fort of stone, the King reserving the

[3] A large stretch of land later in the heart of Montreal that in modern times became of immense value.

[4] *Report on Canadian Archives*, 1899 Vol., pp. 74 and 193–194. At times, the ecclesiastics sold a small part of their land, not long after their acquisition of it. Thus, in 1676, the Bishop of Quebec ceded to Sieur Berthelot the Island of Orleans in exchange for Isle Jesus and 25,000 livres. Berthelot had acquired Isle Jesus from the Jesuit Fathers in 1672.— *Ibid.*, p. 69.

right to take at pleasure all of the oak timber that he wanted on the grant.[5]

Clergy Place Themselves above Civil Law

Professing to be a law unto themselves, the clergy refused to acknowledge the supremacy of any secular tribunal.

Summoned, in 1674, to appear in court, Abbe de Fenelon, Abbe de Francheville and Abbe Remy of the Seminary of Montreal, refused to take notice, on the ground that their priestly character protected them, and that the secular laws could not supplant the Holy Canons, and compel them to give evidence against an ecclesiastic in a criminal matter.[6] The civil authorities refused to recognize the validity of this plea.

On every possible occasion the ecclesiastics attempted to assert their independence of the civil power, and make the Church dominant in civil as well as religious authority — a move which the King's Government contested with cunning weapons. On one occasion, May 1, 1677, the King's Minister wrote to Duchesenau that as he perceived " that the Bishop was assuming an authority a little too independent, it would be perhaps well that he should not have a seat at the [Sovereign] Council. You must seek every opportunity, and on all occasions take every means practicable to wean him from the craving for attending the Council; you must, however, act in this matter with great discretion, taking care that what I write be not divulged." [7]

The exactions and growing wealth of the Church were described in a " Memorial on Canada and the Clergy," written in 1713 by De la March to Pontchartrain, Secretary of State. De la March was a nephew of Boucher, formerly Governor of Three Rivers, and had been in the service of the Seminary

[5] *Ibid.*, p. 194.   [6] *Ibid.*, pp. 62, 65-66.   [7] *Ibid.*, p. 70.

of Quebec for nearly ten years. He described in detail the riches and great revenue of that institution, accruing from its seignories, farms, mills, houses, lands, cattle and vessels, and how it owned all the shore of the river from Montmorency as far as La Baie St. Paul, as well as the Isle of Condre and that of Jesus. " They could do a great deal of good, but stop at no acts of injustice in striving to promote their own interests. They keep in great part for themselves the allowance His Majesty grants for the poorer curés and missionaries, and which is entrusted to them for distribution," etc., etc.[8] It was of the Roman Catholic College of Quebec that De Beauharnais reported later from Quebec to Maurepas that, " It is publicly stated by everybody in this country that the College of Quebec has been built out of the frauds committed in the [fur] trade with the English." [9]

But lands and chattels were by no means the only source of wealth of the ecclesiastics. By a system of tithes every farmer was taxed on his produce, supplying a regular and never-failing income to the priests. An ordinance decreed in 1667 had promulgated a schedule of the amounts in tithes to be levied for the support of the clergy. Not satisfied with this legal rate of tithes, the clergy constantly sought to amplify their exactions.

System of Tithes

The Curés of Beauport and of l'Ange Gardieu exacted tithes not only of grains, but of all products of the soil, whether the land was under cultivation or not, and tithes on cattle, hay, fruits, flax, hemp, sheep and other possessions. " The result has been," the Sovereign Council declared, in 1705, " loud murmurs from the people when leaving the Church." Pro-

[8] *Ibid.*, p. 197.
[9] Paris Docs., *Documents Relating to the Colonial History of the State of New York*, Vol. IX, p. 1071.

hibiting the curés from contravening the tithe ordinance, it ordered them to explain their conduct. Their defense was that they were " reduced to living in a state of poverty which exposes them to the contempt of the people." The protesting farmers replied that " they are able to live in comfort and afford themselves the luxury of a barrel of wine every year." [10] The Royal decision was adverse to the priests.

In urging upon the King, in 1730, measures to enforce regularity on the part of the ecclesiastics in Quebec, Beauharnais and Hocquart wrote that their effect will be " that there will be found no longer in Quebec so many useless ecclesiastics, who, for want of employment, are beginning to engage in worldly amusement, play, feasting and dissipation. The effect of their idle life is that they think nothing of quarrelling amongst themselves and creating discord amongst themselves." [11]

Five years later there was another uproar when, not content with the tithe of the 26th bushel on wheat and other grains, the Bishop of Quebec, in 1735, sought to exact the 13th bushel not only upon grain, but upon all vegetables, hemp, flax, tobacco, and other products. Upon being officially informed that " the farmers would not willingly submit to such an increase," he wisely decided not to change the schedules of exaction already long in force.[12]

Here, then, was the complete ecclesiastical mechanism for extorting a great part of the produce of labor. Some of the priests were sincerely intent upon missionary work, but there was much complaint that extortion was common. Setting themselves up as a privileged class, the ecclesiastics claimed distinct exemptions and immunities. Dire, however, was the punishment inflicted upon the man or woman of " the lower

[10] *Report on Canadian Archives,* 1900 Vol., p. 198.
[11] *Ibid.,* 1887 Vol., p. ccxxvi.
[12] *Ibid.,* 1900 Vol., p. 198.

orders " committing the slightest infraction of the rule of the Church or its regulations translated into civil laws.

For blasphemy a mild punishment was a heavy fine, or imprisonment on bread and water. A Montreal ordinance of 1676 forbade the blasphemy of " the holy name of God or to utter anything against the Blessed Virgin under pain of corporal punishment, and in case of a fourth offense to have the tongue cut off." [13]

The area of 2,096,754 acres granted to the Roman Catholic Church, and constituting nearly one-fourth of the total area granted, was held by a mere handful of ecclesiastics. In 1720, long after most of these grants had been made, and when the population of Canada was said to be 24,434, there were but 24 Jesuits, 32 Recollets, 67 Parish priests and missionaries, 175 nuns, and also 31 priests in what were called foreign missions. Jesuits quarrelled with Sulpicians, and they with other orders, but all upheld the power of the Church, and leagued to prevent any interference with its theological and expanding economic hold.

Seigneurs Get More Than 7,000,000 Acres

Of the 7,985,470 acres, however, granted previous to the British conquest, in 1763, the Catholic Church's share, large as it was — nearly one-fourth — was not nearly as large as that granted mainly to the seigneurs, or feudal landlords. A total of 5,888,716 acres, according to Lieutenant-Governor Milnes, was granted to the laity,[14] comprising less than 400 seigneurs.

Either Milnes' estimate was a moderate one, or the grants

[13] *Montreal Archives,* Sessional Paper, No. 6, Vol. 25, *Que. Sess. Papers,* 1891.

[14] Report of Lieut.-Gov. Milnes to the Duke of Portland, Nov. 1, 1800, (*Canadian Archives,* Series Q, Vol. 85, p. 228;) *Rep. on Can. Archives,* 1892 Vol., p. 14.

to the seigneurs were later irregularly extended. Reporting
to the House of Assembly in 1845, the Commissioner of the
Crown Lands and the Surveyor General stated that the lands
surveyed in seignories in Lower Canada amounted to 9,027,880
acres, and that the lands granted to individuals in fief and
seignory by the Crown of France amounted to 7,496,000
acres,[15] of which about 4,300,000 acres were gradually "conceded" to tenants.

   Up to the year 1763 the old Company of New France or
the various governors had created 376 seignories. This process of creation went somewhat slowly until the years 1671
and 1672. Having attended to his own desires by contriving
to have the Des Islets seignory granted to himself, and erected
by the King into a barony,[16] Intendant Talon was in a proper
mood to begin the grand distribution of seignories.

   In the single year of 1672 Intendant Talon industriously
donated numerous seignorial grants, giving away immense
estates, with full hereditary feudal rights, to favored individuals, some of whom were military officers.

De Martignon and Pottier Grants

   On October 17, 1672, Talon granted to De Martignon a
tract six leagues [17] in front on the River St. John and the
same area in depth. Martignon was vested with the right of
holding the land in fief, with all the rights of jurisdiction and
seignory assured to himself, his heirs and assigns. The grant
was made on condition of homage; he was required to preserve all of the oak timber on that part of his land which he

---

[15] *Journals of the Legislative Assembly of the Province of Canada,*
1849, Appendix B., Vol. III, p. 7. In his report to Lord Durham in
1838, Commissioner Buller's estimate of seignorial estates subject to
obligation to "concede" lands to tenants was 8,300,000 acres, and of
this area about 4,300,000 acres had been "conceded."
[16] *Report on Canadian Archives,* 1899 Vol., p. 252.
[17] A league equalled about 4,428 acres.

should set apart for his principal manor house; in making grants to his tenants he was to reserve all oak timber fit for ship-building; and if mines were discovered, he was to give immediate notice to the King or the Royal West India Company. This extensive domain was considerately granted for no other reason than that Martignon was a creditor of the estate of the deceased Latour, his father-in-law, who had owned more than 50 leagues of land fronting the River St. John, which seignory was in danger of forfeiture to the King for non-settlement and non-cultivation. Talon's opportune grant preserved much of this from threatened forfeiture.[18]

On the next day, October 18, 1672, Intendant Talon presented to Jacques Pottier, Sieur de St. Denis, two leagues in fief and seignory " with all of the hereditary rights of mean and inferior jurisdiction." This grant was given upon the usual conditions of homage and the reserving of oak, and on the condition of cultivation, attending to the fisheries and promoting colonization.[19] To Sieur Dupuy, Talon gave a grant of Heron Island and all adjacent islands in the St. Lawrence River, with the right of fishing; he was to hold it in fief, subject to the duty of paying fealty and homage.[20]

More Generous Land Grants

October 20, 1672, found the high and mighty Intendant Talon in an extremely gracious mood; on that day he made a gift to De Marson, commandant on the St. John " in consideration of military services," of a tract of land four leagues in front and one league deep on the east side of the St. John River, and to De Marson's brother-in-law, Joihert, he gave an

---

[18] *Titles and Documents Relating to the Seignorial Tenure in return to an address of the Legislative Assembly,* 1851, Quebec, pp. 5–6.
[19] *Ibid.,* pp. 7–8.
[20] *Ibid.,* pp. 8–9.

adjoining tract of a league square. Both of these beneficiaries were vested with hereditary feudal jurisdiction.[21]

But on October 29 following, Talon was even more expansively kind; on that day he created ten more seignories. To the eager Governor Perrot of Montreal,— the same who at that very time was deriving large profits from his fraudulent fur trade with the Indians — Talon gave "for services" a whole cluster of valuable islands with all of the rights of seignory and jurisdiction.[22] A gift of an hereditary fief and seignory of two leagues in front by one league in depth on the St. Lawrence River was made by Talon to Sieu de la Boutellerie.[23]

Talon must have stood extremely high in the estimation of the officers of the Carignan regiment (a valuable hold at a time when force swayed everything) after that day's arduous work of signing deeds. To Contrecour, a captain in that regiment, he gave "for military services" an hereditary fief of two square leagues on the St. Lawrence; to another captain in the same regiment he granted a similar large tract; to the widow of still another captain in that regiment he gave a large seignorial estate on the same river; to three other officers estates of large dimensions; and to De Chambly, another captain in the Carignan regiment, a splendid seignorial domain of six leagues in front by one league in depth on the St. Louis River. All of these and other estates granted carried with them full feudal rights.[24]

Further Creation of Seignorial Lords

Officials of all varieties, as well as military officers and merchants, hastened to be transformed into seignorial lords. Not-

[21] *Ibid.*, pp. 9–10.   [22] *Ibid*, pp. 11–12.   [23] *Ibid.*, pp. 13–14.
[24] *Ibid.*, pp. 14–25. These rights, however, did not include titles of nobility which, under ancient feudalism in Europe, accompanied ownership of the land.

withstanding the King's instructions in 1672 to make no more grants until those already granted should have been better settled, Governor Frontenac, May 6, 1675, gave to De Peyras, a councillor in the Sovereign Council, an extensive grant fronting two leagues and the same in depth on the St. Lawrence River, together with three islands.[25] On the same day he handed over to Charles Denis de Vitre the deed for a seignory of the same dimensions on the St. Lawrence, measured from the Metis River.[26] On May 11, 1687, a tract of two leagues frontage was given to Cardonniere and D'Artigny.

March 16, 1691, was a notable date in the chronicles of seignories. On that happy day a number of vast seignories were created. Gobin, a Quebec merchant, was thrown into felicity by the present of a grant of land twelve leagues by ten leagues at the Baie des Chaleurs. De Fronsac's prize was even greater; the gift to him was an immense seignorial fief of fifteen leagues frontage by fifteen leagues in depth at Mirimachi. De Bellefours, a Quebec notary, was transformed into a seignorial lord by the grant of a fief on the St. John River. To D'Iberville was given a seignorial estate of twelve leagues by ten leagues bordering upon the Baie des Chaleurs.[27] Another batch of seignorial estates were given on May 15th following.[28] Certain definite hereditary feudal rights accompanied these estates, too.

The Marquis de Vaudreuil, Governor of Montreal, did not suffer himself to be omitted; his turn came when, in 1702, he was presented with a large seignorial estate at Cascades

[25] *Report on Canadian Archives*, 1899 Vol., p. 67.
[26] *Ibid.*
[27] *Report on Canadian Archives*, 1899 Vol., p. 289. But there were even larger seignorial estates. A Royal memorial of June 14, 1695, complained, for instance, of the Sieurs D'Amours, etc., who, although "owning 30 leagues of rich land in a most favorable climate" on the St. John River, had done nothing to improve their grants but had devoted themselves to trading with the Indians.—*Ibid.*, p. 310.
[28] *Ibid.*, p. 316.

Rapids.[29]   These are some instances of the earlier grants.
After this, most of the seignorial estates granted were in
Labrador, and those given after 1731 were mostly in Lake
Champlain or on the Detroit River.   Some of the seignorial
grants were so extensive that Jacques Hyacinthe Simon de
Lorme (after whom the city of St. Hyacinthe, Quebec, is
named) a contractor for military supplies for the French
army, bought a tract of 108 miles, constituting the estate of de
Rigaud, later seigneur of Vaudreuil.

Feudal Tributes and Servitudes Established

As soon as they were possessed of the seignories, the seigneurs (contrary in many cases, to the " Custom of Paris "—
as the French law which had been introduced into Canada
was called —) established feudal exactions and servitudes of
the most onerous nature.

A few sparse acres were granted to the tenant; to this
day the small rectangular plots into which the seigneurs
divided their farming lands for " concession " to tenants may
still be seen — miles upon miles of these diminutive peasant
farms.   The seigneurs demanded corveĕ or forced statute
labor.   They exacted a ground rent for the use of the common
used as pasture ground.   To themselves they reserved the
privilege of recovering possession of lands granted by them,
whenever they had been sold, on refunding to the purchaser
the amount of the purchase money.   The seigneurs further
reserved the right of taking from the lands sold by them all
of the wood they wanted.   They arrogated to themselves the
preference in buying whatever produce the farmers had for

[29] *Ibid.*, p. 233.   Vaudreuil, it appears, carried on a large fur trade
with the Iroquois Indians; his annual trade, it was reported, reached
1,000 peltries — M. de Clerambault to Ponchartrain, April 27, 1709, Paris
Docs., *Documents Relating to the Colonial History of the State of
New York*, Vol. IX, p. 823.

sale. They reserved as their own property all the pine and oak trees on all land whether held or sold by them. They extorted the eleventh part of the fish caught in the waters adjacent to or in their lands. The tenants were forced to use the seigneur's grist mill; to bake their bread in his oven, and were required to perform many other duties and servitudes and to pay still other plebeian tributes, at the arbitrary will of the seigneur.[30]

Importing Peasantry and Proletariat

Three-fourths of the colonists settled on the seignories had been soldiers.[31] But steps had early been taken by the French Government to ensure a proletariat.

A decree issued in Paris, April 3 and 12, 1669, had, as a means of stimulating large families, ordered a pension of 300 livres a year to all inhabitants of Canada " not being priest, monks or nuns " having as many as 10 lawful children, and directed a pension of 400 livres a year to be paid to those having 12 children.[32] A state fund was later established for the promotion of marriages. In 1671 the King gave orders to ship to Canada thirty bachelors, 20 to 30 years of age, and as many girls of the corresponding age.[33] In 1671 another Royal decree ordered the shipment of " 100 recruits, 150 young women and some cattle." [34] " His Majesty," wrote the Minister from Versailles in announcing the fact to Talon, " has heard with pleasure that of the 165 girls sent to Canada last year only 15 remained unmarried." Talon was commended for having ordered that the volunteers should be deprived of

---

[30] *Report on Canadian Archives,* 1899 Vol., pp. 122–123.
[31] Randot's *Memorial on Affairs in Canada at the Present Time* [1707] *and the Settlement of Cape Breton, Ibid.,* p. 228.
[32] *Report on Canadian Archives,* 1887 Vol., p. ccxxxvii.
[33] *Ibid.,* 1899 Vol., p. 57.
[34] *Ibid.,* p. 251.

the privilege of trading and hunting if not married within two weeks after the arrival of the girls.

Orders had been given that the girls sent to Canada " shall be strong and healthy, and in every way suitable." [35] This assurance had reference to a complaint made to the Archbishop of Rouen that a batch of girls taken from the General Hospital there and shipped off to Canada in 1669 " were found not to be strong enough for the work of farming." [36] The Archbishop was called upon to induce the priests to find about 60 village maids who would consent to go to Canada.[37] In 1671 a hundred hired men were shipped over.[38] Most of the skilled workers were carpenters, ship builders, farmers, shoe makers, iron workers and of some other trades.[39] But the cost of commodities in Canada was so high that skilled workmen could not be induced, without difficulty, to leave France unless assured higher wages and the liberty of returning; instructions came from Versailles, in 1687, that these conditions should be granted.[40]

Such were some of the measures to secure a native white working class, which was supplemented by Negro and also Indian [41] slaves. From the outset the workers and peasants found themselves under the domination of the Church, the feudal seigneurs and the merchants. All three exacted their tribute relentlessly: the Church, its elaborate system of tithes and other exactions; the merchants both in Canada and abroad,

[35] *Ibid.*
[36] *Ibid.*, p. 249.
[37] *Report on Canadian Archives,* 1899 Vol., p. 249.
[38] *Ibid.*, p. 252.
[39] *Report on Work of the Archives Branch,* Dom. Arch. 1910, p. 63, etc.
[40] *Report on Canadian Archives,* 1899 Vol., p. 279.
[41] The right to hold Indians in slavery, and to sell them was decided by Judge Hocquart, May 29, 1733, in the case of an Indian belonging to Decouverte, and hired by him to Radisson. Judge Hocquart decided that this right existed by virtue of an ordinance of April 13, 1709. —*Rep. on Can. Archives,* 1899 Vol., p. 142.

their schedule of usurious prices, often for worthless goods;[42] and the seigneurs their crushing multiple of feudal dues and servilities.

Seigneurs Seek Titles of Nobility

Having assured proprietorship of vast areas of land, the seigneurs sought hard to get titles of nobility. They wanted the hereditary name as well as the substance of an established aristocracy, consistent with the traditions of ancient feudalism.

A patent of nobility was granted to Dupont de la Nouvelle in 1669; Talon received the title of Count to his farm of d'Orsainville; Berthelot, LeMoyne and others were vested with titles,— Le Moyne as Baron Longueuil, named after his seignory; but the greater number of seigneurs petitioned in vain for titles of nobility, although a decree of the Council of State, in 1684, forbade any inhabitant of Canada, other than gentlemen, to assume the title of Esquire, under a penalty of a fine of 500 livres.[43] The King sent word, in 1686, that he did not approve of the proposal to give new titles of nobility in Canada; "there are already too many."[44] A Royal memorial from Versailles, March 30, 1687, declared that, "The poverty of certain noble families [in Canada] is partly the result of their wanting to live like people of rank, without working. I am convinced that letters of nobility must never be granted to any residents of Canada."[45]

But this opposition was not, it is needless to say, intended

[42] Thus, June 30, 1707, an order from Versailles forbad Gitton, a merchant of La Rochelle, to trade in Canada "in order to punish him for sending worthless goods to the Colony."— *Report on Canadian Archives,* 1899 Vol., p. 203.

[43] *Report on Canadian Archives,* 1899 Vol., p. 80.

[44] *Ibid.,* p. 83.

[45] *Ibid.,* p. 277. This seems to have been an irritating subject. Two years previously the King's Minister wrote to De Meulles that he "must curb the audacity of those assuming the status of nobility without being entitled to it."—*Ibid.,* p. 270.

to introduce a more democratic air; it was intended solely to promote the development of resources and trade by preventing too formidable and exclusive an idle class. Already classes in Canada were rigidly fixed in law; in the " great meetings " the population was divided into four classes. First came the clergy, then the nobility, after them the judiciary, and finally the commonalty.[46] The King's Minister, in 1673, informed Governor Frontenac that he must never establish the Estates General for the inhabitants of the country or a body, and that " the syndicate of the settlers must also be quietly suppressed." [47]

Seigneurs' Authority to Punish

Although holding the exclusive rights of trading with the Indians, and also of hunting and fishing, some of the seigneurs looked down loftily upon trade with aristocratic contempt. The extortions of the seigneurs increased with the comparative prodigality of their expenditures, and varied according to personal disposition and extent of rapacity.

The seigneur's right of high jurisdiction (haute justice) gave him power to deal with all criminal cases, including those punishable by death, mutilation or other such extreme corporal penalty. Only such crimes as treason, counterfeiting, and the like, as were considered perpetrated against the royal person or property, were excepted from the seigneur's jurisdiction. In civil cases the authority of the seigneur gave him power to fine or imprison, to award damages and to pass other penal judgments. He could banish obnoxious persons from his seignory, put them in stocks and brand them; and in the case of offenses legally entailing confiscation of property, real or personal, he had the right to appropriate it, excepting in the case of offenses committed against the Crown.[48]

[46] *Report on Canadian Archives,* 1899 Vol., p. 59.
[47] *Ibid.*
[48] Munro's *The Seignorial System in Canada,* pp. 148–149. " This

Outside the chateau the seigneur had his hall for the trying and sentencing of his accused vassals, and he had his prison on the ground floor. For even trivial offenses, according to the answers given later by De Lanaudiere to the Committee of the Council, these were the long-prevailing customary punishments:— "Expressions of resentment, contradiction, ingratitude and scandal, be it by the vassal or subfeudatory, are severely punished by the laws. Besides a confiscation of their lands, there are examples of being obliged to appear in court during its sitting, bareheaded, kneeling, fettered, asking pardon of their offended seigneurs; even imprisonment, put to the galleys, and other unheard-of punishments, at the mercy of the judge. . . ." [49]

Squeezing of the Vassals

Judge Randot, Sr., writing November 16, 1707, to the French Government, at Paris, on the administration of justice in Canada, complained of the spirit of " chicane and cunning," and described how the poor inhabitants were daily obliged to leave the cultivation of their lands in order to defend unjust law suits. *" Many inhabitants have worked on the word of the seigneurs, others on simple tickets which did not express the charges of the grant.* Hence a great abuse has arisen, which is, that the inhabitants who had worked without a safe title have been subjected to *very heavy rents and dues,* the seigneurs refusing to grant them deeds except on these conditions which they were obliged to accept, because otherwise they would have lost their labor . . ." The seigneurs demanded cash payments, which the inhabitants " find very inconvenient, as they frequently have none, for although 30 sous *appear but a trifle,* it is a great deal in this country where

rule," says Munro, " was in full accord with the feudal maxim that 'he who condemns the person confiscates the property.'"
[49] *Seignorial Tenure, Titles and Documents,* etc., Legislative Assembly, Quebec, 1851, pp. 37–39.

money is scarce." Judge Randot enumerated a long list of other abuses.[50]

The cash payments for rent of lands granted was the direct form of taxation exacted by the seigneurs. The indirect form comprised the obligation of maintaining the necessary roads by compulsory labor; the tenant had to yield to the seigneur a pound of flour on every fourteen pounds ground in the mill, of which the seigneur had the exclusive ownership and the monopoly. In a number of other ways the tenant was mercilessly compelled to pay tribute in the form of produce, taxes and fines.

If the tenant or inhabitant failed or refused to fulfill even the slightest of these crushing exactions, the seigneur at once sat, as a judge, inexorably upon him. Exercising certain sovereign powers within the limits of their seignories, and holding the power of high, low and middle jurisdiction, the seigneurs, as we have seen, could hold courts of justice, could confiscate or forfeit property and possess themselves of it, and had the right to all escheated property. Even the act of doing these self-beneficial things was another profitable source, since the holding of courts of justice yielded the seigneurs certain emoluments.[51]

Judge Randot urged in 1707 that statute labor was a cause of trouble — in fact, it had occasioned a riot of workers in Montreal — and suggested other reforms. Ten years later a Royal decree was issued declaring void many of the seignorial exactions and servitudes,[52] but certain odious feudal features remained in force until after the middle of the nineteenth century, causing a series of popular ferments and agitations,

[50] *Ibid.*, pp. 10–11. Italics in the original.
[51] *Ibid.*, p. 47. Also, *Report of the Commissioners Appointed to Inquire Into the State of the Laws and other Circumstances Connected with the Seignorial Tenure,* etc., Laid before the Legislative Assembly, Quebec, October, 1843.
[52] *Report on Canadian Archives,* 1899 Vol., p. 122.

finally, when settlement was made after 1867, costing the public treasury, directly and indirectly, at least $10,000,000 to get rid of them.

Condition of the Peasants and Artisans

While ecclesiastics, seigneurs, officials and merchants were living in such various degrees of elegance as were possible in a newly-settled country, and exercising a differing sway of power, the lot of the working class and its social state were manifestly of the lowliest.

The peasant houses in the rural districts generally consisted of only a single room, lighted by three windows; in this one room the whole family ate, lived and slept.

During the long winters, the rural workers hewed timber, sawed planks or split shingles. "A poor man," wrote Mother Mary, "will have eight children or more, who run about in winter with bare heads and bare feet and a little jacket on their backs, live on nothing but bread and eels, and on that grow fat and stout," which alleged salutary results applied to the stronger constituted only; the weaker died off.[53] The contemptuous manner in which the worker was looked down upon may be judged from this sentence in De la Chesnaye's Memoir: "M. de Lauzon was not liked, because of the little care he took in maintaining his dignity, living as he did without a servant, and eating only pork and pease, like a mechanic or peasant." [54]

Such manufactories as existed were often conducted by the monks,[55] thus placing the Church in the double capacity of theological and employing master. Mendicants and vagrants

[53] Parkman's *Old Régime in Canada*, Vol. II, p. 39.
[54] *Report on Canadian Archives,* 1899 Supplement.
[55] Thus the Hospital Monks of Montreal were given, in 1698, authority to establish manufactories for arts and trades on their premises.— *Ibid.,* p. 97.

were already in evidence. As early as 1674 a decree of the
Sovereign Council prohibited all begging by able-bodied persons in Montreal;[56] vagrants of either sex were, in 1676, prohibited from living in Montreal without special permission;[57]
an ordinance of May 11, 1676, prohibited all poor and needy
persons from begging in Montreal without a certificate from
the parish priest.[58] On May 12, 1686, an ordinance was issued
against vagrants at Port Royal.[59]

Cruel and Barbaric Punishments

Common soldiers were brutally lashed and put to the torture.[60] It was ordered, in 1687, that deporting women of
" bad character " to France was not a sufficient punishment;
they were to be compelled to do heavy physical work such as
drawing water, sawing wood and attendance on masons.[61] For
contravening certain ordinances, offenders were condemned to
kneel with a rope around their necks, holding a lighted torch,
begging pardon of God, the King, and the tribunals of justice
— and then be hung.[62] A soldier of the Montreal garrison and
some shoemakers were accused of " having profaned the sacred
words of the New Testament," and of misbehaving to a cruci-
fix; the soldier was sentenced to be beaten, scourged and to
spend three years in the galleys, and the shoemakers were
also punished, though with a lighter sentence.[63] A Negress
slave found guilty of " setting fire to, and causing the burning
down of the town of Montreal " was hanged and burned.[64]

[56] *Report on Canadian Archives,* 1899 Vol., p. 69.
[57] *Montreal Archives,* Sess. Paper No. 6, p. 94, Vol. 25, *Quebec
Sess. Papers,* 1891.
[58] *Ibid.*
[59] *Report on Canadian Archives,* 1899 Vol., p. 83.
[60] *Report on Can. Archives,* 1887 Vol., pp. ccxlviii and cclix.
[61] *Ibid.,* 1899 Vol., p. 84.
[62] *Ibid.,* p. 61.
[63] *Ibid.,* p. 151.
[64] *Ibid.,* p. 143.

For some slight resistance, law-breaking and violence, one Mathurin Martin was condemned to stand at the main door of his parish church one hour, bareheaded, with irons on his feet, and a placard around his neck inscribed, " A Rebel to the Law! " [65]

Obedience to constituted authority was maintained by branding, lashing, shackling, mutilation and by prisons, the galleys, burning and hanging.

[65] *Montreal Archives*, etc., p. 207.

CHAPTER III

THE HUDSON'S BAY COMPANY

King Charles II found in America an easy way of rewarding servitors and favorites. To one group of these he gave an extensive baronial feudal dominion in Virginia. Another group of intimates and servers composed of Prince Rupert, Count Palatine of the Rhine, Duke of Bavaria, Cumberland, etc., the Duke of Albermarle, otherwise General Monk, who had been instrumental in restoring Charles II to the throne, the Earl of Craven, Lord Arlington, Lord Ashley together with Sir John Robinson, Sir Charles Vyner and other knights and merchants of London, obtained from Charles what turned out to be a far more substantial and enduring gift. This was the charter in perpetuity for the Hudson's Bay Company, granted by Charles II in 1670 to " the Governor and Company of Adventurers Trading into Hudson's Bay."

At the very time that Charles munificently conferred this charter, Canada was claimed as French territory; and in fact the King of France, 43 years previously, had granted a similar charter to a French company. Canada — or at least what was then called Canada — did not become British territory by conquest until more than a century after the granting of the Hudson's Bay Company's charter. It was the asserted illegality of the whole charter that much later caused the most emphatic protests [1] against the alleged usurpations and extravagant claims of that Company. [2]

---

[1] The charter was granted on the nominal condition that a new

[2] In his testimony before the Canadian Legislative Committee of

38

Extraordinary Powers Conferred

The charter granted by Charles II to the Hudson's Bay Company conferred the most extraordinary powers and sweeping privileges.

The Company was endowed with an exclusive and perpetual monopoly of trade and commerce of all the seas, straits, bays, rivers, lakes, creeks, and sounds " in whatsoever latitude they shall be" that lay within the entrance of Hudson's Straits " together with all the lands, countries and territories " adjacent to those waters " not now possessed by any of our own subjects or the subjects of any other Christian Prince or State."

Sovereignty Guaranteed

But these rights and privileges were by no means all. Besides the exclusive trade and commerce, the Company was granted possession of the lands, mines, minerals, timber, fisheries, etc., and was vested with the full power of making laws, ordinances and regulations at pleasure, and of revoking them at pleasure. It could also impose penalties and punishments, " provided the same are reasonable, and are not repugnant to the laws of England"—a superfluous provision considering that little news of what subsequently happened in the vast

passage to the " South Seas " was to be discovered. In 1746, Arthur Dobbs and other petitioners insisted that the Hudson's Bay Company had not carried out this condition, and that its charter was void and forfeited. Dobbs and associates asked in vain for similar powers and privileges.— *Parl. Report of Aug.* 10, 1748, British House of Commons.

1857, William MacD. Dawson, head of the Crown Woods and Forests Branch of the Government at Toronto, stated these facts, and pointed out that the early boundaries of Canada, or New France, undisputedly included the whole of Hudson's Bay. The petition of the Board of Trade of Toronto likewise set forth the same facts.— See *Report from the Select Committee on the Hudson's Bay Company,* etc., House of Commons, 1857, p. 398, and *Ibid.,* Appendix No. XII, p. 435. For fuller details see Chapter IX of this volume.

wilderness controlled by the Hudson's Bay Company ever reached England, although the profits never failed to reach there.

No British subjects were allowed to trade within the Company's territories without leave from the Company in writing and under its seal; if this law was violated all goods of the trespassers brought to England were to be forfeited, one-half to go to the King, and the other half to the Company. No liberty of trade was to be given by the King to any person without the Company's consent. There was to be, it was provided, one vote at the Company's meetings for every £100 put in. All of the territories, forts, factories, agencies, etc., were placed under the absolute jurisdiction of the Company, which was vested with the right of appointing Governors and other officials to preside in its territories, and judge in all causes, civil and criminal, according to the laws of England; it was further provided that criminals could be judged on the spot or be sent to England for trial.

Force Placed at the Company's Disposal

For the protection of its trade and territory the Company was empowered to employ an armed force, appoint commanders, erect forts and take other necessary measures. If any British subject was found trading without the Company's leave, the Company could seize him and pack him off to England for trial. All admirals and other naval and military officers, also mayors, sheriffs and other authorities were obliged, by the terms of the charter, to aid and assist in the execution of the rights, powers and privileges thus granted to " the Governor and Company of Adventurers Trading into Hudson's Bay," otherwise the Hudson's Bay Company of which Prince Rupert was named first Governor.[3]   The only payment

[3] The full text of this remarkable charter is given in *Report*

demanded for these immense powers was that the Company was required to pay two elks and two black beavers whenever and as often as " His Majesty, and his Majesty and his successors " should enter their (the Company's territories), etc.

Thus came into existence a Company of mighty and intrenched powers which since that time to this present day has had the most dominating relation to the economic development and the economic exploitation of Canada. The enormous profits, compounded and invested and re-invested with multifold returning profits which the Hudson's Bay has drawn from Canada during more than 240 years of its aggressive existence, can be traced back to the gratuitous charter in perpetuity that Charles II, in a bold " royal stroke of business " granted for a huge territory to which (so far as strict technical legal jurisdiction went) it is a question whether his government had the remotest claim.

Stock Watering Begins Early

The Hudson's Bay Company had not been long in operation before it began a process of stock-watering. In 1676 its stock was £10,500. In 1690 the stock was trebled, not by subscription but by the creation of a nominal or watered stock, and the capital stock was increased to £31,500. By the same hydraulic process the stock was again trebled and declared to be £94,500, and a subscription was paid in of £3,150, which was also trebled. Of the total capital of £103,950 on December 23, 1720, only £13,150 had been actually paid in.[4]

from the Select Committee on the Hudson's Bay Co., etc. (ordered by the House of Commons to be printed, July 31 and August 11, 1857), Appendix No. XI, Enclosure A, pp. 411–413.

[4] These facts are incorporated in the Report from the Committee Appointed to Inquire into the State and Condition of the Countries Adjoining Hudson's Bay and the State of Trade Carried on There, 1749, contained in Vol. 40 of Imperial Blue Books on Affairs Relating

Manifestly there must have been large profits to justify this successive stock-watering. The profits were, in truth, not merely large but great. In response to a summons from the Lords of the Committee of Privy Council for Trade, J. H. Pelly, Governor of the Hudson's Bay Company in 1838, examined the old books and, in a communication dated Hudson's Bay House, February 7, 1838, informed the committee that: —

Great Profits from the Start

" Between the years 1670 and 1690, a period of 20 years, the profits appear to have been very large, as, notwithstanding losses sustained by the capture of the Company's establishments by the French in the years 1682 to 1688, amounting to £118,014, they [the Hudson's Bay Company] were enabled to make a payment to the proprietors in 1684 of 50 per cent.; and a further payment in 1689 of 25 per cent.

" In 1690 the stock was trebled without any call being made, besides affording a payment to the proprietors of 25 per cent. on the increased or newly-created stock."

Pelly went on to say that notwithstanding losses to the amount of £97,500 in the years 1692-1697 because of the capture of the Company's establishments by the French, and the consequent necessity of borrowing money at six per cent. interest, the Company " were enabled, nevertheless, in 1720, again to treble their capital stock with only a call of 10 per cent. on the proprietors, and, notwithstanding another heavy loss sustained by the capture of their establishments by the French under La Perouse, in 1782, they [the Company] appear to have been enabled to pay dividends of from 5 to 12 per cent., averaging nine per cent.; and showing, as nearly as I am able to judge from the defective state of the books dur-

to Canada. Also see Report from the Select Committee on the Hudson's Bay Company, House of Commons, 1857, p. 344.

ing the past century, profits on the originally subscribed capital stock, actually paid up, of between 60 and 70 per cent. per annum from the years 1690 to 1800." [5] Further large profits, as we shall see, were gathered in after that date.

The Company's System Described

The traffic of the Hudson's Bay Company was then and long remained almost exclusively that of furs. These continuing great profits were extracted, it appears, not only from a systematic exploitation of the Indian tribes but also by a rigorous, tyrannical exploitation of the Company's own employes, or " servants " as they were then called. These facts are not conjecture, but were disclosed in the ample and corroborative testimony given by employes of the Company before the Select Investigating Committee of the House of Commons in 1749.

Matthew Sergeant testified on that occasion that the Indians bartered their furs for brandy, tobacco, blankets, beads and other goods; that the servants of the Company were absolutely forbidden to trade for themselves with the Indians; that he had seen one employe beaten merely for going to an Indian tent to light a pipe; and that these punishments were inflicted at the arbitrary will of the Governor of the Company. Sergeant further testified that he heard frequent complaints of the Indians being beaten by the Governor; that but very few of the Indians would steal, and that they were very civil and good-natured when sober. The chief complaint of the Indians, said Sergeant, was that they were allowed too little for their goods. [6]

[5] *Report from the Select Committee on the Hudson's Bay Co.*, etc., House of Commons, 1857, Appendix No. XIII, pp. 427–428. The Company's ancient motto, " Pro pelle cutem "— skin for skin — certainly produced results justifying both the literal and figurative application of that motto.

[6] *Report from the Committee Appointed to Inquire into the State*

Starvation and Lashing

John Hayter, who had been house carpenter for the Hudson's Bay Company at Moose River, Churchill and Albany (on James' Bay) for six years, testified that the last year he was there the Company's servants " were starved, though there were victuals enough in the storehouse "; that men were lashed for trading with the Indians; and that one man, named Pilgrim, died from want of provisions, although there were provisions enough in the factory [agency].[7]

Edward Thompson, a surgeon, for three years in the Company's service at Moose River, testified that he had seen the Company's officials abuse the Indians. "And being asked, if he knew for what reason the Governors beat the Indians, he said, He remembered an Instance of two Indians almost starved, who came down aboard them to get some bread and cheese; upon which the Governor took an Oar and beat them most unmercifully, saying, ' I'll teach you to go aboard without my leave.' " That the Governor could not imagine that these Indians had been trafficking, since he knew they had not one skin; and the Witness thinks his Reason for treating them in that manner was that they would give the witness and the Rest some Intelligence of the Country." Thompson added that he never knew the Indians to pilfer " except when hard put to it." [8]

Shortweighting Practised

That shortweighting was then practised was shown by the testimony of Christopher Bannister, armorer for the Hudson's Bay Company for 22 years. Asked whether the Company did

and Condition of the Countries Adjoining Hudson's Bay, and the State of Trade Carried on There, Imperial Blue Books on Affairs Relating to Canada, Vol. 40, p. 220.

[7] *Ibid.,* p. 222.
[8] *Ibid.,* p. 223.

not give a better price to the Indians than formerly for their furs he replied that he believed not; " for that he himself had been ordered to shorten the Measure for Powder which ought to be a Pound, and within these 10 years had been reduced to an Ounce or two." [9]

The same fact of cheating the Indians was testified to by Richard White who had been for more than 10 years with the Hudson's Bay Company at Churchill. He stated that the trade with the Indians was fixed by a Company Standard of Instructions, and that the Governors never traded lower than the Standard directed, but on the contrary generally doubled the Standard; —" that is, where the Standard directs one skin they generally take two." Testifying further, White stated that one of the Company's servants had been put in irons and whipped for conversing with Indians; that the Company's men were positively prohibited, on pain of forfeiting all wages, from conversing, trading and trafficking with the Indians, directly or indirectly.[10]

Various other witnesses testified that the Company's governors would not allow them to raise even a little grain and vegetables for themselves. The Company allowed no consideration to interfere with its monopoly or profits; it reserved the exclusive right to itself not only to sell but to raise produce. Accustomed now to the use of guns in hunting, the Indians were forced to depend upon the Company for gunpowder; if denied this, it was often equivalent to consigning them to starvation. This fact, as we shall see in a later chapter, eventually produced conditions of the most tragic character, causing frequent and widespread mortality among various Indian tribes throughout Canada.

[9] *Ibid.*, p. 225.
[10] *Ibid.*, pp. 217–219. Of these and similar long-prevalent practices, the reader will find further ample and corroborated details in Chapters VIII and IX of this volume.

Liquor for Furs

When liquor was first introduced, it was brought over from Europe in large barrels, but in the overland transportation it was found convenient to divide it into small kegs. By diluting the liquor with water, a greater quantity, of course, produced a greater amount of furs. Much later the Indians learned that poured on a fire, good liquor would flame up; but if diluted it would quench the fire. Hence the common usage of the term " fire water " among the Indians.

Writing in 1752, Joseph Robson declared that the Hudson's Bay Company never gave orders for " virtue and sobriety until after several hearings in which its barbarity to the natives and their servants was proved by sundry affidavits," and that the Company " had never attempted to civilize the one or sent over a clergyman for the instruction of the other, nor kept up the least appearance of any factory in the Bay . . ." [11] But this display of reformation was of the most superficial and ephemeral nature, intended for public effect. As we shall have frequent occasion to note in later chapters, the process of unmitigated exploitation was carried on by the Hudson's Bay Company for more than a century later.

Thanks to this early parliamentary investigation, we are able to get some salient details of the methods used in the early years of the Hudson's Bay Company which has been and still is so puissant a factor in the economic life of Canada. The testimony of nearly two centuries ago affords some significant glimpses into the methods employed in the primitive accumulation of capital in Canada. It was estimated that by 1857 the Hudson's Bay Company chiefly had pulled £20,000,000 sterling in profits out of Canada. But this sum

[11] *An Account of Six Years' Residence in Hudson's Bay, from 1733 to 1736 and 1744 to 1747*, by Joseph Robson, Late Surveyor of the Buildings to the Hudson's Bay Co., London, 1752, pp. 55-56.

is by no means to be estimated by the present purchasing power of money. During the decades and centuries when money was of greater value than in its later progressive decline in purchasing power, every pound or dollar was of far greater value than subsequently. Judged by modern standards, this £20,000,000 obviously represented an amount many times greater. Moreover, gathered in as it was during the course of nearly two centuries, it was repeatedly compounded by repeated investments and reinvestments.

Here was one of the prime origins of the capital flowing into England, part of which capital went later into factories, mines and other capitalist concerns at home, and part into investments in Canada and elsewhere. An additional source of the origin of English capital was the profits derived from the traffic in Negro slaves.

Of the later history of the powerful Hudson's Bay Company: — its exploitation of the Indian tribes; its wars with competitive trading companies; its supremacy over a stupendous territory, reaching even to what is now San Francisco; its methods and its profits; its demanding and receiving great sums from the United States and Canada for the surrendering of title to territory which it claimed under the grant of Charles II; and its retention of immense and valuable areas, much of which it still owns — all of these facts will be narrated in subsequent chapters. From the Hudson's Bay Company came officials who developed into land, railroad, steamship, and bank magnates — men promoting or controlling transportation and banking systems and owning vast wealth and resources.

CHAPTER IV

WARS OF THE FUR TRADERS AND COMPANIES

In the long and desperate contest between English and French traders to get control of the fur trade, the supremacy gradually passed to the English. This triumph resulted from the purely economic advantages they possessed, and from their ability to supply rum and cloth cheaper than the French.

As early as 1708 the French Government complained to its officials in Canada that the English gave nearly double the price that the French did for beaver; that, moreover, their articles of merchandise were cheaper, and that a remedy must be sought " for this unfortunate state of things." [1] But no remedy ever came. In a communication dated November 10, 1724, to Governor William Burnett, of New York, Cadwallader Colden, a crown official and later lieutenant-governor of that province, set forth conditions in his " Memoir on the Fur Trade." Of Canada he said that " the Governor and other officers have but a scanty allowance from the King, and could not subsist were it not for the perquisites they have from this Trade. Neither could their Priests find any means to satisfy their ambition and Luxury without it. So that all heads and hands are employed to advance it." [2] Then proceeding to describe the various difficulties of the French in transporting goods via the St. Lawrence, Colden went on : —

---

[1] *Report on Canadian Archives,* 1899 Vol., p. 414.
[2] London Documents, *Documents Relating to the Colonial History of the State of New York,* Vol. V, p. 727. (For purposes of abbreviation these documents are frequently referred to hereafter as *N. Y. Col. Docs.*)

" Besides these difficulties in the Transportation, the French labor under greater in the purchasing of Indian goods proper for the Indian market, for the most considerable and most valuable part of their Cargo consists in Strouds, Duffils, Blankets and other Woolens which are bought at a much cheaper rate in England than in France. The Strouds which the Indians value more than any other clothing, are only made in England, and must be transported into France before they can be carried to Canada.

" Rum is another considerable Branch of the Indian Trade, which the French want, by reason they have no commodities in Canada fit [to exchange] for the West India Markets. This they supply with Brandy at a much dearer rate than Rum can be purchased at New York though of no more value with the Indians. Generally all the goods used in the Indian Trade except Gunpowder and a few trinkets are sold at Montreal for twice their value at Albany, [N. Y.] " The English, Colden concluded, had much the advantage of the French, " and the Indians will certainly buy where they can at the cheapest rate." [3]

English Traders Sell Cheaper than the French

The reports of the French officials confirmed Colden's statements. The English, reported De Vaudreuil and Begon, May 7, 1726, in their memorandum on the " Affairs of Canada," " adopt every means to accomplish their purpose; making presents to the Indians, furnishing them goods at a very low rate, and supplying them with Rum which is their favorite beverage." They added that Sieur de Longueuil, in the course of his voyage to Niagara, met more than 100 canoes carrying peltries to the English and carrying back rum.[4]

[3] *Ibid.*, pp. 729–730. All of the strouds carried by the French into Indian territories, as well as other large quantities of goods for use among the French themselves were conveyed from Albany to Montreal.
[4] Paris Docs., *N. Y. Col. Docs.*, Vol. IX, p. 953.

The British Government issued orders prohibiting the debauching of Indians with rum, but it was impossible to enforce
this order in the great stretches of wilderness far removed
from official eyes.

Moreover, many of the officials not only connived at the
traffic but were themselves financially interested in the trading operations. A petition, in 1764, signed by many of the
foremost merchants in the province of New York — men who
became founders of rich and aristocratic American families —
Henry Bleeker, John De Puyster, Abraham Schuyler, and
sundry others — sent a remonstrance to the Lords of Trade
against the order prohibiting rum. Complaining that the prohibition against rum and other liquors had resulted in a considerable decrease of trade, they protested that the prohibition was an infringement upon the Indians' "liberty of
trade"; highly solicitous were they of the full and unrestricted
right of the Indians to submit to debauchery, cheating and
impoverishment. "Whereas," the petition read on, "when the
Vent of liquors is allow'd amongst them, it spurs them on to
an unwearied application in hunting in order to supply the
Trading places with Furs and Skins in exchange for
Liquors." [5]

Cheap Rum Beats Dear Brandy

The war of the fur traders resolved itself in one aspect,
then, into rum against brandy; and rum, the cheaper drink,
succeeded in winning the Indians' trade in the contested districts.

Of the profits of the French East India Company there
is little available record; dispatches from Canada, in 1749, to
the French Government stated that the "India Company has
experienced no real loss, as it pretends, but even that in the
two years of 1746 and 1747 it has realized a profit from the

[5] London Docs., *N. Y. Col. Docs.*, Vol. VII, p. 613.

Beaver trade of 430,785 livres." [6] Lieutenant-Governor Milnes informed Lord Hobart, in 1802, that the entire value of furs exported by the French East India Company (which had had the sole privilege of exporting beaver peltries), never exceeded £140,000 sterling, and that it was often less, particularly in 1754, when it amounted to £64,000, and in 1755 to £52,000 only, when it was considered a declining trade.[7] It was during this time that Marquis De La Jonquiere (Governor of Canada from 1749-1752), arrogated to himself a monopoly of the peltry traffic, and amassed an immense fortune; an incorrigible miser, he denied himself the veriest necessities of life even in his last moments.

The commercial superiority of the English was rapidly undermining the French traders and merchants everywhere, despite the advantage that the French had of drastic laws and armed forces. This constant process was assisted by the prevalence of widespread corruption and graft among French officials in Canada, which had much to do with preparing the way for British conquest.

Official Graft and Corruption

Heading the band of official pirates was Intendant Francois Bigot. His chief confederate was Joseph Cadet, son of a Quebec butcher. Bigot, in 1756, got Joseph Cadet appointed Commissary General. In the next two years the industrious Cadet, well seconded by his accomplices, P'ean, Maurin, Corpron and Pennisseault, sold to the King, as the State, for about 23,000,000 francs, army provisions and other supplies which had cost them 11,000,000 francs. The audacious plunderers pocketed a profit of about 12,000,000 francs.

But this was only one of their numerous ways of grafting.

[6] Paris Docs., *N. Y. Col. Docs.,* Vol. X, p. 201.
[7] *Canadian Archives,* Series Q., Vol. 89, p. 144.

They accumulated fortunes from the transportation of military stores and in other lines of similar activity, and they speculated in grain and other commodities of which Bigot, by reason of his authority, was conveniently able to raise or depress the price with the most agreeable results.

Meanwhile Bigot was giving sumptuous entertainments at his palace in Quebec and gambling lavishly; he lost 204,000 francs in 1758,— not an irremediable disaster, by any means, since he well knew how to refill his chest. Cadet became the richest man in the colony.[8]

The King's Minister in France soon knew of this great plundering. "I am no longer astonished that immense fortunes are seen in Canada," wrote Berryer to Bigot, January 19, 1759. General Montcalm wrote from Montreal to Versailles three months later, declaring that the Colony was going to ruin because of Governor Vaudreuil's incapacity and the rapacity of Bigot and accomplices who were busy enriching themselves.[9]

Thefts of 24,000,000 Francs

The full thefts of Bigot and his crew amounted to perhaps 24,000,000 francs. The testimony at Cadet's trial in Paris showed that both civil and military officers at all the principal forts had been bribed to attest the legitimacy of his accounts.[10] Bigot and another were banished for life and their property confiscated, and certain other members of the clique were banished for a limited period. The total amount in restitution that the judgment of the court, in 1763, compelled Bigot and his numerous band of confederates to pay was

[8] Parkman's *Montcalm and Wolfe*, Vol. II, p. 28.
[9] *Report on Can. Archives*, 1887 Vol, p. ccxix.
[10] Parkman quotes a writer of the time on Canada: "This is the land of abuses, ignorance, prejudice and all that is monstrous in government. Peculation, monopoly and plunder have become a bottomless abyss." *Montcalm and Wolfe*, Vol. II, p. 29.

11,400,000 francs, of which sum Cadet was condemned to pay 6,000,000 francs.[11]   This crew of grafters could congratulate themselves on their easy sentences; they were not put to the torture, as they had ordered done to common soldiers, and they completely escaped that lashing, shackling, mutilating, branding or hanging to which they, during the very time that they were committing their enormous frauds and thefts, had relentlessly condemned poor offenders whose only crime was that they had committed some petty theft or violated some inconsequential law.

English Become Masters of the Fur Trade

Following the battle of Quebec and the British conquest of Canada, the English became absolute masters of the fur trade.

Reporting, on April 24, 1780, to General Haldimand on the state of the fur trade, Charles Grant, a leading fur trader, estimated that in recent years it had produced an annual return to Great Britain in furs of £200,000 sterling.   There were, perhaps, he stated, 90 to 100 canoes in the fur trade yearly leaving Montreal alone for the Great Lakes; and that besides carrying dry goods, " every canoe carries about 200 gallons of rum and wine." [12]

Lieutenant-Governor Milnes reported to Lord Hobart, in 1802, that, " Since the Conquest the Spirit of British Commerce has brought the Fur Trade into Regular Form; it is now carried on upon System, and a large capital is invested by a Company of Merchants long since known by the name of the North West Company, who have extended the Fur Trade very far into the Interior of the North West parts of this Continent, where they have established numerous Trading

---

[11] *Report on Can. Archives,* 1899 Vol., pp. 187–189.
[12] *Report on Can. Archives,* 1888 Vol., Note E., pp. 59–60.

Houses." [13]   Lieutenant-Governor Milnes, it may be remarked, was extremely partial to the schemes and demands of the powerful fur traders who, in return for his good-will, preserved a discreet silence on the extensive land grants fraudulently given under his administration.   Milnes was not only generous to others in this respect but to himself; he contrived to get 48,082 acres of the public domain by signature of the Duke of Portland, Governor General of Canada. Nearly all of the leading men in the North West Company likewise profited by gratuitous gifts of public land made by Milnes.[14]   We shall have need of referring to these facts more in detail hereafter.

The North West Company

Formed by a number of Montreal merchants and mercantile firms, the North West Company, a distinctively Canadian concern, developed into the most formidable competitor of the Hudson's Bay Company.

Among the original founders of this Company were Simon McTavish, Todd and McGill, Charles Grant, Benjamin and Joseph Frobisher, the firm of McGill and Patterson and five other merchants and firms.   The greater part of the capital used in the later operations of the North West Company was supplied by Alexander Ellice, whose son Edward subsequently became so powerful and leading a capitalist, first in that Company, and subsequently in the Hudson's Bay Company.   A number of Montreal merchants including such firms as Taylor and Forsyth, and Robert Ellice and Company, were, it appears, rolling up fortunes in extortionate charges for goods supplied to the

---

[13] *Ibid.*, 1892 Vol., Note E., p. 135.
[14] *List of Lands Granted by the Crown in the Province of Quebec from 1763 to Dec. 31, 1890.* Printed by Order of the Quebec Legislature, 1891, pp. 8–11. See Chapter V of this volume for fuller details.

British Government for the Indians; Taylor and Forsyth in particular were accused of falsification of accounts and prosecuted.[15]   General Haldiman wrote to Major De Peyster, May 8, 1780, that he had determined to order Indian presents from England " to save the enormous expense caused by the greed of traders." [16]   Much of the capital invested in the North West Company by the Montreal merchants came from this process of charging exorbitant prices on government contracts.

Returns of $250,000 a Year

In 1780 the North West Company estimated its annual returns at £50,000 sterling in furs " which have served to remit to Great Britain in payment of the manufactures imported from the Mother Country." [17]   Basing its application upon its services in discovering and extending trade in new territory, far in the North West, the Company, in 1784, petitioned for an exclusive license.   This petition was favored by Lieutenant-Governor Hamilton on the ground that were the trade " suddenly laid open to greedy and needy adventurers, the returns might be very great for a short period, but the Indians would be drowned in rum, and exclusive of that consideration, it would be the cause of endless quarrels, and bloodshed must be of consequence." [18]

Rum, Violence and Murder

The success of the North West Company, and " the great and rapid fortunes " which many of those in it had amassed, Lieutenant-Governor Milnes wrote in 1802, led to the establishment, in 1800, of a second Canadian Company, called the

[15] *Report on Canadian Archives,* 1887 Vol., pp. 101–116.
[16] *Ibid.,* p. 225.
[17] *Ibid.,* 1888 Vol., p. 61.
[18] *Ibid.,* 1890 Vol., Note C., p. 48.

X. Y. Company, headed by Sir Alexander Mackenzie and
Company. This Company had the command of a capital
equal to that of the North West Company.[19]

Between the two companies a furious competition set in.
Employe often murdered employe in disputes over furs and
territory, and rum was used in the most widespread and shame-
less way to debauch the Indian tribes, each Company seeking
to outdo the other in its excesses in order to get trade, " fear-
less of future punishment, because they know that the Courts
of the Canadas cannot take cognizance of Crimes committed
where they traffick." [20]

The murders and other crimes were so numerous that the
Grand Jury at Montreal, September 10, 1802, handed in a
presentment calling attention to the great disorders in the Indian Country, and calling for a remedy.[21]   At this time the
North West Company had 117 trading posts, and a total force
of 1,058 men.[22]   The number of peltries shipped from Quebec
for the nine years from 1793 to 1801, inclusive, was enormous;
— 137,558 beaver skins, 38,368 martin, 18,349 otter, 11,329
mink, 5,483 fisher, 10,141 foxes, 19,286 bear, 169,811 deer,
144,439 raccoons, 57,151 musk rats, and furs of thousands of
wild cat, elk, wolf, kitt, squirrel, hare, seal and other peltries.[23]

In the war of the two companies, Indians were incited to
pillage and fire upon canoes of the X. Y. Company; attempts
— often successful — were made to debauch and entice away
its employes; and its property was destroyed by treachery
and other underhand acts.[24]   As the force of the North West

[19] *Ibid.*, 1892 Vol., Note E., Milnes to Lord Hobart, " Courts of Justice for the Indian Country," pp. 135–136.
[20] *Report on Canadian Archives*, 1892 Vol., p. 137.
[21] *Ibid.*, pp. 139–140.
[22] *Ibid.*, p. 142.
[23] *Ibid.*, p. 143.
[24] John Richardson to H. W. Ryland, from Montreal, October 21,
1802.— *Ibid.*, p. 145.

Company was two-thirds greater than that of the X. Y. Company, it was not easy for the younger company to retaliate, but it did so when it could. Later — in 1805 — the two companies fused.

Conflict of the Two Large Fur Companies

But this conflict, murderous as it was to both Indians and whites, was insignificant compared to the long and sanguinary war soon breaking out between the North West Company and the Hudson's Bay Company. Here we shall have to turn to the testimony given in 1857 before the British Parliamentary Committee, by Edward Ellice, then loaded with wealth, and a Right Honorable Member of the House of Commons, besides. As Ellice had been connected with all of the companies, his testimony can, perhaps, be accepted as accurate and unprejudiced.

When he went to Canada, in 1803, Ellice testified, "the whole of the Canadian Society, every person of eminence and consequence there, was then engaged in the fur trade, it being the only trade of importance in the Country." Ellice explained that this did not include the seigneurs, and went on: "The trade was carried on with countries that are now civilized regions, and where large cities are established. It was carried on upon the lakes, Lake Ontario, Lake Erie, through the Michigan territory, upon the Ohio, the Missouri, the Mississippi, and in all of the countries to the north of Canada. I was perfectly acquainted with the details of that trade in 1803, and with the persons interested in it."

Carrying on its trade westward of Lake Superior, the North West Company come into acute collision with the forces of the Hudson's Bay Company. The North West Company had the advantage of being directed by aggressive Canadian merchants and traders on the spot; one of its most active

subalterns was Donald Mackenzie, a young Scotchman who
served it eight years, and then became a partner in the United
States of John Jacob Astor who was deriving returns of
$500,000 a year by systematically debauching the Indian tribes
with whiskey and by cheating, impoverishing and indirectly
murdering them.[25]   The Hudson's Bay Company was, on the
other hand, a British concern, directed from London; it had
long since passed into the control of British merchants, although many of the titled aristocracy were among its stockholders.

Indians Complain of Being Wheedled

Bloody collisions between the two companies kept increasing. Ellice testified further that, in 1811, Lord Selkirk, who
brought over a shipload of tenants founded a settlement,
now Winnipeg, on the Red River, and joined the Hudson's
Bay Company. According to a remonstrance sent by Chief
Peguis of the Salteau Tribe, on the Red River, to the Aborigines Protection Society, London, Lord Selkirk had by
dubious methods obtained from that tribe an immensely valuable area of land.

The settlers sent in advance by Selkirk promised the Indians that a great chief who was to follow would pay the
Salteau tribe well for their land, 20 to 24 miles of it, along
the Red River. The tribe then consented to the settlers occupying the land. When the " Silver Chief " (as the Indians
called Selkirk) arrived, he " told us that he had little with
which to pay us for our lands when he made this arrangement,
in consequence of the troubles with the North West Company.
He, however, asked us what we most required for the present,
and we told him we would be content until the following year,

---

[25] See the specific facts in the chapters on the Astor Fortune, Vol. I,
History of the Great American Fortunes, citing government documents.

when he promised to return, to take only ammunition and tobacco.

"The Silver Chief never returned, and either his son or the Hudson's Bay Company have ever since paid us annually for our lands only the small quantity of ammunition which, in the first instance, we took as a preliminary to a final bargain about our lands." This pathetic communication went on to say that this surely was repaying the Indian Chief poorly for having saved the Silver Chief's life, when Cuthbert Grant with 116 warriors had made plans to waylay him — a move frustrated by Chief Peguis and his entire tribe. Peguis bitterly complained that in return for the small quantity of ammunition and tobacco paid yearly to his tribe, the Hudson's Bay Company (which had paid Selkirk's executors £84,111, 18 shillings, 5 pence for his Red River Settlement)[26] now (1857) "claim all of the lands between the Assiniboin and Lake Winnipeg, a quantity of land nearly double of what was first asked from us. We hope the Great Mother [Queen Victoria] will not allow us to be treated so unjustly as to allow our lands to be taken from us in this way." [27]

Selkirk's Heir Gets $420,000

This digression will give an instance of the methods by which a great area of landed property, then of much value, and later of enormous value, came into possession of the Hudson's Bay Company, after enriching the new Earl of Selkirk to the sum of about $420,000, for "proprietary rights" for which (if we may believe the protest of the Salteau tribe), neither he nor the Hudson's Bay Company had actually ever paid. Ellice testified in 1857 that Selkirk, in addition to

[26] *Report from the Select Committee on the Hudson's Bay Co.,* House of Commons, 1857, Appendix No. xviii, p. 449.
[27] *Ibid.,* Appendix, XVI, pp. 444, etc. See sequel later.

being a stockholder in the Hudson's Bay Company, was the proprietor of a large tract of land on the Red River, and claimed that this territory was a free grant made by the Hudson's Bay Company to Selkirk. But Ellice did not touch upon the vital point of when and how the Company had ever bought it from the Indians, and admitted that the alleged grant of the Company to Selkirk was " a private transaction and was never published." [28]

Slaughter in the Trade War

During the course of the sanguinary conflicts between the two companies, an action took place on the Red River, in 1815, between the armed forces, and 16 of them were killed. Selkirk seized William M'Gillivray, principal partner of the North West Company and his property, accusing him of having instigated these murders, and M'Gillivray made counter charges. Kenneth Mackenzie and Simon Frazer were also arrested. Powerful as the Hudson's Bay Company was in England, however, the North West Company was all powerful in Quebec. Its members almost completely controlled the acts of the Government and the Governor in Council, and finally secured acquittal. The well-known Judge Reid, says a biographer, had married M'Gillivray's sister, " and this mighty influence had something to do with the final issue." [29]

Rum the Great Inducement

The methods used in inciting the Indians during this trading war were graphically described by Ellice in his testimony before the Parliamentary Investigating Committee.

" Rum," he said, " was given to the various parties acting

[28] *Ibid.*, p. 323.
[29] Borthwick's *History of Montreal*, p. 398.

in competition, to the Indians and half breeds; the whole country was demoralized; the Indian tribes were in conflict one against the other. In fact, whatever a particular trader carrying on his business at a particular post thought was likely to ruin his competitor and to advance his own interest was done without the least regard to morality and humanity." Ellice further testified that the use of spirits was constantly employed, but blamed its necessity on the American traders. If there was a contest about a trading post on the frontier, he said, "the universal article used to corrupt the Indians is spirits." [30] But, in turn, the United States Government was making indignant remonstrances, charging the Canadians with responsibility for the rum traffic.

The Warring Companies Merge

Such a war was extremely costly, was the conclusion of both companies. Ellice testified that it was he who in 1819 or 1820 succeeded in uniting all interest in the two companies. This merger of the two companies into what has remained the present Hudson's Bay Company was accompanied by two notable incidents. One of these was the claim now advanced by the Hudson's Bay Company (contrary to its previous claims) that its territory extended *west* of the Rocky Mountains. The other incident was the further inflation of the capital stock to £400,000 — an amount still later increased. An Act passed in 1821 gave the Hudson's Bay Company a license for the exclusive trade for 21 years. This rounded out the merger, and assured a definite period of complete monopoly.

From the profits of the North West Company were derived

[30] *Report from the Select Committee on the Hudson's Bay Co.*, etc., House of Commons, 1857, p. 326. Yet during this very time the Hudson's Bay Company was boasting that its missionaries were "civilizing the heathen."

great fortunes which later were conspicuous in banks, steam-boats, railroads, and other capitalist channels. When, for instance, Simon McTavish, one of the heads of that Company, died in 1804, his fortune was estimated at £126,000 sterling, "an immense sum in those days," says a biographer.[31]

[31] Borthwick's *History of Montreal,* pp. 213–214. "The possession of $25,000 in those days," says Borthwick earlier in his work (p. 55), "made a rich man, and $100,000 a very wealthy man."

CHAPTER V

THE LANDED AND MERCANTILE OLIGARCHY

After the British conquest of Canada many of the old French seignories became the property of English, Scotch and Canadian military officers or merchants or of Canadian politicians.

In 1765, General James Murray, Governor, bought from Charest the extensive seignory of Lauzon running six leagues at Point Levy along the St. Lawrence River, and as many leagues in depth, producing in rents and feudal tributes of various kinds an annual revenue of £233 : 15s sterling — a revenue which Murray thought could be increased to £358 : 13s sterling, a year.[1] (This seignory, or parts of it, later became the property of the Government of the Province of Canada; in Chapter XI the details are given of a transaction by which Prime Minister Sir Francis Hincks, James Morris and other high officials formed a syndicate and bought a portion of this seignory from the Government composed of themselves and associates; they did this anticipating that the completion of the Grand Trunk Railway would enhance its value.)

G. B. Hamilton and others became the seigneurs of the De Lery seignory; William Bingham, seigneur of Rigaud; Edward Ellice, with a part of the profits made from the fur trade, bought the seignory of Beauharnais; and William P.

---

[1] *Report of the Work of the Archives Branch,* Dom. Gov't., 1910, pp. 51–53. This seignory contained 387 families, and in produce yielded to the seigneur about 803 barrels of wheat a year.

Christie became the owner of six seignories — the Lacolle, Léry, Noyan, Sabrevois, De Bleury and Repentigny.[2] Simon McTavish, whose fortune of £126,000 sterling came, as we have seen, from his North West Company fur trade, bought the seignory of Terrebonne for the sum of £25,000 sterling in 1803, and there his brother-in-law and associate, Hon. Roderick McKenzie, lived.[3] Other seignories came into possession of still other English or Scotch-Canadian merchants, although not a few of the seignories still were held by the French seigneurs.

These seignories not only yielded annual sums, considerable for the time, in feudal tributes of various and oppressive kinds, but many of them became increasingly valuable for their timber resources and for their privileges of hunting fur-bearing animals.

A New Landed Class Created

Meanwhile, a powerful new landed class was being created by fiat of the British Governors and Government. Under the old seignorial tenure, any individual standing in well with the officials could secure large grants of land, seeing that, according to French law, he was obliged, nominally at least, to concede land to any settler who applied for it in good faith. The various abuses under this custom to which we have referred were evasions, not results, of this law.

In 1763 the British Government abolished the seignorial

[2] *Titles and Documents Relative to the Seignorial Tenure,* etc., Legislative Assembly, Quebec, 1851, p. 175. The value of seignorial estates owned and possessed by British subjects in Canada in 1788 was estimated at £140,000.— *A Review of the Government and Grievances of the Province of Quebec,* etc. (1788), p. 88.

[3] Borthwick's *History of Montreal,'* p. 214. British property in the Province of Quebec, including seignorial estates and the Indian trade was estimated, in 1788, at £1,386,023.— *A Review of the Government and Grievances of the Province of Quebec, etc.* (1788), p. 88.

system of land grants, and in 1791 introduced the system of so-called free grants and free tenure. It was this Act, says Langelier, that "gave rise to the plague of large landholders which has so greatly hindered the settlement and material advancement of the Province [Quebec]." He proceeds to tell that under this system, favored individuals, with the connivance of the Provincial authorities, could obtain a whole township and close it to settlers, and how this had been the result in a considerable portion of the Eastern Townships. "It was under this régime that the system of township leaders and associates originated, which, in less than 15 years, from 1796 to 1809, gave 1,457,209 acres of the best Crown lands into the possession of about 70 persons, one of whom, Nicholas Austin, obtained in 1797 a quantity of 62,621 acres of land in the township of Bolton." [4]

Frauds in Obtaining Large Estates

Describing the secret machinery of the system, Langelier says that, "A person wishing to thus take possession of a portion of the public domain, first came to an understanding with the members of the Executive Council and the persons occupying the highest positions, to secure their concurrence and that of the Governor. He afterwards came to an understanding with a certain number of individuals, picked up at hap-hazard, to get them to sign a petition to the Governor, praying for the granting of land he desired. To compensate them for this accommodating act on their part, he paid his associates a nominal sum, generally a guinea, in consideration of which they at once retransferred their share to him as soon as the letters patent were issued. Sometimes one or two of

[4] *List of Lands Granted by the Crown in the Province of Quebec, 1763 to 1890*, by J. C. Langelier, Deputy Register, Printed by Order of the Legislature, Quebec, 1891, p. 7.

the associates kept a lot of 100 or 200 acres on a grant covering several thousands of acres, but this was the exception,
not the general rule. For that purpose stationers sold blanks
for such retransfers, which forms, as shown in 1821 before
a committee of the Legislative Assembly, had been prepared
and drafted by the Attorney General.

" These frauds were committed with the knowledge of the
Executive Council, several of whose members used this means
to obtain large grants of public lands. Prescott, one of the
Governors of the time, wished to stop this waste of the public
domain, but he brought down upon himself the hatred of the
Executive Councillors, who, headed by Judge Osgood, managed to obtain his recall. Sir Robert Shore Milnes, Prescott's successor, showed himself better disposed towards the
spoilers of the Crown domain, and to give them a tangible
proof of his good intentions, he had a grant given to him of
48,061 acres in the townships of Compton, Stanstead and
Barnston." [5]

Fur Merchants Become Landed Proprietors

As the fur merchants controlling the North West Company
controlled Milnes and the Executive Council, of which some
were powerful members, they, of course, were foremost among
the beneficiaries of land grants.

Simon McTavish received a grant, in 1802, of 11,550 acres
in the township of Chester; and in the same year, Governor
Milnes presented to William M'Gillivray a grant of 11,550
acres of land in the township of Inverness. In 1810 the Ellice family obtained a grant of 25,592 acres in Godmanchester,
and another grant of 3,819 acres in Hinchinbrooke. Five
years later, Governor Lord Drummond granted to Hon. John
Richardson, 29,800 acres in Grantham, and 11,500 acres to

[5] *Ibid.*, pp. 7–8.

Hon. Thomas Dunn in Stukeley. The Frobisher estate comprised 57,000 acres.[6] Langelier says that after about 1806, the system of township associates fell into disuse, and that thereafter almost all of the large grants were made in the name of one individual or of a single family. Every person of eminence, prominence and political influence — which practically meant the all-dominating merchant class from which even the judges often came — rushed to share in the spoils. McGill's possession comprised 38,000 acres; Sir John Caldwell's estate amounted to 35,000 acres. Judge Gale received 10,000 acres; Judges Pyke and Desbarats, 24,000 acres; Chief Justice Sewell, by purchase, 6,500 acres. But it is needless to enumerate further the long and tedious list of beneficiaries set forth in the records.[7] Many of the surveys of these grants, as Commissioner Butler later reported to Lord Durham, were fraudulently made and enlarged.

"These violations of the instructions of the Imperial Government which sequestered the best part of the public domain in favor of a few speculators," adds Langelier, "were encouraged by the Imperial Government itself. Thus, of his own accord, the Duke of Portland gave 48,062 acres to Sir Robert Shore Milnes, and 12,000 acres to each of the members of the Executive Council constituting the Land Commission which had given all the extravagant and scandalous concessions up to that date. Milnes abused his position "to enrich a handful of favorites" none of whom took "the slightest trouble to fulfill the conditions of settlement which were nevertheless in force" so far as the law went.[8]

[6] *Ibid.*, pp. 11–12. See also Lord Durham's Report, *Imperial Blue Books on Affairs Relating to Canada*, Vol. X, p. 63. Here it is stated that the Dunn estate covered about 52,000 acres.

[7] See pp. 15–19, *List of Lands Granted by the Crown in the Province of Quebec, 1763 to 1890*, etc., Quebec, 1891. Further details of the land grants to individuals are given in Chapter VI of this volume.

[8] *Ibid.*, p. 11.

French Seigneurs Loose Their Hold

Probably Milnes considered himself a paragon of moderation in the granting of lands, since as early as 1800 he informed the Duke of Portland that there were 10,000,000 acres in Quebec at the disposal of the Government, and that these " have actually been applied for." [9]

In that long and instructive communication to the Duke of Portland, Lieutenant-Governor Milnes expressed great solicitude lest the power of the aristocracy should not be sustained. Any Constitution granted to Canada, he wrote, " must rest upon a due proportion being maintained between the Aristocracy and the Lower Orders of the People, without which it will become a dangerous weapon in the hands of the latter." He complained that " several causes unite in daily lessening the Power and Influence of the Aristocratical Body in Lower Canada "— the Province of Quebec. Among these causes he specified the indisposition of the French seigneurs " to increase their Influence or improve their Fortunes by trade." " Hence," he declared, the " Canadian Gentry have nearly become extinct."

Another cause, Milnes wrote, was the overshadowing influence of the Roman Catholic Church and the independence of the priests resting upon a sure and solid revenue-producing foundation.

" The Priests," he wrote, " have (in tithes) a 26th of all the Grain, which may be valued at £25,000 or £26,000 a year, which alone must make their influence very considerable, and especially as the Religious Bodies are in possession of nearly One-Fourth of all the Seignorial Rights granted before the Conquest (excepting those of the Jesuit Estates lately taken into possession of the Crown, as will appear by the Inclosure) :

[9] *Rep. on Can. Archives,* 1892 Vol., Note B., p. 13.

there are 123 parishes and 120 Parish Priests." [10]   Milnes
justified the giving of land grants to Protestants on the ground
that it would, in time, if judiciously done, "form in this
Province a body of people of the Protestant Religion that
will naturally feel themselves more intimately connected with
the English Government."

The Commanding "Shopkeeper Aristocracy"

The dominant class at this time in Quebec and Ontario
were the mercantile and shipping merchants — what Judge
Thorpe, in 1806, described as the "shopkeeper aristocracy."
Writing from York (now Toronto), December 1, 1806, to
Sir George Shee, Judge Thorpe said that this shopkeeper
aristocracy, "with great interest in England, composed of
Scotch pedlars" who had so long insinuated themselves into
favor with General Hunter and who had so long irritated
and oppressed the people, were surrounding the new Lieutenant-Governor.   There was a chain of them, he said, linked
from Halifax to Quebec, Montreal, York, Kingston, Niagara
and on to Detroit.   The system pursued was to "get as many
dollars as you can for [from] the Governor by land," and
after themselves, their families and friends were favored with
unbounded tracts of land in the finest situations, at whatever fees they chose to give. [11]

In the next year Judge Thorpe wrote in the same indignant
strain to Sir George Shee complaining of being "surrounded

[10] *Report on Canadian Archives,* 1892 Vol., pp. 9–11.   Milnes stated
that the priests did not consider themselves amenable to any other
power than the Catholic Bishop.   The population of Lower Canada or
Quebec at this time was 160,000, largely Roman Catholic.

[11] *Report on Canadian Archives,* 1892 Vol., Note D., p. 57.   "Those,"
wrote Judge Thorpe, "whom 'the Family Compact' could not intimidate or frustrate in demands for land were sent to a distance in the
wilderness, while favorites and complying members of the House of
Assembly were granted large and convenient tracts."—*Ibid.,* p. 106.

by the vilest miscreants on earth, who have gorged themselves
on the plunder of every Department, and squeezed every
dollar out of the wretched inhabitants."

Denouncing this shopkeeper aristocracy, as he termed it,
Judge Thorpe was elected to the Ontario House of Assembly
under the express promise that he would expose the flagrant
abuses, land granting and other grievances, one of which complaints appears to have been the charge that the subservient
members of the Assembly all were bribed with donations of
public land.[12]

As the head of this discontented popular party, Judge
Thorpe charged that the Governor was surrounded by a few
half pay captains, "men of the lowest origin," and that he
was directed by a half dozen storekeepers "men who have
amassed wealth by the plunder of England, by the Indian Department and every other useless Department, by a Monopoly
of Trade and extortion on the people; this shopkeeper aristocracy who are linked from Halifax to the Mississippi,[13] boast
that their interest is so great in England that they made Mr.
Scott (their old Attorney) Chief Justice by their advocate
Sir William Grant, that they will keep Lt. Governor Gore in
his place, drive me away, and hold the people in subjec-
tion." [14]

Further remonstrances written by Judge Thorpe contained
more references to the extensive ramifications of the " shopkeeper aristocracy " and the power it unscrupulously wielded
throughout Canada.

[12] *Ibid.*, pp. 97 and 101.
[13] Up to 1805, the North West Company had 95 men stationed in
the territory of the United States. To put a stop to this trade a
proclamation was issued by the United States Government, August 25,
1805, forbidding traders, canoemen and others, not citizens of the
United States, from pursuing their traffic on the Missouri River.
[14] *Report on Canadian Archives,* 1892 Vol., Note D., p. 98. Complaint
of the popular grievances, Judge Thorpe insisted, was prevented from
being sent to England " because the members of the House of Assembly were bribed with Crown Lands."— *Ibid.,* p. 101.

Land Jobbing and Corruption

Judge Thorpe also charged that the public lands were bartered openly for private emolument and public corruption; that public money was not accounted for; that the people concluded that it was embezzled by the officials when they heard that General Hunter had sent nearly £30,000 to England; and that the "shopkeeper aristocracy, who rule British North America with a rod of iron, a voracious set," were an all-powerful clique who not only made the laws but they were "universally the Magistrates and enforce the demands of each other." [15] Judge Thorpe added that he was satisfied that his opposition to the illegality of fees, the land jobbing, and the arbitrary system in force, and his exposure of other abuses had raised against him a host of foes, which was true enough.

Accusing Thorpe of being a "factious demagogue," the traders and officials sought in every possible way to intimidate, harass and discredit him, even degenerating into such petty meannesses (as he charged) as to open his letters and to cheat him of part of his salary.

The popular backing that Judge Thorpe received was not one of sentimental agitation or emotional indignation; it arose from the definite and well-understood material interests of a considerable body of settlers who, seeing the abundant natural resources about them, wanted a free hand in developing the fur, hemp, flour and lumber trade and a command of resources with which to engage in manufacturing.[16] In

---

[15] Thorpe to the Secretary of State, August 14, 1807.— *Ibid.*, pp. 105-106.

[16] *Ibid.*, p. 101. Also in his letter to the Secretary of State, August 14, 1807, Judge Thorpe, after telling of the persecutions and calumnies to which he had been subjected by those whom he had exposed and opposed, went on to say, "I strove to cherish what was in infancy, Fur, Flour and Potash, and to bring forth what was in Embryo, Iron, Hemp and Lumber," etc., etc.— *Ibid.*, p. 105.

other words, it was the beginning of the rebellion of the germinating capitalist manufacturing class — an abortive movement that, although then ending in the dismissal of Judge Thorpe, subsequently broke out afresh and culminated in the rebellion of 1837-1838, led by William Lyon Mackenzie in Ontario and by Papineau in Quebec.

It is, however, by turning to the exhaustive and conscientious report of 1839 by Lord Durham, after his appointment as High Commissioner and Governor-General of Canada, that we get a comprehensive knowledge of the circumstances under which tens of millions of acres of the best lands in Quebec, Nova Scotia, Ontario, Prince Edward Island and other parts of Canada were made during these decades to individuals, to the Protestant Church, or to the great land companies owned and controlled by absentee landlords luxuriating in England.

Immensity of the Land Grabbing

Lord Durham reported that of about 17,000,000 acres comprised within the surveyed districts of Upper Canada (Ontario), less than 1,600,000 were unappropriated by 1838, and this 1,600,000 acres included 450,000 acres constituting the reserve for roads. This left less than 1,200,000 acres open to grant; and of this remnant, 500,000 acres were required to satisfy claims for grants founded on pledges given by the Government. The remaining 700,000 acres, in the opinion of Acting Surveyor-General Rodenhurst, consisted, for the most part, of land inferior in position or quality. "It may be said, therefore," concluded Lord Durham as to Ontario, "that the whole of the public lands in Upper Canada have been alienated by the Government." [17]

In Lower Canada (Quebec) of the 6,169,693 acres in the surveyed townships, nearly 4,000,000 acres had been granted

[17] *Imperial Blue Books on Affairs Relating to Canada,* Vol. X, p. 77.

or sold; and there were " unsatisfied but indisputable claims "
for grants to the extent of nearly 500,000 acres." [18]

As for Nova Scotia, nearly 6,000,000 acres had already been
granted, and in the opinion of the Surveyor-General only about
one-eighth of the land, or 300,000 acres remaining to the
Crown, was available for the purposes of settlement.[19]

The whole of Prince Edward Island, about 1,400,000 acres,
Lord Durham reported further, was alienated in one day.[20]

In New Brunswick, 4,400,000 acres had been granted or
sold, leaving to the Crown about 11,000,000 acres, of which
5,500,000 acres were considered fit for settlement.[21]

Protestant Clergy Get 3,000,000 Acres

To whom, and under what conditions, were given these
great areas of land thus alienated from public ownership?
Lord Durham went into this phase of the subject at length.
Of the lands granted in Upper and Lower Canada — that is to
say, in the Provinces of Ontario and Quebec,— fully 3,000,000
acres were granted for the support of the Protestant clergy.
Much of these lands were obtained, it would appear, by irregular methods.

The Church of England clergy had long been scheming to
put itself upon the same solid economic footing as the Roman
Catholic Church, with its enormous land holdings. " Compared," wrote the Anglican Bishop of Quebec to Lieutenant-
Governor Milnes, June 6, 1803, " with the respectable Establishments, the substantial Revenues, and the intensive power
of the Church of Rome, the Church of England sinks into a

[18] *Ibid.*
[19] *Ibid.* Nova Scotia had been ceded by the French in 1713, and it
was long a debatable question whether New Brunswick was included in
the cession.
[20] *Ibid.*
[21] *Ibid.*

merely tolerated Sect; possessing at the present moment not one shilling of Revenue which it can properly call its own . . ." [22]

But already a system of clergy reserves,— as the land grants were called,— had been established by an Act passed in 1791 which directed that in all grants made by the Government, a quantity of land equal to one-seventh of the land so granted should be reserved for the clergy. These clergy grants were generally lots of 200 acres each, scattered at regular spaces over the entire territory of all of the townships. Even this extraordinarily liberal donation was accompanied, it was shown, by the most glaring frauds by which the clergy benefited.

" A quantity equal to one-seventh of all grants," Lord Durham reported, " would be one-eighth of each township or of all of the public land. Instead of this proportion the practice has been, ever since the Act was passed, and in the clearest violation of its provisions, to set apart for the clergy of Upper Canada a seventh of all of the land which is a quantity equal to a sixth of the land granted.

Illegally Get an Excess of 527,559 Acres

" There have been appropriated for this purpose 300,000 acres which, legally it is manifest, belong to the public. And of the amount for which clergy reserves have been sold in that Province, namely £317,000 (of which about £100,000 have already been received and invested in the English funds) the sum of about £45,000 should belong to the public." [23]

[22] *Report on Canadian Archives,* 1892 Vol., Note C. " Ecclesiastical Affairs in Lower Canada," p. 17.
[23] *Imperial Blue Books on Affairs Relating to Canada,* Vol. X, p. 78. Previous to 1827 the lands reserved for the benefit of the Church could only be leased, not sold, but an Act passed that year gave power to sell one-quarter of the land, and not more than 100,000 acres a year.

But this extensive irregularity in land grants for the benefit of the clergy of great areas of the public domain was by no means confined to Upper Canada. " In Lower Canada " [Province of Quebec] Lord Durham's report continued, " the same violation of the law has taken place, with this difference — that upon every sale of Crown and clergy reserves, a fresh reserve for the clergy has been made equal to a fifth of such reserves. The result has been the appropriation for the clergy of 673,567 acres, instead of 446,000, being an excess of 227,559 acres, or half as much again as they ought to have received.

" The Lower Canada fund already produced by sales amounts to £50,000, of which, therefore, a third, or about £16,000, belong to the public."

" If, without any reform of this abuse, the whole of the unsold clergy reserves in both provinces should fetch the average price at which such lands have hitherto sold, the public would be wronged to the amount of about £280,000; and the reform of this abuse will produce a certain and almost immediate gain to the public of £60,000." [24]

Having thus exposed these flagrant frauds, Lord Durham, probably to avoid the appearance of being too severe upon the all-powerful clergy, allowed them the grace of his mitigating comment that " the clergy have had no part in this great misappropriation of the public property, but that it has arisen from needless misconception, or some other error of the civil Government of both Provinces."

But the documents of the time go to show that not only were the clergy fully aware of the frauds perpetrated for their benefit, but that high Episcopal prelates, such as Bishop Mountain of Quebec and Bishop Strachan of Toronto, obtained large land grants for themselves individually. There is not a scrap of evidence that the clergy ever called attention

[24] *Ibid.*, p. 78. Lord Durham's surprisingly penetrating and comprehensive investigation and report followed the rebellion of 1837.

to the excess land that they thus fraudulently or erroneously acquired or sought to restore it; they maintained a discreet silence, taking with a serene conscience all the land and funds that came their way, and subsequently, as we shall see, protested vigorously when an attempt was made to compel forfeiture or restitution.

Crown Lands Commissioner Dismissed for Corruption

Moreover, the Upper Canada Crown Commissioner of Lands conducting the disposition and sale of certain of the clergy reserves and other lands during a considerable part of this time was William B. Felton who later — in 1836 — was impeached by the Quebec House of Assembly for fraud, corruption, oppression, peculation and extortion, and dismissed from office.[25] The House of Assembly standing committee reported that he had "corruptly and fraudulently" received large sums of money from settlers by representing that he was the proprietor of a great extent of land which was really public land that the settlers should have received gratuitously, and that Felton had caused to be fraudulently granted to himself and members of his family much of a total of 31,475 acres.[26]

Different Sects Squabble

At first intended exclusively for the Church of England in Canada, certain of the proceeds from the sale of clergy reserves eventually had to be apportioned among other Protestant creeds, so vociferous and insistent an outcry did the clergy of the other denominations make to have their recognized share in the distribution of the bountiful spoils.

[25] *Imperial Blue Books on Affairs Relating to Canada,* Vol. No. VII, pp. 141–142. Also *Report on Canadian Archives,* 1899 Vol., pp. 930–932 and 1064.
[26] *Imperial Blue Books,* etc., Vol. No. VII, p. 142.

The Presbyterian clergy, in 1820, had demanded that they be given their share. They pointed out that the Roman Catholic clergy and the Episcopal, or Church of England, clergy were already well provided for, and that the State should come promptly to their assistance.[27] The Methodists made the same demand.

Indisposed to yield even a portion of the largess to these denominations, the Episcopal clergy made a bitter opposition. But the other denominations gained the favorable ear of a select committee of the Ontario House of Assembly, in 1828. This committee rebuked Bishop Strachan for his insinuations against the Methodists, and pointed out that, apart from the clergy reserves, the Church of England always had peculiar advantages in Ontario. " It has been the religion of those high in office and had been supported by their influence and countenanced more than any other church by favor of the Executive Government. Its clergymen have had the exclusive right of marrying persons of all denominations indiscriminately," etc., etc.[28] The committee further dilated upon the enormous gift of 225,994 acres of the public lands and an additional £1,000 a year for 16 years, that had been granted to King's College, controlled absolutely by the Church of England clergy with Bishop Strachan at their head.

Although the clergy of the various Protestant denominations made a great noise, and were able by reason of their influence and compact organization to arrange meetings and concoct petitions, there was a comparatively immense body of men, including those of their own creed, antagonistic to their land-grabbing projects. Church of England clergy completely forgot their 39 articles of creed in order to fight to hold the clergy reserves exclusively, and keep the Methodists and Presbyterians from having any part of those blessed pre-

---

[27] *Report on Canadian Archives,* 1899 Vol., Note A., *Clergy Reserves.*
[28] *Ibid.,* pp. 6, 7, etc.

serves. In turn, Methodists and Presbyterians fought back energetically.

The Landed Proprietors Enter the Contest

Another aggressive element now entered the contest. This was the individual " Landed Proprietors "— men who had got together immense estates in various sections, and who wanted the Government to spend large sums building a system of roads, so that their estates could be made accessible, and lumber and produce hauled.

These proprietors cared nothing about the 39 sacred articles when they conflicted with roads, and in this view they were supported by the mass of settlers who were intensely exasperated that so inordinate a part of the best lands, reserved for the clergy, should have been thus withdrawn from settlement entry to lie uncultivated for years. A petition, signed by more than 10,000 Ontario settlers,[29] was sent to the British House of Commons in 1831. From this petition, a pointed and voluminous one, some extracts only can be quoted here.

Demanding that the proceeds from the sale of clergy reserves be applied to the purposes of general education and various internal improvements, the petition declared that " any kind of ecclesiastical establishment, situated as this province is, is essentially anti-christian and baneful to every interest of humanity." The Church of England, the petition asserted, was really in the minority. Yet the enormous land grants given as clergy reserves were controlled by a body of between 50 and 60 Church of England clergy not responsible to anyone.

These clergy, the petition charged, were intent upon avoiding public investigation, and committed to private and secret

[29] Considering the population of Upper Canada at that time — 400,000 — this number of signatures was proportionately very considerable.

measures to bring about their ends. " The Clergy reserve
lands of this Province," the petition read on, " have been
brought from a nominal to a real and rapidly increasing value
by the labor, industry and enterprise of the population generally; and to appropriate the avails of these lands to the support of the clergy of a minor church or churches, will be converting the labors of the many to the undeserved aggrandizement of a few." [30]

Holding the high political offices in Canada, the Church
of England or Episcopal men treated such petitions dis-
dainfully. Just before quitting office, in 1835, Sir John Col-
borne established 57 rectories for the benefit of the Church
of England — an act that, according to Lord Durham, was
bitterly resented by Methodists, Presbyterians and Irish
Roman Catholics.[31]

The contest was a long and acrimonious one, but the revenues of the clergy reserves could not be loosened from the
hold of the ecclesiastics. In the end the Presbyterians and
Methodists accomplished their purpose, although their share
of the proceeds was not nearly as large as that of the Church
of England. The amounts named in Lord Durham's report
as paid to the clergy from the sale of the reserves were only
those paid up to 1838; the total amounts, it may here be
remarked, paid to the clergy of the various denominations,
from 1814 to after the final settlement, subsequent to the
abolition of the clergy reserves in 1854, were $3,843,997 —
an impressive, even formidable sum for those times,[32] and
constituting the chief foundation on which the economic
power of the Protestant churches was erected.

[30] *Report on Canadian Archives*, 1899 Vol., Note A., " Petition Respecting Clergy Reserves."
[31] *Imperial Blue Books on Affairs Relating to Canada*, Vol. X, p. 66
[32] The specific sums paid to each denomination are set forth in
Chapter VII of this volume.

CHAPTER VI

THE LANDED PROPRIETORS

During this period Canada was dominated by what was popularly called the " Family Compact,"— a term that might be supposed to describe a clique joined and interjoined by ties of family relationships. Lord Durham, however, did not find the term a very appropriate one, considering that there was very little of family connection among the officials, functionaries and other individuals thus united.

Composition of " The Family Compact "

" For a long time," Lord Durham reported, " this body of men, receiving at times accessions to its numbers, possessed almost all the highest public offices, by means of which, and of its influence in the Executive Council, it wielded all the powers of Government. . . . Successive Governors, as they came in their turn, are said to have submitted quietly to its influence, or, after a short and unavailing struggle, to have yielded to this well-organized party the real conduct of affairs.

" The bench, the magistracy, the high offices of the Episcopal Church, and a great part of the legal profession, are filled by the adherents of this party: by grant or purchase, they have acquired nearly the whole of the waste lands of the Province; they are all-powerful in the chartered banks, and till lately, shared among themselves almost exclusively all offices of trust and profit. The bulk of this party consists, for the most part, of native-born inhabitants of the colony, or of emigrants who settled in it before the last war with the United States; the principal members of it belong to the Church of England, and the maintenance of the claims of that Church has always been one of its most distinguishing characteristics." [1]

"The Family Compact" in Nova Scotia, however, seems to have been, as it were, much in the family. Two family connections comprehended five of the members of the Executive Council of that Province; and until almost 1837, when two of them retired from the firm, five were co-partners in one banking house. [2]

Lavish Distribution of Land in Ontario

The granting of vast acres of land to ecclesiastics was only one of sundry effective ways of giving away territory. Another of the methods was granting lands for so-called "public services"— a form that in both Quebec and Ontario, Lord Durham reported, had been carried on with reckless prodigality, in violation of instructions from the Secretary of State. [3]

In Upper Canada 3,200,000 acres had been given to what were called "United Empire Loyalists" or to their children; these loyalists were refugees from the United States who had settled in Ontario before 1787. Many of their descendants, it may be here commented, are today living in affluence upon the increment of the land then given, especially in Toronto. To militiamen, 730,000 acres were given. Discharged soldiers and sailors received 450,000 acres. Grants totaling 255,000

---

[1] *Imperial Blue Books on Affairs Relating to Canada,* Vol. X, p. 53.
[2] *Address of Nova Scotia Assembly to the Crown,* April 13, 1837, *Imperial Blue Books on Affairs Relating to Canada,* Vol. A., "Confidential," 1828–1837, Appendix, p. 30.
[3] *Ibid.,* p. 78.

acres were distributed among magistrates and barristers. To
executive councillors and their families 136,000 acres were
donated.

Five legislative councillors and their families received 50,-
000 acres. To a handful of powerful clergymen, 36,900 acres
were given as their personal private property. Titles to a
lump of 264,000 acres were handed over to persons contracting to make surveys. Certain officers of the army and navy
received 92,526 acres. For the endowment of schools, 50,000
acres were set aside.[4]

To one individual, Col. Talbot, 48,520 acres were given;
to the heirs of General Brock, 12,000 acres, and another 12,-
000 acres were presented to Dr. Mountain, formerly Anglican Bishop of Quebec.[5]

Added to the clergy reserves, these land grants, Lord Durham reported, comprised nearly half of all of the surveyed land
in the Province.[6]

The Same Prodigality in the Province of Quebec.

In Lower Canada, otherwise the Province of Quebec, the
land grants (exclusive of those to refugee loyalists, as to the
amount of which the Crown Lands Department could not

[4] *Ibid.*, pp. 78–79.

[5] *Ibid.*

[6] In his *Reminiscences,* Charles Durand, barrister of Toronto, wrote
that the leading people in Ontario "were land grabbers and were
scions, or principals of the Family Compact, and the worst of them was
Dr. James Strachan," Bishop of the Episcopal Church and one of the
three members of the Executive Council of Ontario. "They wanted to
get as much land as they could, keep it for a rise, let others settle
around it, and increase the value of the vacant land monopolized;
and then, of course, make their fortunes." When, in 1827, Francis
Collins, publisher of *The Freeman* at York, criticised the official
aristocracy of York, and referred to John Beverley Robinson, then
Attorney-General of Upper Canada, as "His native malignity," Robinson (Durand says) caused Collins to be indicted and tried for criminal
libel, and Collins was fined heavily and sentenced to imprisonment.
"This severity caused great sensation and clamor."

give any information to Lord Durham) were: 450,000 acres granted to militiamen; 72,000 acres to executive councillors; 48,000 acres to Governor Milnes; 100,000 acres to Mr. Cushing and to another "as a reward for giving information in a case of high treason"; to officers and soldiers 200,000 acres; and to "leaders of townships" 1,457,209 acres.

These totals, added to the clergy reserves, made altogether somewhat more than half of the surveyed lands originally at the disposal of the Crown.[7] Less than a tenth of the land granted in the province of Ontario had been, up to 1837, occupied by settlers, much less reclaimed and cultivated; and in the Province of Quebec nineteen-twentieths of the grants (excepting a few townships on the American border) were still unsettled and in a primitive, wild state.[8] The lands were simply held pending the time that they could be sold at a large profit.

Governing Officials as Land Speculators

Most of the lands granted to the "loyalists" and their children were sold by them for trifles to speculating officials. The price for 200 acres was variously from a gallon of rum to six pounds,— seldom the latter.

Among the extensive purchasers of these lands were Mr. Hamilton, a member of the Legislative Council, who bought about 100,000 acres; Chief Justices Emslie and Powell, and Solicitor-General Grey, who bought from 20,000 to 50,000 acres (each?); and many other members of the Executive and Legislative Councils, as well as of the House of Assembly, were "very large purchasers."[9] As to the militiamen's land grants, Lord Durham reported that they were often disposed

[7] *Imperial Blue Books on Affairs Relating to Canada*, Vol. X, pp. 78–79.
[8] *Ibid.*, p. 79.
[9] *Ibid.*

of for a mere trifle to land speculators who never settled.[10] The fraudulent means by which the "Leaders and Associates" in Lower Canada obtained 1,457,209 acres were described by Lord Durham at length.[11]

Of the large landed proprietors in Lower Canada, many were absentees; in fact, 219,700 acres were owned by absentee proprietors. The remaining proprietors lived generally in the cities of Montreal, Quebec and Three Rivers, "and were men of affluence and of the most influential class." [12]

Almost All of P. E. I. Given Away on One Day

The 1,400,000 acres of remarkably potential rich agricultural soil on Prince Edward Island given away to a handful of individuals was a striking instance of the land jobbing carried on with such flagrant and arbitrary high-handedness. Nearly the whole of this island was alienated in a single day; and the grantees were mostly absentees living in Great Britain.[13] Sir James Montgomery and Sons owned several townships. Lord Selkirk, Lord Westmorland, the heirs of John Cambridge, Rev. J. Macdonnell, Sir J. F. Seymour and others all owned large landed properties.[14] While in the office of Provincial Treasurer, Thomas Haviland (as he testified himself) acted as the resident agent for the properties of Seymour and another large absentee landlord.[15]

These grants were made upon certain conditions, one of

[10] *Ibid.*, p. 81.
[11] *Ibid.*, pp. 79–80. An investigation conducted by Commissioner Buller, in 1838, under instructions from Lord Durham, revealed that 105 individuals or families owned 1,404,500 acres "outside" the seignories — that is, not included in the seignories.
[12] *Imperial Blue Books on Affairs Relating to Canada*, Vol. X, p. 63.
[13] Testimony of Robert Hodgson, Attorney-General for Prince Edward Island, *Appendix B. to Lord Durham's Report*, p. 169.
[14] Testimony of Thomas Haviland, Provincial Treasurer of P. E. I., *Ibid.*, p. 174.
[15] *Ibid.*

which was settlement duties. Lord Durham reported that these conditions were totally disregarded. The Government neglected to enforce them " in spite of the constant efforts of the people and the legislature to force upon its attention the evils under which they labored."

Lord Durham's report continued: " The great bulk of the island is still possessed by absentees, who hold it as a sort of reversionary interest, which requires no present attention, but may become valuable some day or other through the growing wants of the inhabitants. But, in the meantime, the inhabitants are subjected to the greatest inconvenience, nay, to the most serious injury, from the state of property in land. The absent proprietors will neither improve the land, nor will let others improve it. They retain the land, and keep it in a state of wilderness." [16]

On the entire Island only 100,000 acres were under cultivation. Such settlers as came over were mostly English and Lowland Scotch, and these had to pay prices ranging from six shillings, three pence (Halifax Currency) [17] to 20 shillings per acre, or take out long leases.

Two Land Companies Get Millions of Acres

Besides the extraordinarily large land grants given to individuals, enormous areas were obtained by land companies. The Canada Company, headed by John Galt, was one of these. In 1826 it secured 3,500,000 acres in Ontario, for which land it paid the nominal price of from 50 cents to $1 an acre. This Company, it was charged in the Provincial Parliament, then fraudulently evaded taxation by not taking out a patent until it sold the land to individuals, and then the buyers had

[16] *Imperial Blue Books on Affairs Relating to Canada*, Vol. X, p. 86.
[17] Halifax currency: The English pound sterling was $4.85; the pound Halifax currency was $4.

to pay the tax.[18]   The wealth taken by this Company from
Ontario during the nearly 100 years of its existence has been
extremely large, running into many millions of dollars.   The
Company still owns about 100,000 acres of land in Essex,
Kent, Lambdon, Middlesex, Huron and other counties in
Ontario, and is directed from London, England.

The British American Land Company was another land corporation.   Its operations were mainly in Lower Canada,
where it bought from the Government 847,661 acres and subsequently the remainder of 1,044,272 acres for £170,321, 9
shillings, 5 pence, of which sum, £60,000, it was provided,
could be used for improvements.   One of its first directors
was Russell Ellice, and its Commissioners in Canada were
Hon. Peter McGill and Hon. George Moffett.   Although the
Company surrendered part of its purchase in 1841, the
holdings it retained were enormous, and a source of
large and increasing revenues.   From 1844 to 1854 Sir A.
T. Galt, son of John Galt, was its Commissioner in Canada,
and he was succeeded by Richard William Heneker.

These latter details, seemingly merely a record of forgotten
names, are of importance since both the British American
Land Company and many of its officials, as well as other land
speculators, subsequently used part of the capital (thus acquired in selling lands at exorbitant prices to settlers) in
promoting or getting control of banks, railroads, cotton and
woolen factories, mines and other concerns.   John Galt became the president of the Buffalo, Brantford and Goderich
Railroad Company.   The British American Land Company
was instrumental (as we shall see) in founding the textile
mills at Sherbrooke, and likewise were A. T. Galt and Heneker.   To A. T. Galt's multifold later railroad and other activities we shall have frequent occasion to advert;[19] as for

[18] The Toronto *Mirror,* February 3, 1838.
[19] For the present, it may be here stated that A. T. Galt was an

Heneker he became president of the Eastern Townships Bank, was one of the promoters and a director of the International Railway Company, and he became a promoter and director of numerous manufacturing concerns, one of which was the Paton Manufacturing Company — a large textile establishment — at Sherbrooke.[20]

Canada a Dumping Ground for Paupers

Owning such huge areas of land in Canada, it was now to the interest of the titled and other absentee proprietors in England and Scotland to stimulate emigration. Every new settler meant an increase in the increment certain to flow from their land holdings. At the same time, the parishes of England found Canada a convenient dumping ground for their overflow of paupers.

From 1815 to 1830 a total of 168,615 immigrants arrived at the port of Quebec, according to the records of the immigration agent.[21] In his report of 1839 Lord Durham stated that in the previous nine years 263,089 immigrants had landed at the port of Quebec, and that if certain facts had been known, the immigration of the poorer classes would have ceased. Reduced to pauperism by the results of centuries of plundering, extortion and exploitation of the ruling class at home, these emigrants were herded in foul ships and packed off to Canada under the most inhuman and horrible conditions.

active promoter of the Grand Trunk Railway of Canada and of the St. Lawrence and Atlantic Railway (which soon became a part of the Grand Trunk system). As Commissioner of the British American Land Company he subscribed for $100,000 of St. Lawrence and Atlantic Railway stock, and later loaned it a similar sum.

[20] The Sherbrooke Cotton Factory was chartered March 29, 1845, by A. T. Galt and others. The Sherbrooke (Cotton) Manufacturing Company was incorporated with a capital of £50,000, May 27, 1857, by Galt, Heneker and associates. See, *Statutes of Canada*, 1857, p. 815.

[21] *Report on Canadian Archives, Report of the Archivist*, 1899 Vol., p. xiv.

Condition of the Immigrants

Dr. John Skey, Deputy Inspector General of Hospitals, and president of the Quebec Emigrant's Society, testified that the emigrants with families from the South of Ireland in particular, as well as the pauper emigrants sent by parishes from England, arrived in large proportions, in a state of great poverty, although the voluntary emigrants from England had a little money.[22]

Dr. Charles Poole testified that " the poorer classes of Irish and the English paupers sent by parishes, were, on arrival of vessels, in many instances, entirely without provisions, so much so that it was necessary immediately to supply them with food from shore; and some of these ships had already received food and water from other vessels with which they had fallen in. . . . This destitution, or shortness of provisions, combined with dirt and bad ventilation, had invariably produced fevers of a contagious character, and occasioned some deaths on the passage, and from such vessels numbers varying from twenty to ninety each vessel, had been admitted to hospital with contagious fevers immediately upon arrival." For lack of proper food, the immigrants " fall into a state of debility and low spirits by which they are incapacitated from the exertions required for cleanliness and exercise, and also indisposed to solid food, more particularly the women and children; and on their arrival here I find many cases of typhus fever among them." [23]

The testimony given by Dr. Joseph Morrin, Inspecting Physician of the Port of Quebec and a Commissioner of the Marine and Emigrant Hospital, was to the same effect. With few exceptions, he said, the condition of the ships was abom-

[22] *Imperial Blue Books on Affairs Relating to Canada*, Vol. X, Appendix B., p. 83.
[23] *Ibid.*, p. 89.

inable, so much so that the pestiferous odors could be easily distinguished (in a favorable wind or in a dead calm) when an emigrant ship arrived. "I have known as many as from thirty to forty deaths to have taken place, in the course of a voyage, from typhus fever on board of a ship containing from 500 to 600 passengers; and within six weeks after the arrival of some vessels and the landing of the passengers at Quebec, the hospital has received upwards of 100 patients at different times from among them." Children of sick or dead parents were left without protection and wholly dependent on the casual charity of the inhabitants.

Landed Destitute and Turned Adrift

But what was the fate of those immigrants who had escaped sickness?

Even those who had sailed with a little money were often destitute; the extortions of the ship captains on the passage had robbed them of their last shilling.[24] Of these particular emigrants Dr. Morrin reported that they were generally forcibly landed by the masters of vessels, and without a shilling in their pockets to get a night's lodging. "They commonly established themselves along the wharves and at the different landing places, crowding into any place of shelter they could obtain, where they subsisted principally upon the charity of the inhabitants.

"For six weeks at a time, from the commencement of the emigrant ship season, I have known the shores of the river along Quebec, for about a mile and a half, crowded with these

[24] The captain usually told the emigrants that they need not lay in provisions for more than three weeks or a month, well knowing that the average passage was six weeks, and often eight or nine weeks. Laying by his own stock of provisions, the captain, after the emigrants' supplies had run out, obliged them to pay as much as 400 per cent. on the cost price for food, and of nauseating quality at that.— *Ibid.*, p. 90.

unfortunate people, the places of those who might have moved off being constantly supplied by fresh arrivals, and there being daily drafts of from 10 to 30 taken to the hospital with infectious disease. The consequence was its spread among the inhabitants of the city, especially in the districts in which these unfortunate creatures had established themselves. Those who were not absolutely without money got into low taverns and boarding houses and cellars where they congregated in immense numbers, and where their state was not any better than it had been on board ship. This state of things existed within my knowledge from 1826 to 1832, and probably for some years previously." [25]

According to Sir James Kempt, who reported on one particular shipload of immigrants arriving at Quebec, in 1830, those immigrants were described in a letter from the magistrates of a parish in England as industrious people who had been trained to some branch of woolen manufacture, but who would "cheerfully accept any employment that might be offered." [26] It appears that Kempt remonstrated in the strongest terms on the cruelty of attempting to relieve the English and Irish parishes by sending such hordes of paupers to a distant colony when they arrived destitute among strangers. [27]

A Swarm of Impoverished Workers

Few of these people had agricultural knowledge; numbers who took to "the bush" found that they could not make a living, and thronged to the cities. "Many resort to the large towns in the Provinces, with their starving families to eke out by day-labor and begging together a wretched existence," while such others as could go, tempted by a more genial cli-

[25] *Imperial Blue Books on Affairs Relating to Canada,* Durham's Report, Vol. X, Appendix B., pp. 86–87.
[26] *Report on Canadian Archives,* 1899 Vol., p. xiii.
[27] *Ibid.*

mate and higher wages, went to the United States.[28]   The many, forced by stern necessity, remained in Canada.   The Toronto *Mirror,* in an editorial of May 20, 1842, and in numerous other editorials, complained that Toronto was crowded with laborers and mechanics who had completed the railroads and canals in Great Britain, and that large numbers of these impoverished workers were seeking employment.

Famine in Europe soon drove greater numbers of emigrants, many of whom were agriculturalists, to Canada and the United States; and of these, great numbers perished during the passage.   The report of the Commissioners of Immigration for the year 1847 showed that in that year of famine and disease, 17,445 British subjects died on the passage to Canada and New Brunswick, or in quarantine or in the hospitals. This mortality did not include those perishing from contagion disseminated in the principal Canadian cities and settlements.[29]   In 1858 is was reckoned that of the European emigration, three-fourths were agricultural and common laborers whose wages (provided that they obtained work) ranged in Canada from $10 to $20 a month with board and lodging.[30]

Here, then, was an enormous and continuing influx of workers which, added to the proletariat already in Canada, formed a dependent body of surplus labor.   It constituted to a considerable extent the very kind of labor needed at that time in lumbering, building roads, canals and railroads and in agricultural pursuits.   The era of native manufacturing on any important scale had not come, but the era of land clearing, building of roads, canals and railroads was creating fortunes for contractors or owners.   From the swelling vol-

[28] Lord Durham's Report, *Imperial Blue Books,* etc., Vol. X, p. 92.
[29] *Ibid.,* Vol. 27, p. 56, Joseph Howe to Earl Grey, Jan. 16, 1851. Howe stated that perhaps an equal number died on the passage to the United States.
[30] *Canada Directory,* 1857–1858, p. 628.

ume of cheap labor the capitalist could have his pick, employing them at the lowest possible wages.

Cruelty of the Laws

The laws were pitilessly barbaric and cruel. Theoretically, these laws applied to all offenders, but the prosecuting attorneys, magistrates and judges enforcing them were all of the upper class. These officials visited the severest punishment upon poor offenders.

In Ontario the laws were cruel enough. But in the Province of Quebec they were more so. In Montreal 54 persons — some mere boys — were hanged between the years of 1812 and 1840 for various offenses, mostly of minor character. Seven were hanged for murder; twelve for burglary; one for robbing; two for shoplifting; two for larceny; thirteen for stealing horses, cattle or sheep; one for forgery; two for sacrilege; twelve for high treason and two for rape.[31]   In addition, 239 more offenders during this period were sentenced to be hanged but were "graciously" reprieved; of these cases, 39 were for burglary, 15 for robbery, 23 for larceny, 46 for horse, cattle and sheep stealing, 93 for high treason, etc.[32]

For petty larceny, a woman's punishment was often 25 lashes on the bare back; and men, for the same offense, often received 50 lashes on the naked back. If a soldier committed any breach of discipline, his sentence varied from 100 to 500 lashes, and sometimes it was 1,000 lashes. Even during the first decades of the nineteenth century grand larceny was

[31] Borthwick's *History of Montreal*, p. 94. Until its abolition in the reign of George IV, the ancient privilege of "benefit of clergy" remained, by which influential criminals claimed the right of trial by clergy instead of by the civil authorities. Even boys were hanged for the most trivial offenses; in 1813, B. Clement, a boy not quite 14 years old, was executed for stealing a cow.

[32] *Ibid.*

punished by branding the palm of the hand with a red hot iron. Negro slavery was abolished in Ontario in 1793, but remained in force in the Province of Quebec until 1833; if a slave, man or woman, pilfered the least article, 50 lashes on the naked back were publicly given. The pillory was long also a common method of punishment for offenders of all ages and races.[33]

In Nova Scotia, any servant quitting a master or mistress without leave, was subject to arrest, and upon capture was required to serve double the period of his or her bonded term; the term " servant " comprised not only domestic menials but many varieties of laborers. No one could leave the Province without a pass, and any ship captain taking away any such " fugitive," was subject to a fine of £50. Poor children were torn from their parents, and bound out as apprentices by the overseers of the poor. Beggars and wanderers were summarily arrested, and by force hired out for a term not exceeding seven years. Idle persons or tramps were treated " as rogues and vagabonds," and imprisoned. For even the most trivial " felonies " the letter " T " was burned on the offender's left thumb, and the commission of the pettiest larceny entailed a prison term of " not more " than seven years at hard labor. Stocks and lashing were applied for misdemeanors.

Atrocious Jail Conditions

Such were some of the punishments inflicted, early in the nineteenth century, upon the propertyless, no matter what the extenuating circumstances, however young or old, feeble or sick. Driven by poverty into some violation of the minute and drastic laws enacted for the protection of property, they were ruthlessly punished according to the rigors of the prevailing code.

[33] *Ibid.,* pp. 87-94.

Even after this code had been somewhat altered, the penal laws and the prisons continued to be instruments of cruelty and terror.

In their report for 1846, the Inspector for the Provincial Penitentiary in Canada related how "youths of so tender an age as eight years old are sent to the Penitentiary, the rules of which impose constant hard labor and silence, and who are subject to the same punishment as mature convicts." At the same time Prison Chaplain R. J. Rogers reported upon "the extraordinary fact of a convict, only eight years old, having lately been introduced into the Penitentiary; and further that at the present moment, three convicts are under 12, and twelve under 16, years of age." [34]

The varieties and species of abominable tortures and other cruelties inflicted by the keepers of the Provincial Penitentiary at Kingston upon the convicts were graphically described in a legislative report.

For the most trivial offense they were flogged mercilessly with a rawhide or put to the torture of the "Box" or the "Water Cure." Frequently the keepers amused themselves firing arrows at the convicts while those unfortunates were at meals. The bread-and-water and dungeon punishment was extremely common, and if a convict complained of the starvation diet, he was starved still more as a punishment for his presumption. For speaking and laughing, convicts were rigorously punished.[35]

It was at about this time that what was styled a "highly moral sentiment" developed into an agitation against general solitary imprisonment. The reason was by no means exclusively humanitarian. The solitary system was supplanted

[34] *Legislative Council Sessional Papers,* 1846, No. 2, Vol. 5, Appendix G.
[35] *Legislative Assembly Sess. Papers,* 1849, Vol. VIII, Appendix B. B. B. B. and *Ibid.,* 1850, Vol. IX, Appendix R. R.

by the contract system under which convict labor was hired
out to manufacturers who, profiting greatly, were strong in
their praise of the humanitarian spirit which had done away
with solitary confinement.[36]

The Jails and Prisons

Not only were the jails and prisons physically loathsome,
but offenders of all ages and degrees were indiscriminately
herded together in the most demoralizing proximity. We
shall here simply give one instance, as related in the annual
report, in 1849, of Walter C. Crofton, secretary of the Prison
Registration Board:—

"I take the liberty of stating to the Board an instance
which came under my own observation, as one of a case too
numerous, I fear:

"E. D., a girl of about 15 years of age, the daughter of a
very respectable farmer, hired as a servant in a gentleman's
family. She was accused of having stolen some trifling article to the value of 3s., 6d., as laid in the indictment, and
the evidence being very strong against her, she was found
guilty, and sentenced to six months' imprisonment. Many
exertions were used to obtain a mitigation of the sentence,
but owing to the obstinacy of the prosecutor they proved in
vain; she remained the period of her sentence in the ward with
two depraved characters, and came out one of the worst persons I ever met, addicted to every species of vice and infamy.
She had lost all her self-respect, and her parents had cast her
off. She met every attempt to reason with her by the expression that ' she had been sent innocent to jail and that the
law had forced her to become a vagabond '; and true enough
innocent she was, for the very articles she had been convicted
of stealing were found. I can have no hesitation in assert-

[36] *Ibid.*, 1850, Vol. IX, Appendix R. R.

ing my belief that such cases are too common, and yet with a knowledge of such facts, no effort has been made to introduce a system of classification in our District Jails." [37]

The horrors of the penal code were supplemented by those of the civil; under the imprisonment for debt laws, the jails were crowded with the poor whose only crime was that they owed a little money to some landlord, shopkeeper or merchant.

[37] *Journal of the Legislative Assembly of Canada,* 1849, Appendix No. 1 to Vol. VIII. (The pages in these records were not numbered.) "Our gaols," Crofton said further, "are little better than nurseries of crime; old offenders are kept, as it were, to instruct the younger ones how they may best succeed in their profession."

CHAPTER VII

REVOLT AGAINST FEUDALISM

The insurrection, in 1837-1838, led by William Lyon Mackenzie in Ontario and by Papineau in Quebec, was intrinsically one of upspringing capitalist forces, but superficially its character was composite, blending a variety of factors and elements. It is not the purpose here to give any perfunctory chronological or personal narrative of that movement, but to present an outline of the vital economic causes and results.

Grievances of the Rebels

The proclamation issued by Mackenzie, as Chairman pro tem of the insurrectionary Provincial Government of the State of Upper Canada, began by denouncing the "blighting influence of military despots, strangers from Europe ruling us, not according to laws of our own choice but by the capricious dictates of their arbitrary power.

"They," read on the proclamation, "have taxed us at their pleasure, robbed our exchequer and carried off the proceeds to other lands — they have bribed and corrupted ministers of the Gospel with the wealth raised by our industry — they have, in place of religious liberty, given rectories and reserves to a foreign priesthood, with spiritual power dangerous to our peace, as a people — they have bestowed millions of our lands on a company of Europeans for a nominal consideration, and left them to fleece and impoverish our country — they have spurned our petitions, involved us in their wars, excited feelings of national and sectional animosity in counties, townships and neighborhoods, and ruled as Ireland has been ruled, to the advantage of persons in other lands and to the prostration of our energies as a people. . . ."

Then declaring the movement a separatist one, the proclamation enumerated the reforms sought. These included a legislature chosen by the people, free press, civil and religious liberty, free education and other changes not the least significant of which was that of " freedom of trade — every man to be allowed to buy at the cheapest market and sell at the dearest." [1] — the very quintessence of rising capitalism, the moving principle of which was abolition of monopoly and of all feudal restraints, and the assurance of unfettered access to all resources and markets and of unhindered competition.

Abolition of Feudalism Demanded

In Lower Canada the proclamation issued by Dr. Robert Nelson, president of the insurrectionary party, declared for repudiation of all allegiance to Great Britain and provided for 17 different reforms.

Among these were: A Republican form of government; all citizens to enjoy the same rights, and Indians were to be no longer disqualified civilly; dissolution between Church and State; abolition of feudal or seignorial tenure of land " as if such a tenure had never existed in Canada "; imprisonment for debt no longer to exist except in such cases as should be specified by Act thereafter; sentence of death no longer to be passed or executed except in cases of murder.

[1] This proclamation was published in full in the Toronto *Mirror*, Dec. 30, 1837. The tempting reward of 300 acres of the best public lands was held out as an inducement to each volunteer. "Tens of millions of these lands, fair and fertile, will be speedily at our disposal with the vast resources of a country more extensive and rich in natural resources than the United Kingdom and old France."

Other reforms called for were freedom of the press, trial by jury, general and public education, elective franchise and the like. Another provision of the proclamation declared that " all Crown lands, also such as are called Clergy Reserves, and such as are nominally in possession of a certain company of landholders in England, called the ' British American Land Company,' are of right the property of the State of Lower Canada," except such parts as were bought by persons and held in good faith.[2]

Capital to Have a Free Hand

One of the main pleas of the insurrectionists was that capital should have a free hand, especially in the line of development of resources, the establishment of manufactories and of modern systems of navigation and transportation. They pointed to the astounding development of transportation, trade and manufacture in the United States, and asked pointedly why it was that Canada should be so backward? Answering themselves, they replied it was because of the surviving feudalistic conditions which, variously in both Quebec and Ontario placed monopolies of trade and of land in the hands of the Church, seigneurs, officials and companies (largely absentee), and because of the feudalistic laws incompatible with the requirements of an age, the spirit of which was individual enterprise and full personal freedom of trade.[3]

[2] Republished from the Montreal *Herald* in the Toronto *Mirror,* March 17, 1838.
[3] The mercantile community in Montreal and elsewhere, many of whom catered to the seigneurs and other landed proprietors, opposed the insurrection. " The *Daily Advocate,*" read a letter of the times, " has ceased to exist, all the mercantile community having withdrawn their support on its change of front; its staff has now joined the revolutionary journal, the *Vindicator.* The destruction of the British American Land Company is one of their principal objects."— *Rep. on Canadian Archives,* 1899 Vol., p. 877.

In his elaborate report, Lord Durham enumerated some of the grievances. By an Act passed in 1837, he wrote, difficulties were thrown in the way of the employment of capital in banking, and that the banking laws tended to preserve the monopoly held by the few chartered banks in Canada.[4] No man had a right to vote at elections until he paid the whole of the purchase money for public or Clergy land, and as it generally took a period of from four to ten years, he had to wait long before he could vote.[5] There were complaints of great impediments to industrial progress.[6]

Old laws prohibiting the importation of particular articles except from England — laws which originally had been passed to protect the privilege of monopoly in Canada — still prevailed, although the English monopoly had been removed; the result was that almost all of those particular articles used in Ontario were smuggled across the frontier.[7]

But interwoven with this general character of the insurrectionary movement were a diversity of other factors which, although extraneously religious or sentimental, were in reality largely of a distinct economic nature.

Other Causes of the Uprising

Irritated at the refusal of the Church of England clergy to recognize them as an established Church, the Scotch Presbyterians gave much support to Mackenzie; this anger at the Church of England clergy was based not upon the mere refusal of a formal recognition, but because of the absence, of such recognition, which manifestly would have been a *prima facie* admission that the Presbyterians had an equal right in the allotment of the Clergy Reserves.

---

[4] *Imperial Blue Books on Affairs Relating to Canada,* Vol. X, p. 61.
[5] *Ibid.*
[6] *Ibid.,* p. 66.
[7] *Ibid.,* p. 67.

The middle and the working classes complained that the district assessment law was expressly devised to tax them and favor the rich; that the rich not only did not pay their due proportion of the taxes but actually paid less than did those in "middling circumstances." [8] There was a close monopoly of the professions which turned many of the professional newcomers in favor of the insurrection. A British surgeon, licensed in England, could not practice without the consent of the Ontario Board of Examiners. An attorney coming from elsewhere, had to submit to an apprenticeship of five years before he was allowed to practice. Barristers, too, hailing from other parts complained of the discriminations put upon them by Ontario laws.[9]

During the course of the insurrection, the clergy of the favored denominations, professing to speak in the name of God, made the strongest efforts to break down the movement, exhorting the people that they must yield submissively to constituted authority.

At a dinner given on July 25, 1837, to 140 of the Roman Catholic clergy, the Roman Catholic Bishop of Montreal was reported to have said that the clergy "were to represent to their parishioners that it is never permitted to revolt against lawful authority, nor to transgress the laws of the land; that they are not to absolve in the confessional any indication of the opinion either that a man may revolt against the Government under which *he has the happiness to live,* or that it is permitted to break the laws of the country." [10] So ran on this admonishing address.

These were, to be sure, traditionally hierarchic instructions, but they were a curious product considering that when feu-

---

[8] From the Upper Canada *Herald,* republished in the Toronto *Mirror,* Dec. 27, 1839.

[9] Lord Durham's Report, *Imperial Blue Books,* etc., Vol. X, p. 61.

[10] *Imperial Blue Books on Affairs Relating to Canada,* Vol. A, " Confidential," 1828–1837, Unnumbered Doc., p. 4.

dalism was in its last stages a little later, and capitalism rising triumphantly, the Roman Catholic Church and clergy were among the original native investors in capitalist enterprises. With the various reforms demanded, including the abolition of the death sentence for all except capital crimes, the clergy evinced no sympathy.

The insurrection was put down, but it produced many changes, some immediate, others gradual. Imprisonment for any debt under £10 was not abolished until 1849, and other reforms were slowly enacted.

Emigration of Peasants and Workers from Canada

One of the immediate results of the insurrection was the great increase of emigration from Canada to the United States, beginning principally after the insurrections of 1837 and 1838. This emigration included both agricultural population as well as that of the workers of the cities; and the exodus increased year after year.

The lumber market was vastly overstocked; thirteen millions more feet of lumber were produced in 1846 than the market demand justified.[11] Large fortunes had been made in the lumber trade, and the activity had continued on the supposition that further great quantities would be required in the construction of railroads abroad and at home.

Workmen of the cities of Quebec and Montreal, formerly engaged in lumbering, now left in considerable numbers for the United States; there were few manufactories in Canada to employ this labor, and, perforce, they had to drift elsewhere. The same cause led to the exodus of laborers and raftsmen. Another class of emigrants from the Province of

[11] *Report of Select Committee on the Lumber Trade,* Legislative Assembly of the Province of Canada, 1849. In 1846 the quantity of square timber brought to Quebec was 33,300,463 feet; the quantity exported was 24,242,689 feet.

Quebec were young men " of good families " who could not afford to buy land at the prevailing high prices. These families were subject to the indignities of the caste system and to the " exactions of the landed proprietors who impose even heavier conditions than the seigneurs. They hire themselves in the manufactories or on the farms of the United States."

Still another division of migratory workers were the poor families settled on the seignories. These families were forced by debt to emigrate after having sold their lands and moveables, or after their paltry effects had been sold by officers of the law. Such workers, too, sought work on the farms or in the factories of the United States, " frequently at heavy, hard and bodily labor." [12]

More than three-fourths of the Canadians in the United States belonged to the working class. There they were employed in mills, manufactories or as simple laborers, and were living " in a state of degradation really humiliating to our country." Dismayed at losing so many of their parishioners, the priests bitterly complained that many of the seigneurs had refused and still refused " to encourage the establishment of profitable works and useful manufactures for the country, in order to retain exclusively without profit to themselves or the public, the numerous water powers owned by them, and for which they are offered reasonable prices." [13] The committee investigating the startling migration depended much upon the testimony of priests, who, it was critically pointed out in some quarters, had nothing to say of the exactions of the Church.

Yet another matter disquieting to the shippers was the fleeing

[12] *Report of the Select Committee Appointed to Inquire into the Causes and Importance of Emigration*, etc., *Appendix to the Eighth Vol. of the Journals of the Legislative Assembly, Province of Canada,* 1849, Vol. I, Appendix A. A. A. A. A. (The pages of this document are not numbered.)
[13] *Ibid.*

of large numbers of seamen to the United States. Of 20,-
164 seamen at the port of Quebec in 1846, there were 3,549
desertions. The ship masters, studiously seeking to throw
the blame upon anybody other than themselves, accused the
taverns and tippling houses of luring the seamen, getting them
drunk and robbing them. But between the exactions of crimp
and shipping master, the seamen were effectively despoiled
before any other agency plundered them; if in debt, as they
usually were, they were imprisoned; if they deserted, the force
of a special police hunted them down, and if they were de-
tected, threw them into loathsome jails.[14]

At this time, it would appear from a legislative return, the
seigneurs or the owners of seignories owned 7,496,000 acres
of land in Lower Canada, and the Jesuits' estates, not appropriated by the Government, covered 664,080 acres. In 1831
one in every 399 persons in Lower Canada was living upon
alms; in 1844, one in every 151 of the population was a recognized pauper subsisting upon alms. "This shows a fear-
ful increase in pauperism," said the report. The number of
illiterate children was astonishing.[15]

Despite the rebellion of 1837-1838 the Clergy Reserves were
extremely safe from forfeiture or confiscation, and likewise
the lands of the Canada Company and the British American
Land Company.

But the contesting Protestant denominations gained their
point. The legislature of Upper Canada in 1840 passed an
Act distributing the lands among the various Protestant sects,
but this Act was disallowed (or vetoed); and in the same
year an Imperial Act decreed that the funds from the sale of

[14] *Report of the Special Committee on the Act for Regulating the
Shipping of Seamen, Journals of the Legislative Assembly*, etc., 1849,
Appendix to the Eighth Vol. (Pages not numbered.)
[15] *Report of the Board of Registration and Statistics*, etc., *Journals of
the Legislative Assembly of the Prov. of Canada*, 1849, Appendix to the
Eighth Vol., Appendix B, Vol. III.

the land were to be distributed in the proportion of 2 to 1 between the Episcopalians and the Presbyterians. As for the remainder of the Clergy Reserves to be sold, one-third of the proceeds were to go to the Episcopalians, one-sixth to the Presbyterians, and the remainder to be divided among the other denominations. Originally, it may be said, the Presbyterians had been excluded, but, contesting the case in the courts, had obtained a favorable decision in England.

Clergy Denounce Alienation of Their Land Reserves

This proposed arrangement by no means satisfied the large party intent upon obliterating the Clergy Reserves. This party comprised settlers and lumber and other capitalists.

When, in 1850, a Bill was introduced in the Legislative Assembly of Canada to alienate the vested interest held by the Clergy in the revenue from the sale of the reserves (although insuring them stipends), the prelates of the Episcopal Church raised a mighty protest, vociferously calling the measure an "infidel" one. In a circular to the Clergy, Archdeacon Stuart of Kingston, and the Archdeacon of York, denounced the move as one "of direct spoliation of the Church," and as "flagrantly wicked and unjust." The clergy were advised to get together impressive petitions, and were told that if the Church members would "rise and speak in the might of their righteous cause . . . their voice would soon drown the cry of the evil-minded and ungodly faction which aims at her destruction." The petition read that "your petitioners would regard the success of such an attempt as a national sin of the deepest dye and a grievous moral degradation." These petitions were to be forwarded to the Lord Bishop of Toronto before he left for England.[16]

[16] *Imperial Blue Books on Affairs Relating to Canada,* Vol. XVIII, pp. 2-3, of enclosed document, *Clergy Reserves in Canada.*

On September 17 and October 18, 1852, Mr. Brown moved
a motion in the Legislative Assembly that inasmuch as the
Protestant Clergy had got by fraud or error 300,000 acres of
land in Upper Canada, and 227,559 acres in Lower Canada
— in all 527,559 acres — that measures should be taken to
recover the funds paid for these particular lands.[17] Whereupon, the Episcopal Bishops of Quebec, Toronto and Montreal successfully protested against this " proposed confiscation." [18]   In 1854 an Act was finally passed alienating from
the Church all vested rights in the Reserves, but leaving the
clergy certain stipends and allowances " during their natural
lives and incumbrances."

They Get Nearly Four Million Dollars

From 1814 to 1854 the clergy had received $2,181,319 from
the revenues from the Clergy Reserves. Of this sum the
Episcopalian Church in Upper and Lower Canada pocketed
much the greater share — £309,482 sterling in round figures.
To the Presbyterian Church and Synod, £90,891 sterling had
been paid, and to the Roman Catholics in Ontario about £40,-
000.   The Methodists were allotted £21,855 sterling.

After the passage of the Act of 1854, abolishing the Clergy
Reserves, a further sum of $1,662,678 was paid to the clergy.
Of this sum the Episcopalian Church at Toronto received
£188,342 sterling,[19] the share of the Presbyterians was £127,-
448 sterling, and the Roman Catholics received £20,932 currency.

[17] *Ibid.,* pp. 30–31. *Further Correspondence on Clergy Reserves in
Canada.*
[18] *Ibid.,* p. 32.
[19] Bishop Sweatman of Toronto so stated it, but Archdeacon Dixon
of Niagara estimated the amount at £184,342. It was paid to the
Church Society of Toronto (the Church of England clergy). See
History of the Church of England in Ontario, by Bishop Sweatman of
Toronto, and the Rev. William A. Clark, in *Canada; An Encyclopedia of*

The total in dollars of all payments to the clergy from 1814 to the final settlement after 1854 was $3,843,997.[20]

Thus passed away the vested right of the Protestant clergy in those munificent grants of land the retention of which and the revenue from which they had so long held to be all-essential to their orthodox activity. By no means was the abolition of the Clergy Reserves a pleasant matter for the Protestant clergy; they pathetically complained that it left them without solid, revenue-producing property, while the economic power of the Roman Catholic Church was left unimpaired.

Seminary of St. Sulpice Retains Its Estate

This plea was, indeed, true. The force of the insurrection had come and gone without derogating in the slightest from the power of that Church.

Against the Seminary of Montreal (or St. Sulpice) there had long been a bitter undercurrent of opinion in Montreal and elsewhere. Frequently — in 1789, 1804, 1811, and in other years — the legal opinions of the high law officials of the Government were adverse to the claims of the Seminary. But some powerful influence intervened; these adverse opinions were never enforced in the form of judicial decisions.[21]

The Seminary claimed to own, and it held, the seignory of

the Country. Sweatman wrote that, "by a noble act of disinterestedness, all of the clergy but one agreed to leave their shares as a permanent endowment of the Church, receiving the interest only for their lifetime." (P. 334.)

[20] *Editor's Notes on the History of the Clergy Reserves,* by Castell Hopkins, in *Canada; An Encyclopedia,* etc., Vol. III, pp. 154–155.

[21] In their fifth report to the British Government, Lord Gosford, Charles Edward Grey and George Gipps, Lower Canada Commissioners, reported in 1836 that all of them were agreed in the opinion that after the British Conquest, the Seminary of Montreal had no valid title or standing, but was dependent wholly upon the pleasure of the Crown. But they recommended that the Seminary's title be confirmed.— *Imperial Blue Books on Affairs Relating to Canada,* Vol. A, 1837, pp. 145–146.

St. Sulpice in Assumption County, and the Seignory of the Lake of the Two Mountains on the Ottawa; while in the city of Montreal it held three properties of 1,280 acres of land in all — then mostly on the outskirts of the city or at the back of the Island, but in more modern times largely in or near the very center of that city. The Seminary was run by twenty members, " all in Holy Orders," and had four attached priests. Its college contained 1,511 scholars. It exercised feudal rights and demanded payment of feudal burdens; it had an income of about $33,500 a year; and there were also (in 1836) debts of £34,000 or $170,000 due it. The inhabitants of Montreal complained of its exactions and usages, and remonstrated that its farm of St. Gabriel of 300 acres on the western border of the city was used for tillage, thus checking all improvements on that side of Montreal.[22]

An Act of Incorporation

By the stroke of a pen, the priests of the Seminary of St. Sulpice obtained full legal title to their real estate holdings, much of which are untaxed and which, as we have said, are of such great value today.

This confirmation was secured by the passage of an Act, in 1839, during Lord Sydenham's administration as Governor-General.

The Act created the Ecclesiastics of the Seminary of St. Sulpice into a corporation, confirming their title, and provided that the Seminary should commute, at certain prescribed rates, with their censitaire tenants whenever required for all seigno-

[22] *Imperial Blue Books*, etc., Vol. A, 1837, p. 145. Many years before this, the value of the estates of the Seminary of Montreal was calculated at £2,000 a year, besides large tithes in grain and seignorial dues on mutations of property " which, in the Seignory of Montreal, comprehending the whole of the Town, must amount to a large sum." *Report on Canadian Archives*, 1899 Vol., Note C., p. 55.

rial rights, dues and burdens, thus gradually extinguishing seignorial or feudal dues. The Act further required the Ecclesiastics of the Seminary to invest surplus funds derived from these settlements or from sales of lands in public stocks of Great Britain or its Colonies, but allowed £30,000 to be applied in the purchase of houses, lands and other immovable property for income purposes. Finally, the Ecclesiastics of the Seminary of St. Sulpice were to furnish, whenever required, a statement of its estate, income, debts and expenditure to the Governor, Lieutenant-Governor or other person administering the Government [23]— a provision which, so far as we can ascertain, has never been carried out; a public statement of the revenues, income, expenditure and investments of the Seminary of St. Sulpice would undoubtedly disclose some highly edifying facts as to the present wealth and investments of this holy incorporated institution.

Revenues of the Catholic Church

The stripping of the Episcopal clergy of their vested rights in ecclesiastical land grants caused far more trepidation among that clergy than if their entire 39 articles of faith had been abolished.

Sadly, Bishop Strachan had, by way of comparison, pointed out the great intrenched wealth of the Roman Catholic Church left unimpaired by the changes in process. It had, he said, its regular system of tithes and dues, with parsonages, glebe and other endowments; hence had increased in efficiency, wealth and importance. He estimated that the Roman Catholic Church in the Province of Quebec had a revenue of £125,000 a year, a sum then representing a money capital of £2,500,000. At the very low price of six shillings and eight pence an acre, he further said, its extensive land ownings rep-

[23] *Ordinances of the Special Council, Lower Canada,* pp. 520-524.

resented a capital of £700,000. He complained of "the readiness with which Lord Sydenham gave title to a few monks of St. Sulpice, covering the whole city and island of Montreal, with the consent of the Imperial Government, received or implied. . . ."

At the same time that the vested rights in the Clergy Reserves were blotted out, measures were also taken to abolish feudal rights and dues in Lower Canada.

The Onerous Feudal System

It had long been seen that unless this was done, the full unshackled development of capitalism would be greatly impeded. A committee of the Legislative Assembly inquiring into the operation of feudal tenures had reported in 1843 that the system was " in many respects vicious and productive of extreme injury." The feudal tenant not only had to pay heavy dues, but the many reservations to which he was compelled to submit by his lord deprived him of the free use of his land as proprietor. In many instances he was subjected to fines for neglect of certain feudal services,— in some cases, services of mere form. Thus his condition was fettered.

" Instead," went on the committee's report, " of being able to add to his resources by developing such advantages as his soil or its natural position may present in the free exercise of mechanical skill, he is bound to the land for the mere purpose of cultivation, and is dependent on its return for a precarious substance."

Thus, the committee added, if he possessed a mill site, or a spot of land favorable to the construction and operation of machinery, he was prohibited from using it. The reservations in his deed of concession deprived him of the advantage of it, except at a heavy cost. If his crop failed him, he would have to remain in a state of indigence, although able and willing to better his condition by mechanical pursuits. Hence, he was kept in a perpetual state of feebleness and dependence. " He can never escape from the tie that binds him and his progeny forever to the soil — as a cultivator he is born, as a cultivator he is doomed to live and die."

By this means, the committee commented, " all progressive improvement in the country is checked; its resources for advancement in.the arts of civilized life are in the hands of the seigneurs, and they may alone reap the advantage." Every time that land property was sold, the seigneur had to receive his feudal mutation fines of one-twelfth, one-eighth or one-quarter on the price. This fine was levied also on the tenant's improvements, " thereby taxing his industry to an unlimited extent." The committee said of the mutation fine that " although principally oppressive in the towns and villages, it paralyzes the whole country by its influence, for, by affecting property in the towns and populous villages, the seats of wealth and intelligence, its baneful influence is extended in every direction."

Persisting Feudal Servitudes

There were also exercised the feudal rights of preëmption, retrait and that of corveë,— or forced day's labor,— hindering the improvement of the country. The retrait, when misapplied, prevented free conveyance or transfer of property — thus negativing an absolute essential of the development of capital and resources. The corveë was " odious, and humiliating to man, a badge of servitude "; in many instances, the committee reported, corveës had been illegally superadded to the original deeds of concession." [24]

[24] The above are some extracts from the *Report of the Commissioners Appointed to Inquire into the State of the Laws and Other Circumstances Connected with the Seignorial Tenure,* Laid before the Legislative Assembly, Quebec, October, 1843, pp. 69–70.

Lording it completely over their possessions, many of the seigneurs, at the same time, profited richly by the large sums they received for the right that they gave to lumber firms or companies to cut and saw logs on their seignories. But the lines of the seignories and other timber concessions were often indefinite; and when competing forces of lumbermen tried to lumber on disputed territory, "most of the parties were left to fight the matter out by physical force — the forces being brought on the ground for the purpose." [25]

That the seigneurs, both French and English, enforced every iota of their feudal rights against their tenants is evident from the statement of the number of executions lodged in the sheriff's office at Montreal at the instance of the seigneurs. From October 5, 1839, to October 5, 1842, there was a total of 3,440 executions.[26] In turn, the sheriffs extorted fortunes in fees from the misfortunes of these impoverished peasants and manual workers. A committee of inquiry reported in 1849 that Sheriff Coffin of the District of Montreal had a "prodigious income." Likewise other sheriffs reaped fortunes wrung from the scanty means of the poor and unfortunate, whose chattels and other goods were pitilessly seized by the bailiffs at the command of the sheriffs "who charged 20, and often 30 shillings for a writ, although five shillings would have been enough." [27]

In other official reports further facts are set forth as to the merciless rigidity with which hard laws were enforced against the poor; at every turn the impoverished peasant and laborer were harshly proceeded against.

[25] *Report of the Select Committee on the Lumber Trade, Appendix to the Eighth Vol. of the Journals of the Legislative Assembly of Canada,* 1849, Vol. I, Appendix, P. P. P.

[26] *Titles and Documents Relative to Seignorial Tenure,* etc., 1843, p. 175.

[27] *Appendix to Eighth Vol., Vol. I, Journals of the Legislative Assembly of the Province of Canada,* 1849, Report of the Committee, A. Gugy, Chairman.

Feudal Rights Abolished

All of the aforesaid feudal rights and privileges of the seigneurs were abolished by successive measures and means, beginning with an Act passed by the Legislative Assembly in 1854, providing for the suppression of feudal tenures and duties. Surviving in Canada more than 60 years after its abolition by the French Revolution, feudalism had to break down under the irresistible advance of its successor, capitalism. But there was a marked difference between the fate of the French feudal lords, and the good fortune of the Canadian seigneurs. The one faced confiscation and exile or the guillotine; to the other a sum of more than $10,000,000 has been paid,[28] directly and indirectly, since 1867 for the taking away of those " ancient rights " which for more than two centuries had prevailed intact.

[28] Sir John George Bourinot's *Lord Elgin,* pp. 187–188.

CHAPTER VIII

SOVEREIGNTY OF THE HUDSON'S BAY COMPANY

To the individual (or as they were termed, the "independent") traders and to the merchants, factory and mill owners, commercial and railway men, there still remained a large and irritating survival of feudalistic times. In that era when full and unrestricted competition in trade and the widest latitude for the exercise of trading, manufacturing and commercial operations were increasingly considered indispensable to the unhindered development of capital and individual enterprise, the interest of these elements demanded that all feudal barriers be removed.

This particular survival was the monopoly and exclusive powers claimed and enforced by the Hudson's Bay Company. We have seen how, after a long and furious contest, signalized by extensive competitive debauching of the Indian tribes with rum, and by fraud, force, and bloodshed, the North West Company had merged into the Hudson's Bay Company. We have seen also how the Hudson's Bay Company then had secured an exclusive license of trade for 21 years. In 1838 this exclusive license was renewed for 21 years more. The Company now sought to have this monopoly renewed again.

Company Seeks a Renewal of Its Monopoly

The chief argument that it advanced, in 1857, why its monopoly should be renewed was that when there was competition the result was the widespread use of liquor to stupefy and defraud the Indians, and the impossibility of the missionaries peacefully carrying on their work of diffusing civilization and Christianity among the aborigines.

Thus, despite its persistent record of nearly two centuries, the Company, it was sharply pointed out, thrust itself forward in the sanctimonious guise of an errant of colonization and civilization, claiming morality and religion as its chief aims. Concurrently, it never neglected an opportunity, however, of insisting upon and reiterating its ancient exclusive rights and privileges derived from Charles II — rights and privileges which, it declared, were still valid and binding.

But times had greatly altered. The Company now found itself confronted by numbers of hostile small capitalists who, banded in associations and boards of trade, saw clearly that if the resources of the country were to be developed by individual initiative and enterprise, the exclusive sway of the Hudson's Bay Company would have to be terminated and its monopoly effaced, as was happening to the feudalism of the seigneurs and the Church. These aggregated individual capitalists, with all the fresh and determined aggressiveness of their age, set out to fight the claims of the Hudson's Bay Company and to rid themselves of its monopoly. Supporting them were the independent small traders and the proprietary farmers.

They did not lack ample material with which to expose what they energetically charged was the hollowness of the pretenses put forward by the Hudson's Bay Company that by its monopoly it had been able to suppress the use of liquor and to carry on its christianizing operations among the Indians. In the elaborate investigation made by the British Parliamentary Committee, in 1857, the evidence as to the long-continued practices of that Company was so thorough and so conclusive that it seems a matter of great wonderment how it happened that such damaging testimony was allowed to be embedded in the permanent records, considering that many of the British aristocracy, including members of Parliament, were at that very time shareholders in the Hudson's Bay Company.

Treatment of the Indians

The principal witness for the Company, Edward Ellice, himself a member of the House of Commons and of the Select Parliamentary Committee, took great pains in his attempt to show that the merger of the two companies had been extremely salutary. The effect, he said, " has been beneficial to every party interested. It has been beneficial to the Indians; quiet has been universally restored."

Q. " Might not the necessary effect of the whole of the fur trade being in the hands of a single company be to place the Indians entirely at the mercy of that Company with regard to the price which is given them for their furs?"

A. " Of course, it must be so; it must either place them at the mercy of this Company, or leave them at the mercy of whichever competitor for the trade shall give them the most gin or rum, to set them at war one with the other."

If competition should be restored, Ellice added, the employment of rum would be so inevitable that it would be impossible to prevent it; the Hudson's Bay Company, he averred, had taken every possible precaution to prevent the introduction of spirits, but (said he) if an American came across the border, and if there was a trade contest, the article invariably used to corrupt the Indians was spirits.[1]

On the other hand, a protest made by the United States Government, in 1850, against the debauching of the Indians on the frontier by the Hudson's Bay Company, was laid be-

---

[1] *Report from the Select Committee on the Hudson's Bay Company,* etc., House of Commons, London, 1857, p. 326.

fore the Committee. This protest, handed to Lord Palmerston by Abbott Lawrence of the United States Legation, at London, had stated that, " Representations have been made to the Government of the United States from reliable sources that the Hudson's Bay Company annually furnished to the Indians on the north-west frontier of the United States, large quantities of spirituous liquor, endangering thereby the peace of the border, as well as corrupting the Indians themselves."

Lawrence enclosed a letter, dated December 8, 1849, from Congressman Henry W. Sibley, reading: " There exists on our north-west boundary a state of things which calls imperatively for the interference of the Government. I refer to the immense amount of spirituous liquor which is imported by the Hudson's Bay Company annually, not only for their trade in the British possessions, but which is furnished to the Indians who reside and hunt within the limits of the United States. That this evil exists to a very great extent, and renders null all of the efforts of our Government to prevent the introduction of ardent spirits into the Indian country, is a fact which can be established by incontestable testimony, and has already been made the subject of memorials to the proper department. . . ." [2]

The Hudson's Bay Company, through its governor, Sir John Pelly, replied throwing the blame upon the American traders. But it was a significant coincidence that a year and three months after the protest of the United States Government, the Council of the Hudson's Bay Company for the southern department of Rupert's Land, issued an order, May 30, 1851, that after that date no liquor was to be sold from Moose Depot to the Company's officers or servants, or to Indians, or to strangers. [3]

[2] *Ibid.*, Appendix No. 2, p. 369.
[3] *Ibid.*, p. 368. This order was entered in the Council's Minutes.

Widespread Use of Rum

The drenching of the Indian tribes with liquor seems to have gone on as briskly and indomitably in the east of Canada as in the remote stretches of the west. In the vast western expanses, the Hudson's Bay Company was law-maker and law-enforcer, and its officials were supreme dictators. In the older-settled Eastern Provinces it likewise violated laws, and when it did so, it often commanded the support of the very officials whose duty it was to enforce the law.

This was instanced in a notable case in 1831 in the proceedings of the Legislature of Lower Canada (Quebec) against James Stuart, Attorney-General of that Province. One William Lamson had a lease of a stretch of 95 leagues of land, with the exclusive right of trading with the Indians. According to the report of the Legislative Committee on Grievances, the partners and employes of the Hudson's Bay Company assaulted, drove out, arrested and imprisoned Lamson's men, destroyed their huts, then plied the Indians with liquor, debauching and intoxicating them, and seized and took away their furs. When Lamson went to bring criminal action he found, " to his great surprise and mortification " that Attorney-General James Stuart had been retained as private counsel and attorney for the Hudson's Bay Company, and that he had constituted himself as their advocate. The Assembly passed resolutions calling for Stuart's dismissal; he was suspended, March 28, 1831, by the Governor-in-Chief, Lord Dalhousie.

Liquor Indispensable to Trade

Many of the tribes on the Lower St. Lawrence were employed by the Hudson's Bay Company; and as to conditions among the Nipissing, Algonquin and Iroquois tribes, a special Quebec Commission reported in 1858 that, " The unlimited use of ardent spirits, however, seems to be the great check to their advancement. On returning to their settlements with their peltries, everything is sacrificed to the gratification of this passion, and the whites even find it to their advantage to follow them into remote hunting grounds, in order, by pandering to their infatuation for liquor, to obtain, at an almost nominal rate, the fruits of months of toil." [4]

At the same time Fathers T. Hannipeaux and M. Ferard, Roman Catholic missionaries on Manitoulin Island, reported, in August, 1857, that, " Our Indians are not of themselves addicted to drink, but they are supplied with liquor . . . The greater part of these bands subsist by hunting and fishing, and by selling their furs to the Traders of the Hudson's Bay Company. . . . To all who have at all studied the history of the Tribes formerly inhabiting these tracts of land, now so depopulated, it is as evident as that two and two make four that whiskey has destroyed a greater number of Indians than either war or disease." The report went on:

". . . About 20 or 25 years ago, before the appearance of Missionaries in these regions, no barter took place between the Trader and the Indian without the first offering the other whiskey. Frequently even the Trader paid the Indian with liquor. Then could be seen the disgusting spectacle of a whole lodge, from the decrepitude of old age to the child barely out of his cradle, plunged for days and nights in the stupor of a brutish drunkenness."

The missionaries said that they tried hard to bring about a reform, so that there were now few habitual drunkards, but "the heartless trader, who knows their unfortunate propensity, again causes their downfall. The vice of drunkenness is here detested even by those who are addicted to it;

---

[4] *Report of the Special Commissioners, Appointed September 8, 1856, to Investigate Indian Affairs in Canada, Appendix No. 21, Vol. XVI, No. 6, Appendix to 16th Vol. of the Journals of the Legislative Assembly of Canada,* 1858, p. 3.

but the Trader, who looks to his own interest, is pitiless, laughs at the misery and degradation of the Indian, and offers him the fatal draught whenever he can do so with impunity. In the central villages, particularly those more remote from the center,[5] the abuse of strong drinks is more common, but we also remark that the Spring and the Autumn, at the time when the Traders make their appearance for the purposes of trade, are the periods when the evil re-appears periodically, and it is easy to surmise the cause."

The traders, reported the missionaries further, gave the Indians worthless but garish objects in trade; they paid the Indians ruinously low prices for vegetables and fish which they resold at large prices; and by their credit system kept the Indians in a state of slavishness and dependence. The culmination was that the Indian led "a miserable existence, and has nothing but wretchedness in perspective before him."[6]

These reports are merely a few of those in the Canadian archives, and were not part of the voluminous mass of evidence submitted to the British Parliamentary Select Committee. The fact was brought out in evidence in 1857 that the Hudson's Bay Company imported in its ships about 4,900 gallons of spirituous liquors annually. It was notorious that the Hudson's Bay Company exchanged spirits in barter for fur; at the time, on the Pembina River, when Norman W. Kittson of Minnesota, and the American Fur Company, (John Jacob Astor's Company) and the Hudson's Bay Company were in opposition (competition), "the liquor was the principal item of goods which went out to supply the Indians.

[5] Manitoulin Island is 135 miles long, lying in Lake Huron.
[6] *Report upon the Present State of the Great Manitoulin Island, and upon that of the Nomadic Bands of Tribes on the Northern Shore of Lake Huron, Appendix No. 21, Vol. XVI, No. 6, Appendix to 16th Vol., Journals of the Legislative Assembly, Prov. of Canada,* pp. 15–16.

to get the furs." [7] Rev. Griffith Owen Corbett testified that he had traveled 1,000 miles in the Hudson's Bay Company's territories during three years; that he had personally seen the demoralizing effects of ardent spirits on the Indians; that he had seen Indians intoxicated within the gates of Upper Fort Garry (Winnipeg); and that this liquor must have come from the Hudson's Bay Company, inasmuch as there was no other source in the immediate vicinity. He related instances within his personal knowledge of where rum was traded by the Company in exchange for furs.[8]

Independent Traders Suppressed

The point frequently arose that if these practices were committed in the settled regions, what must have been the enormities in the isolated and distant stretches where none but the company's representatives and traders were?

At the same time, so it would appear, the Company took every measure to keep out or suppress individual traders. The Company tried in every way to close up the old traveled routes which would have pointed the way to other traders; if an independent trader ventured to establish himself on Lake Superior or on the other lakes, or in the interior, he was driven out and his property destroyed; he could get no redress; even in 1857, with more modern facilities of transportation, when the Country was somewhat opened up to the jurisdiction of courts not as far distant as in decades previously, "outrages are committed by the Hudson's Bay Company with impunity." [9]

[7] *Report from the Select Committee on the Hudson's Bay Company,* etc., London, 1857, Testimony of John McLaughlin, p. 274.

[8] *Ibid.,* pp. 147–148.

[9] Testimony of Allan MacDonell, *Report of the Select Legislative Committee Sitting in Canada to Receive and Collect Information as to the Rights of the Hudson's Bay Co.,* etc. (embodied in *Report of British Parliament Committee,* 1857) p. 387.

Settlers and Indians Intimidated

Absolutely controlling supplies of every description, the Hudson's Bay Company refused to give even the bare necessities of life to settlers and Indians if its interests demanded that they be denied them. Testifying that he had seen an Indian hung when he was on the Pembina, John McLaughlin was asked by the House of Commons Committee whether he did not know that the Company, by Act of Parliament, was prohibited from trying or executing cases of capital punishment. He knew it, he said, and so did all of the other settlers in the Red River Settlement.

Q. "How is it that the Colonists resident on the spot did not remonstrate against this execution?"

A. "It is impossible for them to remonstrate there; they are too much under control of the Company; the Company would stop supplies." [10]

As to the intimidations practiced upon the Indians by threatening them with starvation, the testimony was overwhelming. Chief Justice William Henry Draper, of the Court of Common Pleas of Upper Canada, agreed that the system established by the Hudson's Bay Company was such as to place the Indians in a state of utter dependence. "If what I read," he testified, "is true, that a silver fox skin, or some other valuable skins, are obtained for three or four tin kettles, of course, it must be so, but I have no knowledge of it as a fact myself." [11]

The principal articles traded were blankets and cottons, some ammunition and tobacco. If an Indian sold furs to settlers, the Company seized the furs and impounded them,

[10] *Report from the Select Committee on the Hudson's Bay Co.*, etc., 1857, p. 280.
[11] *Ibid.*, p. 228.

and imprisoned the Indian.[12]   The Company also refused supplies and provisions to Indians who did not comply with the most minute of its numerous regulations; in such cases, the consequence was starvation.[13]   The Indians had become dependent upon the Company for their powder and shot; they had lost their original mode of hunting; the gun had replaced the bow and arrow.   "To make an Indian really a hunter with the bow and arrow — a deer stalker — takes a whole life; you cannot reteach the present generation; it takes a whole life to approach at that distance the animal for which the bow and arrow came into use.   Of course, that is one of the main causes of their decline."   And if they could not get ammunition the Indians could no longer obtain furs, and in turn provisions and supplies; well knowing this, the Hudson's Bay Company used the fact as a lever to hold the Indians completely under their control.[14]

The Hudson's Bay Company even prevented Indians from trading with Indians, or making presents of furs to one another, or wearing furs, "and tried to use missionaries to

[12] *Report from the Select Committee on the Hudson's Bay Company,* etc.   Testimony of John McLaughlin, p. 263.

[13] *Ibid.*   Notwithstanding such testimony, and the memorials of both Indians and settlers, all of the current so-called histories seek to represent the Hudson's Bay Company as a benevolent corporation.   A typical instance is Begg's work, *History of the Northwest.*   Referring to the Indians he wrote (Vol. I, p. 219) : — " But sometimes disease and death would come among them, and at others, *through their own improvidence,* starvation would stalk in their midst.   It was then that the *kindly offices* of the Hudson's Bay Company's servants would be felt — hungry mouths would be filled as far as the resources of the post would allow, medicines and clothes would be furnished, *and the grateful Indians would feel themselves bound to their white brothers by the greatest of all ties, that of gratitude.*   It was this fatherly care of the Indians that gave the Hudson's Bay Company their great influence over the savage tribes of the North West," etc., etc. (The italics are mine.— G. M.)

[14] *Report from the Select Committee on the Hudson's Bay Co.,* etc., p. 315.   Testimony of Richard King, M. D., who was in the North West for three years.

tell Indians that the anger of God would follow wearing a foxskin." [15]

Of the misery and degradation of the Indians of Lake Superior when dependent upon the Hudson's Bay Company's posts for all of the necessities of life, Allan MacDonell testified that he could give many instances. The Company's system, he declared, was one calculated to destroy the capabilities of the Indian trying to emancipate himself from the bondage "of an avaricious community of trading monopolists." He related a particular instance at Penetanguishine, of how the Hudson's Bay Company agent had forbidden the Indians from gathering cranberries, which were sold at a very remunerative price to a white who had engaged them. The Company threatened that, if they did not stop, their supplies would be cut off during the long winter months. The object of the Company "was to prevent the Indians learning that there was another pursuit whereby they would become independent of the Company, and cease to be its hunters." [16]

They "Rob and Keep Us Poor"

"The Traders," petitioned Peguis, Chief of the Salteau Tribe, at Red River settlement, "have never done anything but rob and keep us poor, but the farmers have taught us how to farm and raise cattle. . . .

"We have many things to complain of against the Hudson's Bay Company. They pay us little for our furs, and when we are old we are left to shift for ourselves.

"We could name many old men who have starved to death in sight of many of the Company's principal forts.

"When the Home [British] Government has sent out questions to be answered in this Country about the treatment of

[15] *Ibid.,* p. 265. Testimony of John McLaughlin.
[16] *Ibid.,* p. 389.

Indians by the Company, the Indians have been told that if they said anything against the Company they would be driven away from their homes.

"In the same way, when Indians wished to attach themselves to missions, they have been both threatened and used badly. When a new mission has been established, the Company has at once planted a post there, so as to prevent Indians from attaching themselves to it. They have been told that they are fools to listen to missionaries, and can only starve and become lazy under them. We could name many Indians who have been prevented by the Company from leaving their trading posts and Indian habits when they wished to attach themselves to missions," etc., etc.[17]

Starvation and Cannibalism

A pathetic and restrained petition, this, it must be admitted. But far in the barren east of Canada the same practices had been going on. A letter on the condition of the Indians in remote Labrador, that had been written by William Kennedy to Lord Elgin, Governor-General of Canada in 1847-1854, was produced before the British Parliamentary Select Committee in 1857. In this letter, Kennedy quoted from a letter that had been received by him.

"You will be grieved," read a passage in this letter, "to learn that the curse which had effect in the old country has extended here, though arising from causes of more frequent occurrence than even the failure of crops.

[17] *Report from the Select Committee on the Hudson's Bay Company,* etc., British Parliament, 1857, Appendix No. XVI, p. 445. Chief Peguis sent with his petition a letter he had received from the "Silver Chief" (Lord Selkirk) dated Fort Douglas, July 20, 1817, highly commending his (Peguis') services to the whites and his influence in favor of the settlers. A similar letter dated Jan. 1, 1835, from Sir George Simpson, Hudson's Bay Company's Governor of Rupert's Land, was enclosed, in which letter Simpson guaranteed Peguis an annuity of £5 sterling a year.

" Starvation has, I learn, committed great havoc among your old friends, the Nascopies, numbers of whom met their death from want last winter; whole camps of them were found dead, without one survivor to tell the tale of their sufferings; others sustained life in a way most revolting, as using as food the dead bodies of their companions; some even bled their children to death, and sustained life with their bodies!"

In another quoted letter of Kennedy to Lord Elgin was this announcement, " At Fort Nascopie the Indians were dying by dozens of starvation; and among others, your old friend Paytabais." In a third quoted letter Kennedy stated, " A great number of Indians starved to death last winter, and —— says it was ——'s fault in not giving them enough ammunition." [18]

It is probable that the William Kennedy here referred to was Captain William Kennedy. He was a son of Alexander Kennedy who had been a Chief Factor of the Hudson's Bay Company. The dates of William Kennedy's letters to Lord Elgin are not given in the records. Judging from the context of his correspondence, in which references are made to the famine of 1847 in Europe, his letters were written a year or two years later.

Sir George Simpson, Governor of the Hudson's Bay Company, who at the time was dubbed " King of the Fur Trade " and " Emperor of the Plains," styled these statements exaggerated, although admitting that there had been some recent cases of cannibalism in the Athabasca country.[19] But little

[18] The above correspondence is included in the *Report from the Select Committee on the Hudson's Bay Company,* etc., British Parliament, 1857, pp. 82–83. The blanks in the final sentence appear in the Select Committee's report: we are, therefore, unfortunately not able to determine the name of the person responsible for these atrocities.

[19] *Ibid.,* p. 82. See his full testimony in the Select Committee's Report. Simpson was in reality the viceroy, if the term may be used, of the Supreme Council or Committee of the Hudson's Bay Company

or no weight, it was not unreasonably pointed out, could be given to Simpson's word considering that he testified that Fort Nascopie was on the Labrador Coast *when in fact it was 400 miles inland.*[20]

Lord Strathcona Begins His Career

At this point authentic historical narrative requires that it should be noted that it was in this identical Labrador territory, and at this time, that the greatest and richest Canadian capitalist of present times — Lord Strathcona and Mount Royal — served his apprenticeship of 13 years with the Hudson's Bay Company, and made his first start on the road to wealth. He was then Donald A. Smith, a young Scotchman, and had been assigned, in 1838, to the Labrador post — " the bleakest corner of the earth "— by Sir George Simpson.

" Some years before Mr. Smith's arrival," says Beckles Willson, Lord Strathcona's laudatory biographer, " the attention of the Company had been directed to this bleak district as a possible field of lucrative enterprise. The Moravian mission-

---

in London. He had full authority over all their Colonial possessions, and held the office until he died in 1860 — a period of nearly 40 years. He was also a powerful bank magnate, first of the Bank of British North America, and from 1859 of the Bank of Montreal.

[20] *Report from the Select Committee on the Hudson's Bay Co.,* etc., British Parliament, 1857, p. 83. During Sir George Simpson's examination, a passage in Thomas Simpson's *Life of Thomas Simpson* was pointed out to him. Thomas Simpson was a distant relative of Sir George Simpson, and for a time had been his private secretary. Dealing with conditions among the Indians in the country between Winnipeg and Lake Superior, the passage in question stated, " Parents have been known to lengthen out a miserable existence by killing and devouring their own offspring." Sir George Simpson in reply reflected upon Thomas Simpson's judgment. Evidence was also placed before the Committee from Ballantyne's book entitled *Hudson Bay.* Ballantyne stated that cannibalism existed among the natives at the Hudson's Bay Company's posts, and instanced the case of conditions at Peel's River, a post in the Arctic circle. Sir George Simpson's chief defense was to characterize these statements as exaggerated.— *Report from the Select Committee on the Hudson's Bay Co.,* etc., p. 84.

aries among the Esquimaux had issued a pamphlet in which, after describing the state of the natives, it was stated that the furs of the fox, mink and martin had been obtained." At first, the trade did not seem promising, but Simpson resolved to persist. Willson tells of the wretched life led by the Esquimaux in hunting for the Company, and describes how, as a reward for all their toil and hardships, after some of them had spent two years on their hunting journey, all that they received " was a little tobacco and a few strings of beads, very few having the means of procuring guns and ammunition."

Willson proceeds to narrate the following important particulars, evidently not knowing of the facts brought out before the British Parliamentary Committee of 1857, or if knowing them, choosing to omit them: " Donald [Smith] came ultimately to be stationed at Hamilton Inlet, where the Company then had two posts. . . . He and his comrades at the post spent most of their time trading in furs with the Indians — particularly the Mountaineers and the Nascopies." After thus placing Mr. Smith's early activities among these tribes, Willson goes on to say that before Smith had left Labrador the Esquimaux had all but totally vanished from the lower coast. Willson tells how the Nascopie tribe had become greatly reduced, but explains the appalling mortality by saying that it was due partly to natural causes and partly to diseases contracted by contact with modes of living of the whites inducing respiratory diseases.[21]

Strathcona in Labrador

Dr. Grenfell relates that it was at the North West River post of the Hudson's Bay Company that Donald A. Smith spent his early 13 years in Labrador. This post was a con-

[21] See Beckles Willson's *Lord Strathcona,* pp. 21–31.

siderable distance in from the coast, and was reached via Hamilton Inlet. Fort Nascopie lay some hundreds of miles northwest. "Early in the last century," says Grenfell of the North West River post, "this was an important place, the residence of the Chief Factor in charge of Labrador." Although the barren lands of Labrador were supposed to be unproductive, yet, Grenfell relates, "this post had a large farm where oats and vegetables were grown." The remnants of the Nascopie tribe still come to that post to trade their furs.[22]

George Gladman, whose father was a Chief Factor of the Hudson's Bay Company and who himself had been associated 31 years as Clerk and as Chief Trader with that Company, testified before the Select Committee of the Canadian Legislative Assembly, in 1857: "No agricultural settlers (properly so-called) are permitted at or near the Company's trading stations, except Red River. Their stations are occupied solely by the officers and employes of the Company and their families, the Indians being the only other residents near the station."[23]

If Willson had read the testimony before the British Parliamentary Committee of 1857, he would doubtless have been more cautious in too conspicuously locating Lord Strathcona and Mount Royal among the Nascopie tribe, and in admitting the extraordinarily large mortality among those Indians; for, as we have already cited, it was those same Nascopie Indians who were terribly reduced by starvation, and who were forced to the awful extremity of eating the dead bodies of their companions, and even to kill and eat their own children!

It was in such a time and place that Donald A. Smith, later created Lord Strathcona and Mount Royal — Strathcona, the

[22] Grenfell's *Labrador, the Country and the People,* p. 142.
[23] *Journals of the Legislative Assembly of Canada, Appendix to the 15th Vol.,* 1857, Vol. XV, No. 4, Appendix No. 17.

most powerful Canadian capitalist of these times — began and flourished. According to Willson, quoting from another writer, Smith was rated a highly valuable employe of the Hudson's Bay Company during the 13 years he was in service in Labrador "learning the secrets of the Company, how to manage the Indians, and how to produce the best returns." He showed, Willson relates further, an "invaluable knack of turning everything to account. ' No matter,' it has been heard of him, ' however poor the post might be, Donald Smith always showed a balance on the right side of the ledger.' He was rewarded, first by a chief tradership, and after ten years more spent on the shores of Hudson's Bay . . . he was appointed a Chief Factor." [24]

Fortune From a Wilderness

In 1856, when Smith was 48 years old, he was chosen to fill the post of Chief Executive Officer of the Hudson's Bay Company in North America, and was stationed at Montreal.[25]

By this time, it would appear, Donald A. Smith's personal fortune amounted to £10,000 or nearly $50,000.[26] It need not be explained that such a sum at that period represented very considerable wealth; in purchasing power it perhaps equaled much more than ten times that amount reckoned by present standards. That in so desolate a country as Labrador, Donald A. Smith should have been able to accumulate the greater part, if not all, of £10,000, was regarded as convincing demonstration of his tenacious capacity. He was, in 1857, it appears, a stockholder in the Bank of Montreal, as were other

[24] Ellice testified in 1857 that the Chief Factors and the Chief Traders of the Hudson's Bay Company were paid in shares. The Chief Factors were virtually dictators in the territory over which they ruled.

[25] Beckles Willson's *Lord Strathcona*, p. 36.

[26] Bryce's *The Scotsman in Canada*. This is a highly eulogistic work.

officers of the Hudson's Bay Company;[27] this was the same Bank of Montreal in which 15 years later he became so dominating a personage, and as to one of the transactions concerning which details are related later in this work.

Of the further career of Donald A. Smith, the supereminent Canadian magnate and distinguished member of the peerage, we shall relate more hereafter in its chronological and proper place.

[27] *Journals of the Legislative Assembly of Canada, Appendix to the 15th Vol.*, 1857, Vol. XV, No. 4, Appendix No. 11.

CHAPTER IX

PASSING OF THE HUDSON'S BAY COMPANY'S SOVEREIGNTY

At this point the essential question incisively thrusts itself: What were the definite results, in concrete currency form, of these long-continued methods? In plain, understandable commercial language, what were the profits of the Hudson's Bay Company, which was directed from London by a sovereign quintet of merchants and aristocrats?

The answer to this question offers no difficulty. Doctor Sir John Rae, who, for 20 years, had been in the Company's service as medical officer at Moose Factory and in the Arctic region, asserted in his testimony that the Company's employes were forced to pay, on goods for their own use, 50 per cent. more than the London price. As for the Indians, they were charged (in furs) more than 200 per cent. in excess of the price that the Company paid in London for the goods which it sold them. The Indians, he said, possibly were forced to pay 300 per cent., but it was clearly established that they had to pay more than 200 per cent.[1]

David Gunn, writing March 6, 1857, from the Red River Settlement to Philip Vanhoughnet, President of the Executive Council, at Toronto, stated that the price of goods sold at the

---

[1] *Report from the Select Committee on the Hudson's Bay Co.*, etc., British Parliament, 1857, pp. 34 and 500 of Report and Testimony. The story has long been current that the Hudson's Bay Company in exchange for old, long obsolete muskets compelled the Indians to pile the most valuable furs as high as the musket. This fact, however, does not appear in the evidence.

Hudson's Bay Company's stores there varied from 100 to 400 per cent. on the prime cost. Gunn further described how by decreeing prices for produce, the Company had the helpless agriculturalist, who had no other market, at its mercy; if the farmer was suspected of infringing any of the Company's many privileges, he was cut off from selling to the Company, and there was no market whatever for him.[2]

Company's Large Profits

But what of the Company's annual profits? Ellice testified, in 1857, that the average annual profits for the previous 17 years had been £65,573, of which £39,343 had been appropriated to the profit of the Company in England, and £26,229 had been annually appropriated to the Factors and Traders in the interior of Canada; the general profits of the Company during that period had averaged 12 per cent. upon the capital.[3]

These profits, however, were simply those extracted from the fur traffic. They did not include the profits from the Hudson's Bay Company's asserted ownership of stupendous areas of land, and from its grain, cattle, horse, sheep, produce, fishery and timber lines of business. Immense quantities of timber in British Columbia and Oregon were cut and sawed and exported by the Company. It had at this time 156 establishments or posts, of which 12 were in Washington Territory and Oregon, in which territory it claimed proprietary or rather possessory rights; and, indeed, it subsequently was able

[2] *Ibid.*, Appendix No. VII, p. 383.
[3] *Report from the Select Committee on the Hudson's Bay Co.*, etc., British Parliament, 1857, p. 326. From these annual profits each Chief Factor received about £617 yearly, and each Chief Trader about £308. It may be said that never has there existed a concern which made economy such a science as did the Hudson's Bay Company. Agnes Laut tells in her *Conquest of the Northwest* (Vol. II, p. 392), how it saved nails when it could use wooden pegs.

to get $450,000 in gold from the United States, in 1870, as payment for the surrender of those asserted rights, under a treaty executed in 1864.[4]

From Newfoundland, thousands of miles to the Pacific Coast, the Company had its chain of trading posts, and it even had a trading post in distant Honolulu.[5] Some of its trading posts were forts, surrounded by grim, high palisades, flanked by bastions, and armed with cannon and with blunderbusses on swivels, with round shot and cannister handy, always ready for instant action. Strong gates guarded the forts; and in the bastions, which were usually three-storied, were ports and loopholes near which abutted stands containing muskets, bayonets and ammunition ready for use. The most rigid discipline, almost military in character, prevailed for even the most menial employes.[6]

Hosts Killed Off or Turned Into Vagrants

The fate of vast numbers of Indians was graphically described in a memorial dated May 18, 1857, from the Committee of the Aborigines Protection Society to Henry Labouchere, Chairman of the British Parliamentary Select Committee on the Hudson's Bay Company.

The Committee of that Society stated that the Indians were the real producers of the huge wealth from the fur trade,

[4] See *U. S. Ex. Doc. No. 220, Forty-first Congress, Second Session,* pp. 1–3. The Commissioner for Great Britain was John Rose, a banker and Canadian politician, to whom frequent reference will be made hereafter.

[5] See enumeration of trading posts in *British Parl. Report of 1857,* Appendix No. 2, pp. 365–367.

[6] All officers and employes had to get up with the ringing of the Fort bell at 5:30 A.M.; at 6 A.M. instructions for the work of the day for the various employes were given by the officer in charge; at 8 A.M. breakfast was served, etc., etc. Every Sunday morning, "all hands" had to attend "divine service," clergymen of different denominations alternating.— See descriptive reminiscences in *British Columbia Year Book* for 1897.

estimated on competent authority at £20,000,000, which had already gone to England. The aborigines were rapidly wasting away, said the memorial, and it cited the statement of Dr. McLaughlin, superintendent of the Hudson's Bay Company's affairs west of the Rocky Mountains, that he believed that nine-tenths of the entire Indian population there had been swept away by disease, principally fever and ague.

" The malignancy of these diseases," the memorial said, " may have increased by predisposing causes, such as intemperance and the general spread of venereal [diseases] since their intercourse with the Europeans, but a more direct cause of mortality was their mode of treatment."

Then describing how immense numbers of animals had been killed, and the increased difficulty of the Indians getting furs, the Committee of the Aborigines Protection Society stated that necessarily the Indians had a harder time getting the necessities of life; and when they did get supplies from the Hudson's Bay Company it was under a credit system so devised as to keep them in debt to the Company.

It was a fact, said the Committee further, that although under the system in force " we have given unlimited scope to the cupidity of a Company of traders, placing no stint upon their profits, or limits to their power, the unhappy race we have consigned to their keeping, and from whose toil their profits are wrung, are perishing miserably by famine, while not a vestige of an attempt has been made on the part of their rulers to imbue them with the commonest arts of civilized life, or to induce them to change the precarious livelihood obtained by the chase for a certain subsistence derived from cultivation of the soil."

The Hudson's Bay Company — so concluded the memorial of the Committee of the Aborigines Society — had been in rigid, exclusive, supreme control for two centuries with every opportunity to uplift the Indian. " And yet what has been

the result? The system which has made the Company pros-
perous and powerful, has made the Indian a slave and his
country a desert. He is at this day wandering about his
native land, without home or covering, as much a stranger
to the blessings of civilization as when the white man first
landed on his shores. . . ." [7]

Of the great numbers of Indians that had once inhabited
Canada, few remained in many Hudson's Bay Company sections in 1857, compared to the original population. The Esquimaux were reduced to 4,000; in the older parts of Canada
there were but 3,000 Indians frequenting the establishments
of the Hudson's Bay Company. The whole of the tribes on
the plains numbered only 25,000. On the east side of the
Rocky Mountains the Thickwood Indians, preserving themselves in their mountain recesses, were much more numerous,
totaling 35,000; and in British Columbia and on the North
West Coast, where exploitation was but comparatively recently begun, there were 80,000 Indians. This made a total
of 147,000 Indians in the Hudson's Bay Company's territory.
Adding 11,000 whites and half breeds, the full total of the
Company's " subjects " was 158,000. [8]

Enrichment of British Shareholders

The £20,000,000 sterling that the fur trade had yielded to
British capitalists was distributed among a noted array of
titled aristocrats, church prelates and clergymen, politicians,
merchants and others. On the list of the Hudson's Bay Company's stockholders in or about 1856, appeared the names of
the Earl of Selkirk, Countess Lydia Cavan, Baron Wynford,

---

[7] *Report from the Select Committee on the Hudson's Bay Co.*, etc.,
British Parl., 1857, Appendix No. XVI, pp. 441–444.

[8] *Ibid.*, Appendix No. II, pp. 365–367. These were the estimated
figures as nearly as was compatible with the difficulty of getting accurate returns.

Viscount Folkestone, Sir George Sinclair, Sir Edmund Antrobus, Bishop John Banks Jenkinson, Rev. Oswald Littleton Chambers, the Ellice family and scores of other notables.[9]

Considering that the £20,000,000 from the fur trade were profits flowing in during a long period, it is easy to see that by a multiplying series of investments and reinvestments compounding continually, that sum really represented a far larger sum; and it may be said, too, that with the extraordinarily large purchasing power of money then — far greater than now — £20,000,000 was a prodigious amount, much greater intrinsically than even such a large sum would be in these present days. It has been estimated that at least one-half of the revenues of the stockholders of the Hudson's Bay Company have come back to Canada for investment.

What the Company's profits were from land and its various other lines of business it is not possible to say. We have seen in an earlier chapter of this work by what means the Hudson's Bay Company, through the Earl of Selkirk, was alleged to have obtained the far-reaching and valuable lands of the Salteau Indians near Winnipeg. Vast areas of the finest agricultural lands were secured — fraudulently, as the Salteau tribe asserted — by the payment of some scraps of tobacco and some grains of ammunition.

For this very land, it would seem, the Hudson's Bay Company charged settlers five shillings sterling per acre; and later — in 1829 — more than doubled the price. But the settlers threatened armed trouble, and the Company considered it expedient to reduce the price to seven shillings six pence, at which price it remained for 30 years or more.[10] This was

[9] The full list is given in *Ibid.*, Appendix No. XVII.
[10] David Gunn of the Red River Settlement, March 6, 1857, to Vanhoughnet, President of the Executive Council at Toronto, *Ibid.*, Appendix No. VII, p. 383. "Fear," wrote Gunn, "made the rulers of the land pause on the brink of the precipice to which they had been hastening."

the identical land, some 20 or 24 miles in extent, of which Chief Peguis complained that his tribe had been defrauded.

If any settler was in arrears for land, the Company (to which, perforce, he was compelled to sell all of his produce), deducted one-fifth for payment for the land, at the same time selling the same produce to the Indians for ruinously exorbitant sums, and charging the settler (as we have seen) from 100 to 400 per cent. advance on the prime cost of all goods that he bought. Every employe of the Company, in fact, was forced to pay for 50 acres of land before he could come to the Red River Settlement; if he could not pay cash, he had to go to Europe or remain in the Company's service until he had saved money enough to pay for the land.[11]

Petition of 575 Settlers

In 1849 the settlers rose in armed revolt against the Company which, insistently proclaiming its rights under the Charter granted by Charles II, had " ruled with a hard and heavy hand." The Company mollified its extortions, yet nevertheless, despite the Company's persistent claims that it was treating the settlers fairly, the settlers still bitterly complained that extortion in various ways was continuing.

In 1857 a petition signed by 575 settlers at the Red River Settlement was sent to the British Parliamentary Select Committee. The petitioners told how the flattering promises of the Earl of Selkirk had induced emigrants to settle there.

" We have paid large sums of money to the Hudson's Bay Company for land," the petition read, " yet we cannot obtain deeds for the same. The Company's agents have made several attempts to force upon us deeds which would reduce ourselves and our posterity to the most abject slavery under that body. . . .

[11] *Ibid.*, p. 383.

Penalties Against Freedom of Trade

" Under what we believe to be a fictitious Charter, but which the Company's Agents maintained to be the fundamental law of Rupert's Land [the whole of the West and North West Territory], we have been prevented the receiving in exchange the peltries of our Country for any of the products of our labor, and have been forbidden giving peltries in exchange for any of the imported necessaries of life, under the penalty of being imprisoned, and of having our property confiscated; we have been forbidden to take peltries in exchange for food supplied to famishing Indians.

" The Hudson's Bay Company's clerks, with an armed police, have entered into settlers' houses in quest of furs, and confiscated all they found. One poor settler, after having his goods seized, had his house burnt to the ground, and afterwards was conveyed prisoner to York Factory.

" The Company's first legal adviser in this Colony has declared our navigating the lakes and rivers between this colony and Hudson's Bay with any articles of produce, to be illegal. The same authority has declared our selling of English goods in this colony to be illegal.

" On our annual commercial journeys into Minnesota we have been pursued like felons by armed constables, who searched our property, even by breaking open our trunks; all furs found were confiscated."

Payments of 100 to 400 Per Cent. Advance

The petition went on to say that, " Thus, we, the inhabitants of this land, have been and are constrained to behold the valuable commercial productions of our country exported for the exclusive profit of a company of traders who are strangers to ourselves and to our country. We are by necessity compelled to use many articles of their importation for which we pay from 100 to 400 per cent. on prime cost, while we are prohibited exporting those productions of our country and industry which we could exchange for the necessaries of life."

Then the petition proceeded to describe how the governors, legislators, judges and other authorities were all Hudson's Bay Company functionaries — governors, chief traders and chief factors —; how they were appointed by the Company, and arbitrarily imposed and enforced such taxes and prices and decreed such offenses and punishments as suited the Company's interests. They made the laws, judged the laws, and executed their own sentences.[12]

Individual Freedom of Trade Demanded.

In an age when steam machinery and factories had already been established in Canada, when railroads were being built, when the owners of the thousands of lumber, grist and other mills in Eastern Canada were looking for the widest outlet for their products, and when ambitious traders were demanding the free right to trade, it was a logical development that nascent capitalism should indignantly complain of such feudal and arbitrary restrictions upon the freedom of trade, as their interests conceived and demanded it.

The Toronto Board of Trade vehemently protested against what it termed this assumed, usurped power of a single corporation — and " foreign " at that — to enact tariffs, collect customs' dues and levy taxes. It derided what it styled the pretended rights by which the Hudson's Bay Company, under a charter granted by Charles II, nearly 100 years before Canada had passed from French control, assumed sovereignty

---

[12] This petition appears in full in Appendix No. XV, *Report from the Select Committee on the Hudson's Bay Co.*, etc., British Parl., 1857, pp. 437–438.

over the North West Territory and arbitrarily exercised the power to grant away and sell lands belonging to the Government.[13] The Toronto Board of Trade's petition dwelt with emphasis on this point.

When testifying before the Canadian Legislative Select Committee, in 1857, Allan MacDonell gave a long list of facts tending to prove the illegality of the Company's charter. " The very foundation for the Charter is a grant of territory presumed to have been made in the year 1670. Now as Charles II could not grant away what the Crown of England did not possess, much less could grant away the possessions of another power, the very words of the charter itself excludes from the operation of the grant those identical territories which the Hudson's Bay Company now claim."

These further representations were brought out in the Parliamentary Investigation: — The Hudson's Bay Company did not enter the valley of the Saskatchewan until about the year 1793, and did not plant its establishments in the valley of the Assiniboine until about 1805, more than a hundred years after the date of its charter. It did not set up exclusive rights until 1814.[14] William Mac D. Dawson, head of the Woods and Forests Branch of the Crown Land Department at Toronto, testified that his investigations had disclosed that the Hudson's Bay Company had no real title in the Red River and the Saskatchewan country; that " it was a monstrous imposition and was first assumed under Lord Selkirk." Dawson also testified that when the Company carried their trade into the interior, " they also gave out that it was their country (a fiction which the license of exclusive trade helped them to maintain); and they industriously published and circulated maps of it as such, which being copied into other maps and

[13] *Appendix No. XII, Ibid.*, p. 435. Petition of Board of Trade of Toronto to the Legislative Council of Canada, April 20, 1857.
[14] *Ibid.*, Appendix No. VIII, p. 387.

geographical works, the delusion became very general, indeed." [15]

Promises to Reform

The disclosures laid bare by this accumulation of testimony, letters, petitions, memorials and other evidence produced before the Parliamentary Select Committee, made the deepest kind of a public sensation.[16] For nearly two centuries the Hudson's Bay Company had represented itself in England as the grand evangel of religion, colonization, and civilization among the Indians; for nearly two centuries it had assiduously spread abroad its pretended reputation; and by insisting long enough upon its assumed virtues had been credited with them by the large mass of unknowing. Now the truth was revealed, and bad as it was, yet it was regarded as undoubtedly only part of the whole.

Imminently threatened, as the Hudson's Bay Company now was, with judicial and legislative extinction, it had to adopt some hurried expedient to save itself. Thereupon, with the most solemn assurances and the most plausible address, it announced that such " abuses " would be no longer countenanced, and it pledged " its faith " to the British Parliament, in 1857, that it would at once institute certain definite reforms in its territory in Canada. What these promises came to we shall soon see.

With its powerful ramifications of interest among merchants, clergy, bankers, politicians and titled aristocrats in

[15] *Ibid.*, p. 394.

[16] By " public sensation " is meant merely among that part of the people having no direct pecuniary interest in trade and commerce. The trading class, with all its aristocratic auxiliaries, sought to minimize the horrors, and to justify the " exigencies of trade " on the score of their " adding to the wealth of England." While one branch of the English trading class was benefiting from the exploitation in Canada, other branches were pocketing profits from that in India and elsewhere, from the opium traffic in China and from the horrors of the factory system in England itself.

England, the Hudson's Bay Company was even able to get, on the whole, by no means unfavorable recommendations from the Select Parliamentary Committee. This Committee recommended that Vancouver Island be given up by the Hudson's Bay Company; that its privileges west of the Rocky Mountains should cease, and that just as soon as Canada could make arrangements to take over the Government of that immense northwestern area of land called Indian Territory, that territory should be ceded. But, "to avoid the demoralization of Indians by rival traders" that country was meanwhile to be left in control of the Hudson's Bay Company.

Waters Its Stock

To narrate the immediate sequel we shall now turn to the communication of Sir George E. Cartier and William Macdougall, Commissioners in London for Canada, to Sir F. Rogers — a document dated February 8, 1869. This communication showed how the Hudson's Bay Company, in exchange for the proposed relinquishment of its antiquated title, tried to get from Canada the sum of £2,000,000 sterling ($10,000,000) and *one half of all of the territory* that it was to surrender. This communication further revealed that the Company was subjected to a peremptory refusal, but that it did succeed in getting £300,000 sterling ($1,500,000) and *one-twentieth of all of the extraordinary fertile expanse from the Red River to the Rocky Mountains*. In addition, it was allowed to retain the land around its trading posts — an incalculably rich present, as we shall see, of itself.

Commissioners Cartier and Macdougall reported that Ellice was for many years "the ruling spirit of the Company," and that the Company had avowed its belief "that colonization and the fur trade could not exist together." It was not astonishing "that the Company had always cherished the latter, which was profitable, and discouraged, and as far as possible, prevented the former."

The Company, the Commissioners went on, was reconstructed in 1863 with loud promises of a new policy; great assurances were held out by it that it would reform its practices. "The stock of the old Company, worth in the market about £1,000,000, was bought up and by some process which we are unable to describe, became £2,000,000. A show of anxiety to open postal and telegraphic communication was made, and 'heads of proposals' were submitted to the Governments of Canada and British Columbia, which on examination were found to embrace a line of telegraph only, with the modest suggestion that the two Governments should guarantee the Company a profit of not less than 4 per cent. on their expenditure! A proposal so absurd could only have been made to be rejected, and it was rejected accordingly." The Commissioners continued:

Promises Never Carried Out

"The surplus capital of the reconstructed Company, which was called up for the avowed purpose of opening their territories to 'European colonization, under a liberal and systematic scheme of land settlement' has never been applied to that purpose. Five and a half years have passed since the grand scheme was announced to the world, but no European emigrants have been sent out, no attempts to colonize have been made." The Commissioners added that by a formal vote of the Company's shareholders in November, 1866, the policy of colonization was absolutely and definitely condemned.

When the matter of the relinquishment of its territory by the Hudson's Bay Company came up definitely, this, according to the report of Canada's Commissioners, is what happened: —

Terms Demanded by the Company.

The Company wanted, in 1863, " in fee simple, *half of the land proposed to be surrendered with various conditions, including a guarantee by the Governments of Canada and British Columbia of an annual profit on the Company's expenditures for improvements on their own property!*

" In 1864," the Report went on, " these conditions took the form of a demand, first, to be paid £1,000,000 sterling from sales of lands and mines, with large reservations ' to be selected by them,' etc.; and secondly, to be paid £1,000,000 sterling in cash with other terms and restrictions favorable to the Company.

" In 1868, these conditions for the surrender of territorial and governing rights over the *whole* territory, remained at £1,000,000, as in the first proposition of 1864, with large reservations of land at ' selected points,' specially exempted from taxation, with full liberty to carry on their trade free from the export and import duties, to which all other subjects of Her Majesty in that country would be exposed." Commissioners Cartier and Macdougall described the grave doubts existing as to the legality of the Company's charter.[17]

Gets £300,000 and Vast Areas of Land

After the foregoing proposals had been rejected, an arrangement was finally made in 1868-1869. The Hudson's Bay Company received £300,000 ($1,500,000) in cash. It also was allowed to retain the land — an area of 50,000 acres — around the various trading posts, and, in addition, two sections in every township, making *a reservation of one-twentieth*

[17] The full communication of Commissioners Cartier and Macdougall was published in *Sessional Paper, No. 25, Sessional Papers,* Dom. Parl., Vol. II, No. 5, 1869.

of the entire region in the fertile belt from the Red River to the Rocky Mountains. For this cash payment and land grant the Company consented to surrender to the Government its trade monopoly and all its claims. In 1870 Manitoba, Rupert's Land and the North West Territories were formally declared part of the Dominion of Canada.

Meanwhile, however, the rebellion of Half Breeds and Indians had begun. There were those who openly charged that furious at not being consulted on the terms of settlement, certain officers and factors of the Hudson's Bay Company in Canada (who were, in a sense, partners and who were opposed to the settlement as it meant considerable loss to them), were secret abettors of this rebellion in 1869-1870. This rebellion, led by Louis Riel, centered about Winnipeg. Thither Sir Donald A. Smith — he was now a Sir — the head officer of the Hudson's Bay Company, was sent by the Canadian Government as Special Commissioner. Although there were distinct economic causes behind this rebellion, it may be added here that Smith later had to face serious taunts in the Dominion House of Commons when he was a member of that body.

It was during the debates in the Dominion House of Commons, in 1875 and 1876, that Smith, then a member of the House, felt called upon to answer certain charges. In a published statement, W. B. O'Donohue, one of the leaders of the insurrection, in effect charged that while employed on a confidential mission for the Canadian Government, Smith had betrayed his trust. O'Donohue further specifically charged that " the insurrection was advised by Governor William Mac-Tavish, who, with other officers of the Hudson's Bay Company, also aided and abetted it from its inception to the very hour it ceased to exist," and that Donald A. Smith had recognized the Rebel Government. Smith, on April 2, 1875, gave a long explanation denying these allegations.

Charged with Aiding Riel's Rebellion

John Christian Schultz who had been on the Council for the North West Territories, who was now a member of Parliament and who later became Lieutenant-Governor of Manitoba, engaged in a very bitter and personal debate with Smith.   It was, said Schultz, the general belief that the papers of the Provisional or Rebel Government had been destroyed by the Hudson's Bay Company, and he (Schultz) believed the statement to be correct.   Smith then gave his explanation, in which he denied that these papers were valuable.[18]   The next year — on March 23, 1876, Schultz returned to the attack, and submitted an affidavit of John Bruce, the first President of the Provisional Government of the North West, in which document Bruce stated that he had been frequently accustomed to go to Governor MacTavish of the Hudson's Bay Company for advice, and that MacTavish had told him that it would be well to resist the Canadian Governor, and " that it was an injustice to the people the Canadians taking possession of the country, and an injustice to the officers of the Hudson's Bay Company, because the Government had given them no part of the £300,000 paid for their country." [19]   Smith again denied that he helped the insurrection.

It was during this day's debate that Schultz said: " The House must be aware that this Company had made a large claim against the Government for compensation for losses during the rebellion.   If the Hudson's Bay Company were not guilty of complicity during the rebellion they were entitled to compensation for their losses the same as anyone else, but it seemed that their guilt was now confessed in the fact that they did not now dare to push their claim; and that even his

[18] *Debates in the House of Commons, Dom. Parl.,* 1875, pp. 1060–1069.
[19] *Debates in the House of Commons,* etc., 1876, pp. 811–812.

hon. friend from Selkirk [Donald A. Smith], brazen as he was in other respects, did not dare say a word about it." [20]

Not until this so-termed rebellion was put down and the transfer completely made, did the Canadian Government pay the $1,500,000 cash to the Hudson's Bay Company. The Company's officials in Canada, thanks greatly to Smith's efforts,[21] succeeded in getting their part of the payment; the English stockholders wanted to monopolize the whole sum, but the Company's officials in Canada carried their point. A sum of £107,000 was divided among them in consideration of the relinquishment of their claims.

Company's Immense Land Possessions

By this final settlement the Hudson's Bay Company was left in possession — or at least with a title to — immense areas of land in Manitoba, Saskatchewan and Alberta and elsewhere — one-twentieth of that entire region of rich and valuable agricultural land. Its land possessions also comprised great and valuable tracts in what are now large cities; the Company's landed estate in Winnipeg, Edmonton and other cities is of enormous value; and it has already derived vast revenues from the sale of only a part of those landed properties.

Leaving aside its revenues from the sale of its farming lands before 1893, its returns since that date to 1912, from the sale of 1,953,567 acres of agricultural lands, were $15,-627,944.[22] The Company's annual report of March 31, 1912, showed that the Company still owned 4,032,860 acres of unsold land, and that it was getting an average of $19.01 an acre for its agricultural lands.[23] It distributes annually among its stockholders the rich sum of an average of $2,000,000, con-

[20] *Ibid.*, p. 813.
[21] Begg's *History of the North West*, Vol. II, p. 402.
[22] *Annual Report, Dep't. of the Interior*, March 31, 1912, p. xxiv.
[23] *Appendix to Canadian Annual Financial Review*, Nov. 1912, p. 130.

stituting the revenues from its fur land and operations; for although the Hudson's Bay Company has gradually evolved into a modern storekeeping corporation to supply the needs of settlers from its department stores in a dozen or more cities, it still is pursuing the fur trade as it did more than two centuries ago. Only recently — in November, 1913 — it added $1,000,000 to its capital stock.

Such is a summary of the operations of the Hudson's Bay Company, still a powerful, aggressive institution, still obtaining wealth from Canada, still ruled from England by a small Council at the head of which is Lord Strathcona and Mount Royal, formerly plain Mr. Donald A. Smith.

The surrender of its sovereignty in 1869 left most of the vast territory over which it had long dictated open to settlement and to unhindered development and exploitation. How, when the ink had hardly dried on the surrender papers, railroad and other capitalists, chief among whom was Donald A. Smith, hastened to reach out and get immense land grants, great coal mines, timber and other resources, we shall presently note in detail.

CHAPTER X

INCEPTION OF THE RAILROAD POWER

The railways of Canada, owned, controlled and ruled privately by individual groups or corporations of capitalists, cover more than 26,000 miles of lines; and expressed in the substance of modern money terms, their capital is about $1,600,-000,000. But the real amount upon which interest and dividends must be paid is $2,918,055,699.

These are the privately-owned railway systems, but this is not to say that their proprietorship has come from the application of private cash. The funds that paid for their construction have come largely, if not fundamentally in whole, from the ever-accessible public treasury which the railway promoters early began to plunder, extending and elaborating the process with time and opportunity.

Vast Gifts of Land, Cash and Guarantees

The public finances have been placed at the disposal of railway promoters in three principal forms. Cash subsidies, comprising either outright cash or loans has been one method; land grants, another; and guarantees of bonds, a third. The first two were the main ways in the early decades of railroad history; the last-named is an outgrowth of the financial methods of more recent years. All three come under the official designation of "Government aid," the tabulated aggregate of which, to this present writing (1913), has reached:

Land grants ....56,052,055 acres
Cash subventions $244,000,000
Guarantees of bonds $245,000,000

According to an estimate made by Mr. R. D. Fairburn in a paper read at a recent convention of the Canadian Manufacturers' Association at Halifax, these 56,052,055 acres, if appraised at $20 per acre, produce a total amount of $1,121,-041,100. In arriving at this estimate Mr. Fairburn pointed out that the Canadian Northern Railway reported an average price for its lands of $45.17 per acre. " Thus," he said, including the cash subsidies granted up to 1912, " we have given to the railways $1,320,113,173 or about $50,000 per mile."

But this estimate hardly expresses the total value of the land grants, which comprised, in some cases, great areas of timber lands; in other cases, the most enormously valuable coal and other mineral deposits. Of the total of the profits drawn from these, and their entire present and potential commercial value, no accurate computation can be given.

These land grants, however, by no means include the city or town terminal land and water facilities donated during the last sixty years by municipalities to railway promoters for stations, freight depots, entrances and exits and other purposes. The aggregate value of these may be reasonably said to be stupendous.

A fraction more than 31,000,000 acres of the 56,052,055 acres in land grants were donated by the Dominion Government; the Government of the Province of Quebec gave 13,-625,949 acres: that of British Columbia, 8,119,221 acres; the New Brunswick Government, 1,647,772 acres; that of Nova Scotia, 160,000 acres, and that of Ontario, 635,039 acres.[1] Of the Dominion land grants one railroad alone —

[1] See 1912 and 1913 *Railway Statistics of the Dominion of Canada,* etc., p. xvi, etc.

the Canadian Pacific — received a present of 25,000,000 acres.[2]

Of the $244,000,000 contributed in cash subventions, or their equivalent in so-called loans, the Dominion Government has given about $190,000,000.[3] The Provincial governments have given nearly $36,000,000, and municipalities $18,000,000 in cash subsidies. This aid has been largely outright cash donations; only a small part has been in the nominal form of loans or subscriptions to shares, which have practically turned into gifts.

As for the guaranteeing of bonds of privately-owned railways by the Dominion Government or the Provincial governments, the guarantees have been:

Dominion	$ 91,982,553
Manitoba	20,899,660
Alberta	45,489,000
Saskatchewan	32,500,000
Ontario	7,860,000
Nova Scotia	5,022,000
British Columbia	38,946,832
New Brunswick	1,893,000
Quebec	476,000
Total	$245,070,045

In the single year of 1912, bond guarantees were increased by the sum of $96,733,688, bringing the amount from $148,-336,357 in 1911 to the above stated total in 1912.

[2] Minus 6,793,014 acres for the relinquishment of which the Canadian Pacific Railway Company received $10,189,521 from the Dominion Government.

[3] See 1912 and 1913 *Railway Statistics of the Dominion of Canada;* p. xvi, etc. To the sum stated in this report, we have added the subsidies voted during the 1913 session of Parliament, including the ten-year loan of $15,000,000 at 4 per cent. to the Grand Trunk Pacific Railway Company which loan may turn out to be a gift.

Besides the foregoing sums, the Dominion Government has spent more than $116,000,000 in constructing the eastern division of the National Transcontinental Railway, of which the Grand Trunk Pacific Railway Company will have the free use for the first seven years of a lease of 50 years.

All of the sums above given are exclusive of the great sums spent on the construction or acquisition of what are Government-owned railways. Of these expenditures the Intercolonial Railway system cost nearly $95,000,000.[4]

The Original Promoters

With this preliminary, we shall now proceed to narrate certain facts pertaining to the inception of Canada's railways.

The prime and first consideration of railway ownership was the ability to get legislation giving certain definite rights and privileges. This legislation conferred what was called a charter of incorporation. Having the power, as the legislative politicians did, to grant to themselves these charters, it was not an astonishing outcome that the promoters should have so often been the politicians themselves. This was particularly so inasmuch as many of the politicians, then so-called, were not politicians in the sense that they exclusively followed politics. Not a few of them were landowners of considerable holdings, and it was not a far step for them to promote railways, the operation of which would increase the value of their timber and other lands. Other members of Parliament were traders, merchants or shippers, as well as land speculators, and had a personal and immediate interest in bringing about modern methods of transportation. Still other members of Parliament were lawyers, who were either connected with landed or trading families, or who were often themselves interested in capitalist undertakings or aspired to become so.

[4] *Annual Report of the Dep't. of Railways and Canals,* 1912, p. 53.

At the same time, the parliamentary railroad promoters were compelled by the exigencies of politics to put on an appearance of great concern for the public welfare while engaged in the very act of seeking to enrich themselves; they assiduously presented themselves as law makers having at heart the development of the resources of Canada and the expansion of its wealth.

To comprehend the large and important part the parliamentary legislators took as personal beneficiaries in the original promotion of railways, it is only necessary to survey the lists of incorporators of the first railroads.

Politicians Were Business Men

The promoters of the London and Gore Railroad Company, chartered in 1834, were headed by Allan N. MacNab, and comprised a large contingent of the most prominent legislative and other politicians. This railroad subsequently developed into the Great Western Railway of which MacNab became president. To this generation, MacNab's name is obscure, but in his day he was a conspicuous personage — member of the Canadian Parliament for many years, Speaker of that body for a long time, created a knight, Prime Minister in 1854, raised to a baronetcy in 1856 — altogether a commanding dignitary whose daughters married into the British titled aristocracy.

The original object of a number of the first railroad companies was neither the settlement of the country nor the transportation of passengers, but was chiefly one of reaching the lumber and other resources of what were then the backwoods regions. In this category of railways was the Cobourg and Peterboro Railway, constructed chiefly to transport lumber, flour and other products, and with specific powers in its charter to build an extension to the Marmora Iron Works.

According to Lord Sydenham, Governor-General of Canada, the proceedings of the Canadian Parliament were far from being characterized by that considerate and polite reciprocity and discretion that might have been expected. " You can form no idea," wrote Sydenham in a private letter to Lord John Russell of the British Government, in 1840, " of the manner in which a Colonial Parliament transacts its business. I got them into comparative order and decency by having measures brought forward by the Government, and well and steadily worked through. But when they came to their own affairs, and, above all, to the money matters, there was a scene of confusion and riot of which no one in England can have any idea. Every man proposes a vote for his own job; and bills are introduced without notice, and carried through *all* their stages in a quarter of an hour! . . ." [5]

Beneficiaries Were Highest Dignitaries

The members of the Canadian Parliament benefiting by charter and other grants were not merely ordinary members. The chief beneficiaries often were the foremost members — men who were leaders, or who evolved into leaders of political parties, or who became Cabinet Ministers or Prime Ministers.

We have already mentioned Sir Allan N. MacNab; he, for a considerable time, was Chairman of the Legislative Assembly Standing Committee on Railroads of which Sir Francis Hincks, J. Cauchon and other conspicuous railway promoters were also members. Another prominent parliamentary rail-

[5] Adam Shortt's biography *Lord Sydenham,* p. 251. Lord Sydenham was, no doubt, impressed by their primitively uncouth methods as compared with those in England, where the most flagrant jobs are put through with polished ease and leisurely equanimity, thus covering them with a nice gentlemanly elegance. Centuries of experience have taught this as a fine art.

road promoter was Malcolm Cameron, who, going to Parliament in 1836, remained there for more than a quarter of a century, varying the parliamentary routine by serving as a Cabinet Minister in various posts, as president of the Executive Council and as a member of the Legislative Council. His colleague, James Morris, another railroad promoter in his own interest, was likewise a seasoned parliamentarian, having gone to the Upper Canada Assembly in 1837, thence to the Canadian Parliament in 1841. From 1844 to 1858 Morris was prominent in some governmental capacity — in the Legislative Council (an appointive body constituting the upper branch of Parliament), as Cabinet Minister in the Executive Council, as Speaker of the Executive Council, and as Postmaster General.

There was John Ross,— member of the Legislative Council in 1848-1849, Solicitor-General of Canada in 1851, then Attorney-General, and subsequently Speaker of the Legislative Council. Sir John A. Macdonald was among the list; from 1844 when first he went to Parliament he stood out with growing conspicuousness, becoming a Cabinet Minister in 1847, long keeping his seat in Parliament.

Grant Each Other Charters

More in evidence among the charter getters was George E. Cartier, of Montreal; he entered Parliament in 1848, and remained for decades, meanwhile having his season of commanding authority as Cabinet Minister in 1856, and Premier in 1858. Another noted promoter was John Young; he was elected to Parliament from Montreal in 1851 and 1854.

Nor should we omit the eminent John Sandfield Macdonald, serving in Parliament for many years from 1841 onward, and filling various high government offices from 1851 to 1858, after which he again displayed his acumen in Parliament.

There, too, were Francis Hincks, Hugh Allan, William Hamilton Merritt, J. J. C. Abbott, James Ferrier, William Allan, Luther H. Holton, and many other notabilities; and last, but by no means least, A. T. Galt who held a seat in Parliament for many years, dating from his first election in 1849.

With rapidity, charters of every description were forthcoming in plethoric succession. Nearly all of them were granted by these men to one another, and to strings of associates. These were the men, who, aiming at creating capitalists or becoming capitalists themselves or expanding their wealth, invested themselves and associates with the proprietary possession of charters for railroad, insurance, canal, banking, gas and water and other companies, all of which charters contained valuable privileges and immunities and exclusive rights.

For purposes of elucidation we shall catalogue a number of these charters.

They Give Themselves Charters

Among the incorporators of the St. Lawrence and Atlantic Railroad Company, chartered March 17, 1845, were A. T. Galt and Peter McGill,— the latter long President of the Bank of Montreal and a member of the Legislative Council of Canada.[6]

The list of incorporators of the Canada, New Brunswick and Nova Scotia Railway, chartered in 1847, with a capital of $2,000,000, reads as though it were largely a roster of Parliament itself. Heading the procession of incorporators was Sir Allan N. MacNab; there were five members of the Legislative Council, including the active John Ross; a long roll of members of the Provincial Parliament; the Mayors of Montreal, Toronto and Kingston, and other office holders. Associated with them were a number of trading and sundry other

---

[6] *Statutes of Canada*, 1845, p. 146.

men of capital — Sir George Simpson, Governor of the Hudson's Bay Company and Paul Fraser of the same Company; several bank cashiers; some seigneurs and various other individuals of note either in politics or trade. The lawyers for the Company were either then conspicuous in politics or became more so later — attorneys such as Henry Sherwood of Toronto and John Rose of Montreal.[7]

In the list of incorporators of the Western Telegraph Company, chartered March 23, 1848, were Francis Hincks and Malcolm Cameron,[8] both variously members of Parliament and of the Canadian Government. It was in this year that the Woodstock and Lake Erie Railway Company — later developing into the Great Southern Railway Company — was chartered; of the malodorous operations and bribery committed by the promoters of this railway, some instructive details are related in the next chapter.

Sir Allan N. MacNab, Malcolm Cameron, John Young and other notables prominent in Parliament or trade or in both, were the incorporators of the Canada Life Assurance Company chartered April 25, 1849.[9] Five days later, another charter was passed by the Canadian Parliament, naming MacNab, Young and others as proprietary incorporators of the Ontario Marine Fire Insurance Company.[10] On the same day, May 30, 1849, the Quebec Warehousing Company was chartered, with Young as one of its chief promoters and incorporated beneficiaries.[11]

It was during this brisk session that the Parliament of the Province of Canada passed an Act with a preamble asserting the principle that in a new and thinly-settled country, where

[7] The full list of incorporators is given in *Imperial Blue Books on Affairs Relating to Canada,* Vol. 27, " Railways," pp. 7–8, and 18–19 of Enclosure " Correspondence," etc.

[8] *Statutes of Canada,* 1848–1849, p. 9.

[9] *Ibid.,* 1849, p. 916.

[10] *Ibid.,* p. 899.

[11] *Ibid.,* p. 1079.

capital was scarce, the assistance of Government could safely be afforded to railway lines, " and that such assistance is best given by extending to Companies constructing railways under charter the benefit of the guarantee of the Government for loans." [12]

One delectable point was omitted in this preamble, namely, that the members of the very Parliament that enacted this law were largely themselves railroad promoters, or planning to become so.

A Long Succession of Charters

From now on charter after charter was rolled out in finished form. Hon. Robert Jones, John Young and associates were vested with a charter, May 30, 1849, for the Montreal and Vermont Junction Railway Company,[13] and on the same day, a charter was presented to Young, Luther H. Holton and partners, empowering them to construct a ship canal from Lake Champlain to the River St. Lawrence.[14]

Louis Massue, Louis Methot, James Bell Forsyth, F. R. Angers and other personages, some of whom ranked as honorables, were incorporated August 10, 1850, as the proprietors of the Quebec and Richmond Railway Company.[15] Forsyth and others obtained a charter for the Quebec and St. Andrews Railroad Company.[16] John A. Macdonald and John Hamilton were among the incorporators of the Kingston Fire and Marine Insurance Company, chartered August 10, 1850.[17]

Equally active and powerful politicians were the incorporators of the Montreal and Kingston Railway, chartered in 1851. This group of promoters was small, but then or later

[12] *Statutes of Canada*, 1848–1849, p. 214.
[13] *Ibid.*, 1849, p. 124.
[14] *Ibid.*, p. 981.
[15] *Ibid.*, 1849–1850, p. 1576.
[16] *Ibid.*, p. 1596.
[17] *Ibid.*, p. 1701.

of great parliamentary power: John Young, George Moffatt, A. N. Morin, L. H. Holton, A. T. Galt, George E. Cartier, and Ira Gould. The charter of this railway, it seems, was repealed at the instance of Sir Francis Hincks, but a railroad of much the same name, the Kingston and Montreal, came into being with a capital of £600,000 currency in shares, of which Galt, Holton and D. L. Macpherson gathered into their ownership almost the whole.[18] This railway, it may be here remarked, later became part of the Grand Trunk Railway of Canada, controlled by much the same coterie of legislators owning the Kingston and Montreal Railway. Often these legislative and other capitalists sold or leased charters to themselves as heads of other railways, profiting exceedingly thereby.

Grand Trunk R. R. Incorporators

The charter of the Grand Trunk Railway of Canada, in fact, was regarded as one of the richest prizes. This was secured, November 10, 1852, by A. T. Galt, Peter McGill, George Pemberton, George E. Cartier, Luther H. Holton and other Parliamentary incorporators, with powers to build a railway from Toronto to Kingston and thence to Montreal.[19]

John Sandfield Macdonald and William Merritt headed the group of incorporators of the Dalhousie and Thorold Railway Company, chartered May 23, 1853.[20].

John Young and Sir Allan MacNab were prominent in the list of incorporators of the London and Port Sarnia Railway Company, chartered in the same year,[21] and MacNab was also among the incorporated shareholders of the Hamilton

---

[18] Trout's *Railways of Canada,* 1870, p. 146.
[19] *Statutes of Canada,* 1852, pp. 103–104.
[20] *Ibid.,* 1853, pp. 522–523.
[21] *Ibid.,* p. 362. Almost immediately after this charter was granted, the London and Port Sarnia Railway was leased to the Great Western Railway of which MacNab was the head.

and Port Dover Railway chartered at the same time.[22] P. J.
O. Chauveau (a prominent member of the Canadian Parliament since 1844, a Cabinet Minister several times, and later
the first Premier of Quebec after Confederation), headed the
promoters and incorporators of the Quebec and Saguenay
Railway Company, which corporation was duly chartered in
the next year.[23]

The directory of the Niagara District Bank, chartered May
19, 1855, comprised James Morris, John Ross, John Sandfield
Macdonald, William Hamilton Merritt and others of note,[24]
and among the incorporators of the Zimmerman Bank, chartered on the same day, were Luther H. Holton and other public men.[25]

Get Bank Charters, Also

A prominent array of men in office headed the list of proprietary incorporators of Molson's Bank, chartered May 19,
1855,— an institution which has since become one of the richest in Canada: there were William Molson, John Molson, Sr.,
George Moffatt, Samuel Gerrard, James Ferrier and other
Montreal notables.[26] Here it may be remarked that the politicians in the United States have long since so well appraised
the value of bank charters, that as early as the years 1799,
1805, 1811 and 1824 bribery had been used to wrest from the
legislators charters for the Manhattan, Mercantile, Merchants'
and other New York City banks.[27] But in Canada, with many

22 *Ibid.*, p. 368.
23 *Ibid.*, 1854, p. 118.
24 *Ibid.*, 1855, p. 851.
25 *Ibid.*, p. 836.
26 *Ibid.*, p. 821.
27 See *Journals of the (New York) Senate and Assembly*, 1805, pp.
351 and 399, and *Ibid.*, 1812, p. 134. See also *History of the Supreme
Court of the United States*, pp. 215–216. The chartering of the
Chemical Bank in 1824, was accomplished by a considerable sum in
bribe money and $50,000 in stock as bribes.— See, *Journals of the
(N. Y.) Senate*, 1824, pp. 1317–1350.

of the bank incorporators themselves leaders in legislative councils,[28] bribery was, in general, superfluous.

More railway and other charters were consecutively enacted. John Young, Sir Allan N. MacNab and associates obtained a charter for the Hamilton and South Western Railway Company, on May 30, 1855.[29] Four members of the Canadian Parliament were the chiefs among the incorporators of the Amherstburg and St. Thomas Railway Company, chartered in the same year.[30] J. J. C. Abbott, George Moffatt, Hugh Allan and other political luminaries secured a charter, July 1, 1856, for the Canadian Marine Insurance Company.[31] William Cayley, J. H. Cameron, John Beverly Robinson and two other members of the Canadian Parliament were among the incorporators of the Canada Western Railway Company, chartered May 16, 1856.[32]

The list of incorporators of the Strathroy and Port Frank Railway Company, chartered June 10, 1857, was headed by Malcolm Cameron.[33] A number of members of the Canadian Parliament were among the promoters and incorporators of the Eastwood and Berlin Railway Company, and of the Brantford and Southwestern Railway Company, both chartered in 1857; and there were five members of the Canadian Parliament among the chartered incorporators of the Toronto and Owen Sound Railway Company, chartered in the same year.[34]

As for the Bank of Canada, chartered in 1858, its incorporated shareholders were headed by William Cayley, John Ross and other Parliamentary notabilities.[35]

[28] See many other instances in *Statutes of Canada*.
[29] *Statutes of Canada*, 1855, p. 761.
[30] *Ibid.*, p. 713. For details as to the particular history of this railway see next chapter.
[31] *Ibid.*, 1856, p. 512.
[32] *Ibid.*, p. 69.
[33] *Ibid.*, 1857, p. 622.
[34] *Ibid.*, p. 638.
[35] *Ibid.*, 1858, p. 690.

More Railroad Charters

Of the North Shore Railway (which later became the Quebec, Montreal, Ottawa and Occidental Railway, some 90 miles long), Sir George Simpson of the Hudson's Bay Company was an early president, and a number of members of the Parliament of Canada were directors.[36] This railroad eventually received 2,700,000 acres of land as a gift from the Quebec Legislature, and $752,000 in cash bonuses and $1,948,600 in loans from the Provincial governments and from various municipalities. The chief pusher of this railway was J. Cauchon, a prominent Quebec politician who was Crown Commissioner of Lands and a member of the Canadian Government Ministry in 1857; in that capacity he assiduously promoted the North Shore Railway Company's demand for a large land grant, and he later became the Company's president.

A notable assemblage of legislators comprised the list of incorporators of the European and North American Railway. Although by the Act of Incorporation, only two of the nine directors were to be elected by the Legislature to represent the Province of New Brunswick, almost the whole personnel of the government of the Province of New Brunswick were among the incorporators — the Speaker of the House of Assembly, the Provincial Secretary, the Attorney-General, and other officials, not omitting 23 members of the New Brunswick Legislature. Three presidents of large New Brunswick banks were also on the list.[37] Certain Maine capitalists were acting in unison. The European and North American Railway Company, by the N. B. Act of March 15, 1851, was allowed a capital of $1,500,000, and miscellaneous privileges

---

[36] *Canada Directory,* 1857–1858, p. 628.
[37] The complete list of incorporators appears in *Imperial Blue Books on Affairs Relating to Canada,* Vol. 27, " Railways," etc., p. 12, of Enclosure, " Further Correspondence Relative to," etc.

such as exemption of its lands, stock, personal property, etc., from taxation.[38] A month and a half later, the promoters gave themselves, by special law, a land grant to the extent of five miles on each side of the railway along the entire route [39] — a modest performance, indeed, seeing that they could as easily have made it ten miles.[40] However, over in Maine they obtained another land grant of 700,000 acres.[41]

Charters to Obstruct Development

The contractors for that part of this railroad running from St. John, N. B., to Point du Chene, were the firm of Peto, Brassey, Betts and Jackson. They were obliged (for reasons hereafter explained) to suspend operations in 1854, because of bankruptcy; and in 1856 the Government of New Brunswick bought the road from them for the sum of $438,000, and completed its construction. That portion of the European and North American Railway is now part of the Government-owned Intercolonial Railway. Other parts of the European and North American Railway were later merged — in 1872 — into the St. John and Maine Railway which received from the government and certain municipalities of New Brunswick $1,240,000 cash subsidies — which was nearly one-half of the entire cost of the road, namely $2,698,589.

[38] *Ibid.*, p. 17.

[39] *Ibid.*, p. 27.

[40] In the case of another railway company, the St. Andrews and Quebec (later called the New Brunswick and Canada Railway, 127 miles in length) the directors at first claimed ten miles of land on each side of the line, but later, in 1852, amiably consented to take the five-mile land grant on each side voted by the Assembly instead of the ten miles as proposed by the board of directors. *Imperial Blue Books,* etc., Vol. 27, "Railways," pp. 90–93 of "Further Correspondence Relative to the Projected Railway from Halifax to Quebec." This railway received subsidies of $575,000 from the government, and $47,500 from the municipalities, of New Brunswick.

[41] See *Seventh Report of the Forest Commissioner of Maine,* 1908, p. 90.

These are but a few examples of members of Parliament voting charters largely to themselves; we shall be under the unavoidable necessity later of specifying many other instances. Some of these charters were obtained without the slightest idea of constructing railroads; it was the general recognized custom to get charters for the purpose of preventing other railroads from entering particular regions and towns, and of compelling such railroad companies as wanted to build there to buy out the charters at exorbitant prices.

In the case of such railroads as were constructed, the promoters frequently formed construction companies, and thus made large profits from railroads the charters and subsidies for which they, themselves, as members of Parliament had voted.

Scramble for Charters

There was thus hardly a member of the Parliament of the Province of Canada or of the other legislative or the executive bodies who was not in some way zealously pushing railway or other projects in which he or his associates were personally interested.

The absence of indirection and the open-handed and deliberate fashion marked by not the slightest circumlocution were the most remarkable features of this general scramble to vest perpetual rights in themselves by their own votes. At a later period, parliamentary members often concealed their identity by substituting the names of relatives, friends or mere go-betweens, but at this particular period this more refined subterfuge was not thought of. Quite the contrary. High government officials and members of parliaments not only openly voted charters to themselves and associates, but in prospectuses, often issued for stock jobbing purposes, advertised their connection as a guarantee of the prominence and stability of these enterprises, and as the best assurance that could be given that the whole power of the state could be infallibly depended upon to pass whatever additional laws were necessary, and to give gratuities in loans, bonuses and land grants.

The Church Subscribes for Stock

Charters were, therefore, easily rolled through the legislative grind, but to get the funds for construction from private sources was often a very different and an arduous task.

The charter of the St. Lawrence and Atlantic Railroad Company, incorporated March 17, 1845, gave specific power to the ecclesiastics of the Seminary of St. Sulpice of Montreal, or any other civil or ecclesiastical body, to lend money to the Company or subscribe for its stock; this was the first instance of authority of this kind given in Canada.

Timmins, secretary of the provisional committee of the Canada, New Brunswick and Nova Scotia Railway Company, wrote from Fredericton, N. B., January 7, 1850, to Earl Grey, at London, that he had been canvassing the parishes contiguous to the line of railway for the purpose of enrolling stockholders.

" The venerable Archbishop Signy," he wrote further, " having supplied me with letters to the Catholic clergy, his name has been like a tower of strength among them. . . . In proof of the zeal shown by the clergy in Lower Canada, I have the pleasure to tell you that the name of every rector, vicar and curé for the whole distance is entered in the Book of Enrollment [of stockholders] and the proposed applications for shares, and the enregistered amount in Canada and this province to the present time, including the £35,000 offered from the Hotel Dieu Nunnery and Seminary of Montreal, and for which the Bishop, Monseigneur Bourget, has entered his name, is £223,500, and the corporations of Quebec have granted £100,000, also, in debentures, to carry on the branch

to Melbourne, making £335,000, which, considering the state
the Country is in, is gratifying. . . ." [42]

It was not from private sources, however, that the railroads
secured much of their capital, but from the Government of
Canada and the Provinces and the municipalities. Controlling, as they did, the legislative and executive bodies and municipal bodies it was a remarkably easy process, they soon discovered, to have laws enacted indirectly allowing them to tax
the whole body of the people. These contributions came in
the form of forced loans, and gifts of money, land and other
modes of bonusing, pouring constant supplies of cash and
donations into the hands of the railway promoters.

[42] *Imperial Blue Books on Affairs Relating to Canada,* Vol. 27,
" Railways " Enclosure, p. 17. Timmins was accused of having no
authority to act for the Company, and Earl Grey refused to communi-
cate with him until this assurance was given.

CHAPTER XI

FIRST PERIOD OF RAILWAY PROMOTERS

Within a few years after the chartering of some of these initial railway projects, their promoters had transferred to themselves from the treasury of the Government of the Province of Canada, then composed of Ontario and Quebec, the aggregate of nearly $22,000,000.

Appropriated first in the form of loans, almost the whole of this sum was either soon or gradually converted into the equivalent of a gift. Nor, judging by current standards, was it a modest gift. Compared to the extremely slim population of those parts of Canada at the time, and the great purchasing power of given amounts as contrasted with the far lower power of today, that $22,000,000 represented a sum perhaps equal to ten times that amount in these more enhanced years. But, as we shall see, this was by no means the only cash bounty. Subsidies totalling nearly $10,000,000 more were, in that infant age of the railways, obtained from counties and municipalities in what are now the Provinces of Ontario and Quebec.

The prodigality of these money advances can be somewhat adequately estimated when the scanty population and the paucity of developed resources of the Canada of that time are recalled. These subsidies, moreover, were merely the cash largess. Many of the railway charters specifically allowed the free appropriation of timber, stone and other necessary construction material from the public domain. Besides the cash subsidies, the railway promoters contrived to get from municipalities extensive gifts of city land for approaches, terminals and stations, all of which land became of ultimate enormous value.

In every direction, by force of law and often out of law, many of the politicians and their allies and associates were grasping economic power, which is to say, means for accumulating wealth.

Railroads Were His Politics

Such contests, frequently carried on by competing individuals or groups, engendered bargaining or bitter animosities and enmities which were transferred to the open political arena, often operating as the secret or open cause in the overthrow of this or that Ministry and other such political changes. Occasionally, some politician more candid than his colleagues, divulged the secret as, for instance, Sir Allan N. MacNab did when he made the blunt declaration, famous in the politics of the period, that *railroads were his politics.*

Admixed with economic aims was the discussion of certain issues affecting religious, racial and other controversies, but these, too, had their underlying strata of definite economic aspects.

To invest the past with the color of legitimacy is a marked characteristic of conventional history. Here, say the apologists, was a vast country, the resources of which had to be developed. The public collectively were not ready to undertake the construction of great railway systems, and therefore private capitalist enterprise had to step forward and consummate this indispensable work. Responding to this legitimate enterprise, the successive Canadian governments as legitimately presented companies of capitalists with the necessary laws and means.

This sounds plausible, but unfortunately the facts at no stage coincide.

Sir Francis Hincks' Mission

To begin with, there is the fact that among the chief beneficiaries of the charters and subsidies were members of Parliament or of the Government. Then presently came a notable Grand Trunk Railway incident involving Sir Francis Hincks. An Act passed in 1850 contained a conditional provision that the Grand Trunk Railway could be constructed as a public work by the Canadian Government joining with the municipalities. This law was, in itself, a clear recognition that private capitalist enterprise was not necessary. Why were the provisions never carried out? Why did Sir Francis Hincks, who, in his capacity of Inspector-General or Finance Minister, was sent as Canadian envoy to England to continue negotiations with the British Government, not insist upon the execution of this particular clause? Why was it that the contract for building the Grand Trunk was turned over to the English contracting firm of Peto, Brassey, Betts and Jackson?

Hincks' change of front was, wrote Thomas C. Keefer, perhaps the most eminent Canadian civil engineer of his time, " in consequence of propositions made to him in England by English contractors of great wealth and influence. . . . It was also believed that a powerful though indirect influence wielded by those contractors, materially contributed to the adverse position assumed by the new Colonial Minister on a question to which the Imperial Government had, by his predecessor, been so far committed. The course of the Canadian envoy can only be defended on the assumption that a refusal was inevitable, and that a proper appreciation led him to appreciate it.

Contractors Set Aside $250,000 of Stock for Hincks

" No more unfavorable impression would probably have remained had not his name subsequently appeared as the proposed recipient of a *douceur* [a present or an intended bribe] from the contractors in the shape of £50,000 [$250,000] of paid up stock in the capital stock of the Company which, however, he repudiated when it was announced." [1]

But this abbreviated account is an incomplete and meager description of the full charges against Hincks. It omits a number of important particulars, and does not clarify the question of precisely why it was that those English contractors, the most thrifty and methodical of men in business matters, should have been so uncommonly generous in thus setting aside $250,000 of Grand Trunk stock in Hincks' name.

That this amount, or to be exact, £50,400 sterling in shares, was credited to Hincks, is an incontestable fact; and it was this very fact, leaking out in 1854, that caused considerable discussion. It pressed seriously for explanation and investigation, more especially as there were eight other specific charges that in various ways Hincks, and, in some cases, certain of his colleagues, had taken advantage of their high positions to speculate in land, the price of which was increased by canal or railway projects and legislation, or to speculate in railway stocks or municipal railway bonds.

To attempt to suppress these charges by a mere denial, or by ignoring them, was an impossibility; they were too grave, and the popular and the political talk was too great. Therefore the course of an investigating committee was decided upon. This committee was chosen by the Legislative Council or upper House, nearly all, if not all, of the members of which had themselves benefited by similar speculations or had similar connections and interests. The Speaker of that body was John Ross, the head of the Grand Trunk Railway of Canada. These facts were not favorably commented upon.

The fact was proved by the evidence produced before this

[1] *Eighty Years' Progress of British North America,* 1781 to 1861, pp. 199–200.

committee that 1,008 shares of Grand Trunk stock, valued at £50,400 sterling, had, on April 25, 1853, been allotted to Hincks, and that a few days later, on May 3, 1853, the sum of £10,080 was paid in cash as part payment on that stock, and a receipt was made out in Hincks' name and in his favor. There was also another £50,400 worth of Grand Trunk shares credited similarly to Alexander Mackenzie Ross. But what anonymous benefactor was it that paid the cash, amounting to one-twentieth of the price of the stock, for Hincks' presumable benefit?

Sources of the Allotted Stock

That was a delicate and difficult point to determine, and it was some time before it was fully solved. John Ross testified that he didn't know who paid the cash; it was popularly remarked that as the head of the Grand Trunk Railway, Ross' innocence of knowledge of certain facts was, indeed, extraordinary, doubly so considering that Ross, in 1852, had, as president of that railway, been sent to England to superintend the completion of the contract for the construction of the Grand Trunk. A. T. Galt, Grand Trunk promoter, also professed the densest ignorance as to this particular transaction; he testified that he knew nothing of who made the original allotment of stock.

Light, however, was obtained from George Carr Glyn and Thomas Baring, English bankers and Grand Trunk directors in London.

In response to written questions, Glyn wrote to the Legislative Council Committee that the allotment of stock to Hincks and to Ross was made by the Grand Trunk directors upon the representations of Sir S. M. Peto, of the contracting firm of Peto, Brassey, Betts and Jackson. Baring's written replies to the committee's queries corroborated this. It was Peto,

Baring informed the Committee, who had paid the first deposit
on the shares, and it was likewise Peto who had caused the
receipts to be made out in the names of Hincks and of Ross.[2]
According to Baring's view, Hincks and Ross had no personal
interest.

Hincks Accused of Bargaining

Called as a principal witness, George Brown, a member of
Parliament, put his answers in the form of a definite charge
that Hincks had made a bargain with the English contractors.
By this bargain, Brown alleged, the contractors were to get
the bulk of the Grand Trunk stock and bonds, and exorbitant
stated sums for the construction of the railway. Brown further charged that by reason of Hincks' influence, the contractors obtained a charter for constructing the Quebec and Trois
Pistoles Railway — a Grand Trunk branch line; that Hincks
was also of service to those contractors in the Quebec and
Richmond Railway contract, and that Hincks had given them
his great influence in promoting through Parliament a Bill for
the amalgamation of these and other railways.

Furthermore, Brown charged that in return for that £50,400
of Grand Trunk stock, Hincks had used his official influence
to get the Grand Trunk contract for the firm of Peto, Brassey,
Betts and Jackson. It was believed, Brown charged, that in
return they had placed the £50,400 sterling of stock in his
name, and had paid £10,080 sterling on account to Hincks'
credit, and that before further installments became payable,
the fact of Hincks' owning so large an amount of stock in-
opportunely became public, and caused the sudden abandon-
ment of the plan.

The general belief was, Brown stated, that Hincks must

[2] *Legislative Council Sessional Papers,* Vol. 13, First Sess., Fifth
Parl., 1854-1855, Appendix A. A. A. A., pp. 25-26. (Although this
document is indexed, the pages are not numbered.)

have known of the transaction; that as chief promoter and a director of the Grand Trunk he must have consulted the allotment list, and could not have been ignorant of the holdings of stock credited to him. There was a belief in other quarters, Brown averred, that the stock was assigned to Hincks and the deposit paid for him so as to enable him to sell it to others, and thus pocket the premium or profit expected from the sale of his shares.

Committee Exonerates Hincks

Despite the plea that it was the practice to admit such testimony as circumstantial and relevant, the majority of the committee by vote would not accept Brown's evidence. Their refusal was based upon the ground that only matters within his personal knowledge would be accepted. They, however, allowed his testimony to be published.

Hincks' own explanation was that the Grand Trunk shares credited to Ross and himself were merely *" held in trust for allotment in Canada* to parties who might be desirous to take an interest in the Company." If this were so, it presented the sight of a Prime Minister acting as an intermediary for the disposition of stock the market price of which depended much upon legislation that he himself caused to be enacted.

It was obviously an incongruous explanation, but it was adopted by the Legislative Council Committee, which went even further and reported that the stock had been put in Hincks' name " without his knowledge," and that he had no personal interest in it. That the report of this considerate committee was of a " whitewashing " character was freely charged; certainly its extenuating treatment of the other charges brought against Hincks seemed to impart much substance to this widely-expressed view. Frankly cynical that report was, too, excusing speculations by Ministers with the off-hand remark that everyone else who could do so was doing likewise. No evidence of corruption could be found — so this committee reported.[3]

Hincks' Friends Get Contract

So the English contracting firm of Peto, Brassey, Betts and Jackson got the contract. Already its members were enriched by their operations in the construction of many railroads in England and elsewhere in Europe. If any curious investigator seeks to know the methods by which the railroads in England were built, he has only to consult the graphic account that Smiles gives in his " Life of George Stevenson." There the informative details will be found of how these lines were " scamped " by improper ballasting and other methods of inefficient construction by which contractors reaped the largest possible profit for the cheapest, hastiest and poorest kind of work. These methods were transferred to Canada.

For their work of construction the English Grand Trunk contractors agreed to take two-thirds of their pay in stocks and bonds — a fact which subsequently led to the ruin of all of them except Brassey, who shrewdly edged out of the mess in time.

The all-potent banking house of Rothschilds, in reality, however, owned an eighth interest in the capital of the Grand Trunk. The Canadian Government's financial agents of the Grand Trunk in England were the big banking houses of Baring Brothers and Company, and Glyn, Mills and Company.

[3] See *Legislative Council Sessional Papers,* Vol. 13, First Sess., Fifth Parl., 1854–1855, Appendix A. A. A. A., giving the report and incorporating the testimony. So useful a document was this report, it may be parenthetically explained, that Sir Francis Hincks, in his *Reminiscences,* published thirty years later, fell back upon it as his vindication notwithstanding the fact that certain other transactions (which are described in this chapter), were admitted both by the committee and by Hincks himself.

Less than six men or concerns in England held most of the Grand Trunk's stock.

The Grand Trunk's Exalted Directors

Of the nineteen Grand Trunk directors, nine were nominated by the Canadian Government for the purpose of safeguarding the public interest. Of these nine, four were Cabinet Ministers, and eight of the nine were really nominees of the English contractors. A number of the government directors were stockholders in this project or other projects at the same time. Whether they were able to reconcile these conflicting interests, and to what extent and in just what manner they responded to the purposes of their appointment, will be seen later in this chapter.

Very impressive, therefore, was the directorate of the Grand Trunk Railway Company. The list comprised not a few of the most powerful and what were considered the most illustrious Canadian public men.

There was John Ross, Member and Speaker of the Legislative Council, Solicitor-General of Upper Canada, and stockholder in the Grand Trunk Railway of Canada; he was appointed president of the Grand Trunk through the all-powerful influence of the English contractors controlling the stock, and he remained president until 1862. There was Francis Hincks, promoter and incorporator, as we have seen, of several railroads, and a stockholder in the Grand Trunk. A merchant and bank manager in early life, Hincks went to Parliament, pushed the Great Western, the Grand Trunk and other railway projects and subsidies, became Inspector-General (a position analagous to Finance Minister), and then became Prime Minister of Canada, and was knighted.

Another of the Grand Trunk directors was E. P. Tache; he had been Cabinet Minister in 1848, and thereafter was

Receiver-General, Speaker of the Legislative Council, and then head of the Government; a Sir, he too, became, in 1858.

A Roll of Honor

In addition, there was James Morris, Member of the Legislative Council and Postmaster-General; Malcolm Cameron, President of the Executive Council; R. E. Caron, Speaker of the Legislative Council; Peter McGill, Member of the Legislative Council, the Executive Council, and for decades President of the Bank of Montreal; he, too, was a Grand Trunk stockholder. Among other notabilities was George E. Cartier, Member of Parliament for Montreal, and later Premier of Canada, the Grand Trunk's chief lawyer. Such were some of the Grand Trunk's directors as listed by the Company's prospectus.

All, or nearly all of these men, as we have previously noted, were among the incorporated proprietaries of various different or interconnected railway or other private companies. For instance, Hincks, Morris and other Government members were, as an investigation in 1855 showed, partners in a syndicate organized to buy from the Government the Domain Farm on the Seignory of Lauzon. They calculated that the completion of the Grand Trunk Railway would increase the property's value. The transaction was duly consummated. Hincks admitted the syndicate's operations, but justified them on the ground that he had not used his official position unduly and had not benefited financially. The same disclosures showed that Malcolm Cameron speculated in Grand Trunk stock.[4]

---

[4] See *Legislative Council Sessional Papers*, etc., 1854–1855, Vol. 13, Appendix A. A. A. A. One of the first witnesses called, Moses H. Purley, agent for Crown Lands in New Brunswick, testified (in replying to a leading question), that he had known a member of the Executive Council to buy at special sales property which that very

Get $15,557,500 of Public Cash

The Grand Trunk Railway came into existence with the impressive capital of £9,500,000, increased a little later to £12,900,000 sterling. The Canadian Parliament was extremely generous. Of this amount it guaranteed £3,111,500 sterling, the several sums of which were granted on different occasions.

When, in 1855, one of these sums of £500,000 sterling aid to the Grand Trunk Railway was being voted through the Legislative Assembly of the Province of Canada, protests were made in that body against votes being cast by Galt and Holton on the ground that they were extensive contractors of the Grand Trunk or its amalgamated lines, and a similar protest was made against the vote of Angus Morrison on the ground of his being a stockholder. Morrison admitted that he had held stock, but denied any present pecuniary interest. Motions to disqualify Galt, Holton and Morrison from voting were defeated.[5] Hincks, Ross, MacNab, Cayley, Cartier and other railroad promoters all joined in voting down the motion.[6]

In consideration of getting the contract on their own terms, the contracting concern of Peto, Brassey, Betts and Jackson had assumed the risk of disposing of the stock and bonds. The prospectus issued by the Company and framed by Hincks, Ross and Galt, was a glowing production. To investors it held out the certainty of dividends of 11½ per cent. But how

member in his capacity of Cabinet Minister had expressly ordered to be sold at a special price.

[5] *Journal of the Legislative Assembly, Prov. of Canada,* 1855. Vol. XIII, Part II, pp. 1030-1031.

[6] *Ibid.* The returns to Parliament in that very year showed that Hincks, McGill, William Allan, John Ross and other members of Parliament or Government were stockholders in either the Grand Trunk or in railways amalgamated with it.— See *Journals of the Legislative Assembly,* 1854-1855, Appendix F. F., Vol. XIII.

such profits could be extracted from a thinly-populated country, with small developed resources, and especially from a country traversed by numerous competitive waterways and canals, was hard to see. Even the English contractors, it was said, were misled by this roseate prospectus.

Manipulating Grand Trunk Stock

After having been manipulated upward, the market price of Grand Trunk stocks and bonds began to decline and continued so. It was freely asserted that this came about largely because of the extravagance, blundering and inefficiency that at every step marked the construction of the Grand Trunk railway.

The staff of officials sent over from England were paid "princely salaries"; the chief of these received an annual salary of $25,000, which, together with his "expenses," brought the whole paid to this official up to $43,000 a year — considered a colossal sum at that period. Other official salaries ranged in lavish proportion.

The St. Lawrence and Atlantic Railway, controlled by Sir A. T. Galt and others, was "unloaded" upon the Grand Trunk Railway Company at cost, notwithstanding the known fact that its stock had been sold at 50 per cent. discount. After getting it at this extortionate price, which had been paid upon the representation that it was complete, the Grand Trunk Railway Company had to spend another $1,000,000 to put that line in some fair degree of shape between Montreal and Portland.[7]

One of the charges of corruption brought against Sir Francis Hincks was that as Cabinet Minister he had obtained secret advance information of this amalgamation, and had

[7] Keefer, *Eighty Years' Progress of British North America,* 1781 to 1861, p. 208.

speculated in the stock. That he did get a telegram from A. T. Galt and did buy stock was admitted, as likewise the fact that the market value of the stock went up after the amalgamation. But the generous Legislative Council Committee reporting on this and other charges, smoothed over the transaction on the ground that Hincks did not buy the stock *until several weeks after* the amalgamation.[8]

"Scamping" the Construction Work

When it became evident that Grand Trunk stocks and bonds were depreciating, the agents and sub-contractors of Peto, Brassey, Betts and Jackson "scamped" construction work whenever they could; most railroad construction was paid for not by the work but by the mile. It was Brassey, it may here be remarked, who introduced the subcontracting system in Canada. Provisions of the contracts were either not enforced or were but meagerly complied with. East of Toronto — the section of the work carried on by the English contractors — the rails were of poor quality, and the ballasting and the placing of sleepers were so flimsily, badly done as to lead later "to a destruction of rolling stock and property . . . which is unprecedented in the history of railways."[9] The entire scheme of construction was grossly and manifestly inefficient. In level country the railroad was not raised so as to keep out snow and water. The gradients in hilly regions were badly arranged and flagrantly defective. Everywhere "the contract-

[8] See *Legislative Council Sess. Papers,* etc., Vol. 13, 1854–1855, Appendix A. A. A. A. See also, Hincks' *Reminiscences,* p. 347.

[9] Keefer, p. 209. "At this identical time," says Keefer, "the contractors wielding a gigantic scheme which traversed every county in the Province, virtually controlled the government and the legislature while the expenditure continued." Keefer might have added, with equal accuracy, that they controlled certain influential newspapers, also, and through them a certain part of what was called public opinion.

ors kept the road as near the surface as the contract permitted, no matter how much it might be smothered in winter and flooded in spring, or how frequent and severe the gradients became." Irrespective of railroad considerations, stations were placed where land was cheapest; this was done to obtain political support, or benefit from a speculation in building lots.[10]

Brassey Holds on to His Fortune

The firm of Peto, Brassey, Betts and Jackson later went bankrupt, but, doubtless foreseeing how affairs were going, Brassey had discreetly withdrawn. He left an enormous fortune said to have been £7,000,000 or nearly $35,000,000, which his eldest son, Lord Brassey, later Governor of Victoria, Australia, largely inherited. Most of this wealth came from the profits of railway construction work; for it was Brassey, as we have said, who developed that vicious system of subcontracting which introduced the sweatshop evils, so to speak, on construction work. Strikes were numerous. The construction camps were in such a condition that cholera found its easy prey among the laborers; in one case in particular, 60 in a gang of 200 men were down with cholera at the same time; it is needless to say that many died.[11]

As for the construction of the western part of the Grand Trunk from Toronto to Sarnia, the contractors were mainly such Parliament members as A. T. Galt, L. H. Holton, D. L. Macpherson leagued with Casimir Gzowski (later a Sir) in the firm of Gzowski and Company.[12] The list of stockholders

[10] *Ibid.*, p. 210. Keefer estimated in 1861 that in addition to the $1,000,000 expended to put the St. Lawrence and Atlantic Railway in shape, the Grand Trunk had to spend $6,000,000 on its main line to make up deficiencies in the carrying out of the contract.

[11] *A True Captain of Industry*, Article on Brassey in the *Canadian Monthly and National Review*, issue of October, 1872, p. 317.

[12] High members of the Government saw no impropriety in making

of the Toronto and Guelph Railway Company, controlled by the Grand Trunk Railway Company, showed that Gzowski and Company were the largest private stockholders, owning 10,398 shares.[13]

Samuel Thompson, one of Toronto's prominent publishers and municipal officials at the time, and secretary of the Toronto and Guelph Railway Company, refers in his *Reminiscences* to a certain contract for laying out the Esplanade for the Toronto terminus of the Grand Trunk. Gzowski and Company succeeded in prevailing upon the officials to supersede the first contract that they had by a second. By this second contract, Thompson relates, the city lost about $50,000, and Gzowski and Company benefited in one item alone to the extent of at least $16,000, that sum representing the difference between the rates of wages in 1853 and 1855 — presumably by the contractors retaining the old scale of wages.[14] But such profits were nothing compared to the immense potential value of the Esplanade property turned over by the city of Toronto to the Grand Trunk and the Northern Railway.

It was at this identical period that, as we shall see, Mayor John G. Bowes of Toronto was a partner with Hincks, the Prime Minister of Canada, in a corrupt bargain in the private purchase and sale of Toronto City bonds issued as aid to the Northern Railway Company.

As to the circumstances of this particular transaction full details are set forth later in this chapter.

fortunes out of construction of railroads. The Hon. L. H. Holton, connected with the firm of Gzowski and Co., which built the western part of the Grand Trunk, was at the same time a member of Parliament, and a director of the Grand Trunk, as also a bank president and director. He later was a Cabinet Minister in various Administrations, and twice Minister of Finance. He remained in Parliament until his death in 1880.

[13] *Appendix F. F., Appendix No. 9, Vol. XIII, Appendices to Journals of the Legislative Assembly,* etc., 1854-1855.

[14] *Reminiscences of a Canadian Pioneer,* p. 281.

Did Governor-General Elgin Take Away £80,000?

Writing cursorily and with a scantiness of detail as to conditions in 1853, Thompson, in his volume, has a curious passage to this effect: "The Ministry then in power was known as the Hincks-Tache Government. . . . People remembered William Lyon Mackenzie's prophecy who said that he feared that Francis Hincks could not be trusted to resist temptation. When Lord Elgin [Governor-General of Canada] went to England, it was whispered that his lordship had paid off £80,-000 of mortgages on his Scottish estates, out of the proceeds of speculations which he had shared with his clever minister. The St. Lawrence and Atlantic transaction, the £50,000 Grand Trunk stock placed in his [Hincks'] credit — as he asserted, without his consent,— and the Bowes transaction, gave color to many stories circulated to his [Hincks'] prejudice. And when he [Hincks] went to England, and received the governorship of Barbadoes, many people believed it was the price of his private service to the Earl of Elgin." [15]

If there was any substance in these charges, the available official documents do not contain any support of them, although much went on that never was disclosed in official reports. Hincks made a general denial.

Members of Parliament "Entertained"

At the same time, railway contractors, "practical men" versed in all of the arts of shoddy construction and bribery, came over from the United States to seize *their* share of the harvest.

"One bold operator," Keefer wrote, "organized a system which virtually made him ruler of the province [of Canada] for several years. In person or by agents he kept 'open house,'

[15] *Ibid.*, p. 290.

where the choicest brands of champagne and cigars were free to all the people's representatives, from the town councillor to the cabinet minister; and it was the boast of one of these agents that when the speaker's bell rang for a division more members of Parliament were to be found in his apartments than in the library or any other single resort. By extensive operations he held the prosperity of so many places, as well as the success of so many schemes and individuals, in his grasp, that he exercised a quasi-legitimate influence over many who could not be directly seduced. Companies about to build a railway or get a municipal loan or other grants were led to believe that if he were the contractor, he could get the sanction of the government to any extent."

Blackmailing Operations

Keefer further wrote that before the English contractors for the Grand Trunk Railway could proceed with their schemes in the Canadian Parliament they were compelled to give this lobbyist-contractor a one-third interest in their contract. He, too, foreseeing Grand Trunk troubles, compromised by exchanging his one-third interest for £12,000 sterling.

When an English contractor was confidently about to swoop upon the contract for the Toronto and Hamilton Railway, up turned this same irrepressible individual; he had to be bought off with £10,000 sterling. "But," Keefer narrates, "he had to disgorge later when seeking the coöperation of this same English contractor for the celebrated but abortive Southern Railway scheme." [16]

The Toronto Northern Railway contract had been turned over to a band of American contractors. As payment they were to receive the Company's bonds and stocks and government guarantee debentures. But before they could get any

[16] *Eighty Years' Progress of British North America,* etc., pp. 222-223.

part of the government debentures, the contractors were required, by the terms of the grant, to complete one-half of the first 75 miles. When their cash was exhausted, they asked the Government for an advance of money, despite their not having completed the necessary work.

"Fixing" Government Officials

"But," so Keefer describes the incident, "the Government found the road so 'scamped' under the American engineer (who subsequently openly became a partner with the contractors), that the Commissioner of Public Works refused to recommend the issue of provincial bonds.

"Here was a fix! But the contractors sent for their American 'brother' who, for a brokerage of $100,000 of the first mortgage bonds of the Company, undertook to obtain the guarantee. He went to his colleague in the government; the Commissioner of Public Works was shunted out of office on a suddenly-raised issue (which was immediately thereafter dropped), and just one week afterward, the guarantee bonds were forthcoming.

"In connection with this incident it is worthy of remark, that a member of the Government shortly afterward paid away nearly £10,000 of the first mortgage bonds of the same company in the purchase of real estate." [17]

The Great Western Railway sought legislation to lay a double track from Hamilton to London. Keefer says that the Company was gravely assured that the Government was powerless to give the Company the right; the American contractor in question, the Company was told, had too much influence in Parliament.

The contractor was accordingly "seen." What was his price? It was the contract for the double tracking. The

[17] *Ibid.,* p. 224.

double-track scheme was later dispensed with by the Company as unnecessary, but other privileges were sought and secured. " Among other favors obtained by the legislation thus bartered for, was the power to disregard that provision of the railway Act which requires trains to stop before crossing the bridge over the Desjardins Canal [near Hamilton]. In less than two years thereafter, a train *which did not stop* plunged through this very bridge, and among the first recovered of the sixty victims to that ' accident ' was the dead body of the great contractor himself." [18]

The particular contractor thus referred to was Samuel Zimmerman.

It is in such authentic accounts that we get real glimpses of some of the methods used at the time; and, as we shall see, we get still other definitely established facts of other methods used by railway promoters.

Rids Itself of the Government Lien

We shall now revert to the Grand Trunk Railway.

Pleading that it was now in a sadly embarrassed condition, the directors of that railway, placing themselves in the legal position of paupers, applied to the Canadian Parliament for " relief."

It promptly came, in 1857, although not without encountering great opposition from the Great Western Railway forces in Parliament, led by Sir Allan N. MacNab and also antagonism from other railway interests. A motion for an inquiry

[18] *Ibid.*, p. 224. This catastrophe happened on March 12, 1857. Keefer could have added that he wrote with authority; he was, in fact, one of the examining civil engineers reporting on the accident. Although planned originally to be built of oak timber, the bridge was constructed of pine, and was in a bad condition. After one theory following another put out by the Company to explain the cause of the accident had been discarded, the Great Western Railway Company declared that Providence was responsible!

into Grand Trunk affairs was voted down. It was during this debate that the Hon. J. Cauchon, Commissioner of the Crown Lands Office and Cabinet Minister, curtly informed Premier Taché that he would not vote for the Grand Trunk Aid Bill unless he (Cauchon) was given assurance that a grant of 1,500,000 acres would be made to the North Shore Railway Company; Cauchon himself read his letters on the subject in Parliament. Although Cauchon did not then succeed in obtaining the land grant, the North Shore Railway Company later secured an even larger land grant, and Cauchon (as already noted), became the Company's president.

An accommodating law was passed (20 Vic. Cap. XI.) by which the Canadian Parliament declared that it would forego all interest in its claims against the Grand Trunk until the earnings and profits of the Company, comprising those of the St. Lawrence and Atlantic Railway Company, should be sufficient to pay *all charges* including:

1. All expenses of managing, working and maintaining the lines of the Company.

2. The rent and interest of the St. Lawrence and Atlantic Railway (acquired by the Grand Trunk), and all interest on the bonds of the Company, exclusive of those held by the Province of Canada.

3. A dividend of six per cent. on the paid up share capital of the Company, in each year in which the surplus earnings should admit of same.

At the same time, the government directors of the Grand Trunk were dispensed with.

Parliament "Too Liberal"

Further legislation favorable to the Grand Trunk Railway was enacted in the following years. On June 9, 1862, a law was passed (25 Vic. Cap. 50.) the purport of which again allowed the postponing the payment of the Government loans, and authorized the Company to issue £500,000 sterling of equipment bonds. Five years later another law was enacted authorizing the Company to issue another £500,000 sterling of equipment bonds to take priority over all other charges, except the bonds allowed in 1862. With all the outstanding issues of bonds and other what-nots, the Government now stood a slim enough chance of ever recovering its loans, and much of them it never did get back. In properly subdued yet indignant language, Swinyard, president of the Great Western Railway, sourly complained of the too " liberal spirit " which Parliament had shown towards the Grand Trunk Railway.[19]

In that era the most bitter competition for privileges, powers, subsidies and traffic prevailed between various of the railroad companies. Each had their sturdy representatives in Parliament; and in the course of this warfare each sought hard to damage, if not cripple the others. If one company was unduly favored with Government grants, loans or other laws or donations more than the others, acid resentment resulted. The same was true with regard to Provincial legislation and municipal by-laws; competing companies used every possible influence to prevent one another from securing bonuses or other grants of public aid.

The two most aggressive foes were the Great Western Railway Company and the Grand Trunk Railway Company of Canada — the one with a line with branches from Suspension Bridge to Windsor, and the road of the other running from Quebec and Montreal to Toronto and other places and with projected lines paralleling certain of the Great Western's territory in Ontario. This sharp competition, it may be said here, continued for many years more until the Grand Trunk absorbed the Great Western.

[19] See *Sessional Paper No. 61, Sess. Papers,* Vol. I, No. 9, 1867-1868, p. 5.

The Great Western's Diversion of Funds

From November, 1852, to June, 1855, the Canadian Government made loans totaling £770,000 to the Great Western Railway Company. " The Company," confidentially wrote Finance Minister John Rose to the Governor-in-Council, February 24, 1868, " was represented in Parliament by the late Sir Allan MacNab for many years its President, and it was he who, in 1852, moved the Resolution in the Railway Committee set forth in the Company's petition "— a resolution aiming to give the Great Western a monopoly in the Ontario Peninsula, but which bill failed to pass,[20] for the very obvious reason that at that time Grand Trunk influences were dominant.

Finance Minister Rose made the accusation that the accounts of the Great Western Railway showed that its promoters appropriated a total of about $1,225,000 of the funds in doing what the Company was never chartered to do and what it had no legal right to do — in constructing a railroad in the United States — the Detroit and Milwaukee Railway. Rose further asserted that fully $4,000,000 of its capital was used thus, and also absorbed in constructing other lines and in steamship investments.[21]

Here the fact may be interjected that so far as cash went, the Commercial Bank of Canada had advanced £250,000 to the Detroit and Milwaukee Railway Company. With accumulated interest this claim amounted to considerably more by 1863. The bank, however, could get nothing, inasmuch as the Great Western had foreclosed two mortgages in 1860 against the Detroit and Milwaukee Railway, and a lawsuit availed

---

[20] See *Sessional Paper No. 61, Sessional Papers, Dom. Parl.,* 1867–1868, Vol. I, No. 9, p. 17.

[21] *Sessional Paper No. 7, Sess. Papers, Dom. Parl,* 1869, Vol. II, No. 3. Rose's communication, June 9, 1868, to Thomas Swinyard, president of the Great Western Railway Co. Rose was a member of a prominent European and New York banking firm.

nothing.   C. J. Brydges was one of the Canadian directors of
the Detroit and Milwaukee line; the two other Canadian directors were those politicians James Ferrier and William Molson. Brydges was appointed receiver, and the road was sold
in 1860 to the Great Western for the nominal sum of $1,000,-
000. Down, therefore, went the Commercial Bank of Canada
in resounding ruin; it was one of the largest banks in Canada,
and its collapse made a great sensation.

A Series of Tragic Accidents

Although millions of dollars were thus advanced from the
public treasury to the Great Western Railway, that line was
so inefficiently constructed that disastrous wrecks, causing considerable loss of life, were frequent.

At Lobo, on June 2, 1854, six passengers were killed, and
14 injured; at Thorold, on July 16, 1854, seven passengers
were killed and 14 injured; a terrible wreck at Baptiste Creek,
on October 27, 1854, caused the death of 57 persons and the
injury or mutilation of 46. These are a few of the many accidents in that single year of 1854, calling forth the appointment of an investigating Legislative Commission.

" We find," the Commission stated in part, " that at the
opening of the road, the embankments and cuttings were in a
dangerous state; that the ties or sleepers were without the stay
or support of gravel on the surface; the road crossings and
cattle grades were unfinished. The trestle works in some cases
substituted for embankments were notoriously insecure, and
in fact neither grading nor superstructure were in a fit state
to hazard the prosecution of traffic in the face of the contingencies of the coming winter and spring in this climate and
in this country." [22]

[22] *Report of Commissioners Appointed to Inquire into a Series of
Accidents on the Great Western Railway*, etc., *Leg. Council Sess.*

The Commission incorporated evidence proving that Managing-Director Brydges of the Great Western Railway had received full warning from a noted civil engineer that the road was in a too dangerous state to open it for traffic, but that he disregarded the warning. No railway official was punished for this continuous loss of life, and indeed it was only three years later that the appalling disaster (which we have already described), happened on the Great Western's system at Desjardin's Canal, near Hamilton.

Extracting Subsidies from the Towns

By 1858, the railway contractors had completed, or professed to have completed, 1,483 miles of railway in Ontario and Quebec. Funds poured into their laps. The most amazing audacity was shown in securing loans from municipalities.

From the town of Port Hope with about only 3,000 population, a loan of $740,000 was squeezed. The town of Niagara with but 2,500 population, was influenced to give $280,000. Brockville, with a bare 4,000 population, yielded $400,000, and Cobourg, with the same number of inhabitants, $500,000. The City of Ottawa, with less than 10,000 population, presented $200,000, and the City of London, having no larger population, $375,400. Brantford, of not more than 6,000 population, was persuaded into voting a $500,000 loan.[23] These are but a few examples of the manner in which small and poor municipali-

Papers, Vol. 13, 1854–1855, Appendix Y. Y. No doubt the conditions as reported by this Commission were true enough, yet it should be noted that the Commission was regarded as subject to Grand Trunk influences. It was a common practice for legislative committees, one or more of the members of which were interested in a particular railway, to disclose the truth as to the workings of a competitive railway, with the object of damaging its reputation and the market value of its stock.

[23] See the itemized table in *Eighty Years of Progress in British North America,* etc., pp. 216–217.

ties were depleted of funds, and corrupted or compelled to mortgage future generations for the benefit of railway contractors and owners, who exacted tribute with the most inordinate and presumptuous insistence.[24]   Keefer tells of one village allowed by the Governor-in-Council (the permission of which body was required under the Railway Loan Act), to borrow $300 per head of the population.

Northern Railway Subsidy Jobbery

As for subsidies procured from the larger municipalities, the Northern Railway scandal, revolving around the issue of Toronto City bonds in aid of that project, revealed the methods often used to get municipal subsidies.

In 1850 the City of Toronto, or rather its officials, voted a gift of £25,000, a valuable site for a station, and the right of way, to aid this enterprise.   The next year the City of Toronto was prevailed upon to loan £35,000 more to the Company, under conditions making it virtually a gift.   One of these conditions was that certain parts of the road had to be completed before these sums were available.   Despite the fact that they did not comply with the required conditions, the contractors, in the very act of " scamping," had the assurance to ask for the full subsidy.   Mayor John G. Bowes had been a director of this same railway company.

An illegal by-law was thereupon passed to hand over £60,000 to the Railway Company.   Advised by " eminent counsel " that this by-law was in fact an illegality, the contractors and their confederates quickly hit upon a plan of circumventing it. A Bill was hurried through Parliament.   This Bill was appar-

[24] Keefer estimated that by 1861 the municipal railway loans in Ontario amounted to $5,594,000 and those in the Province of Quebec to $925,940.   There was also about $3,000,000 more contributed by municipalities which sum was not entered in the railway fund.—*Ibid.*, p. 215.

ently innocent and modest-looking; its sole ostensible object was to allow Toronto to issue a loan of £100,000 of bonds for the purpose of consolidating the City's debt. But it was in the fifth clause of the Bill that the " little joker " cunningly lay. Notwithstanding the fact that the subsidy railway debenture bonds voted by the City's officials did not mature for twenty years, this clause compelled Toronto to pay *at once* to the contractors the debenture bonds *at their face value.* Prime Minister Hincks rushed this Bill in all of its stages through Parliament in a few days, and it became law. None or few of the legislators knew that a few weeks previously Hincks and Bowes had personally bought those very bonds at four-fifths their face value.

Soon revelations were forthcoming that Bowes and Hincks had been in secret partnership, and that they had bought from the Northern Railway contractors, at a large discount, a batch of the identical bonds issued by Toronto to aid that Company. By certain bank manipulations, it appeared, they did this without having to spend a cent of their own money.

Hincks and Mayor Bowes Share Profits

In the Court of Chancery, in 1854, Bowes admitted the transaction, and likewise did Hincks. Each of them, it was disclosed, made a profit of £4,115.

Even the Legislative Council Committee which, in 1855, presented Hincks with so white a bill of moral and political health, admitted that Hincks' partnership with Bowes was fully proved, but asserted that Hincks had not used his influence as a Cabinet Minister to get the money for buying the bonds. The Judicial Committee of the Privy Council, however, denounced the transaction as a corrupt bargain, and Bowes was condemned to pay a judgment of nearly £5,000. Samuel Thompson, who was then chairman of the finance committee of the Toronto Municipal Council, insisted in his *Reminiscences,* published thirty years ago, that Hincks had used his official powers for his private profit, and that deception had been practiced on Toronto's Finance Committee and Municipal Council.[25]

No doubt it was to this incident that Keefer referred in his account (already cited in this chapter), of what he described as the Toronto Northern Railway contract. That, writing a few years after the transaction, Keefer should have made certain definite charges, at a time when most of the people concerned were alive, and that these charges, published in book form, should have called forth neither denial nor libel suit, certainly invests them with weight, corroborated as they were by sworn admissions as to other bargaining.

Keefer's account supplies the finishing touches. He wrote, as we have seen, that the contractors " scamped " the work; that the Commissioner of Public Works, because of that notorious fact, refused to sanction giving them subsidy bonds; that the contractors offered a certain contract-lobbyist a bribe of $100,000 of first-mortgage Northern Railway bonds if he would arrange matters with the Government to hand over the subsidy bonds to them; that the lobbyist immediately got busy and in contact with a certain high Government official; that on a trumped-up issue or pretext the Commissioner of Public Works was summarily dislodged from office; that the guarantee subsidy bonds were then issued in a rush; and that soon

[25] See *Legislative Council Sessional Papers, First Session, Fifth Parl.,* 1854–1855, Vol. XIII, Appendix A. A. A. A. The full transcript of the proceedings in the Court of Chancery is embodied in this document. See also, Thompson's *Reminiscences of a Canadian Pioneer,* p. 283. Thompson was Secretary of the Toronto and Guelph Railway Company until it was absorbed by the Grand Trunk Railway in 1853. Municipal officials of the various other cities were likewise stockholders in different railway companies. That after the exposure of such a transaction Bowes should have been elected to Parliament was characteristic of the elections of the times. The annals are full of election scandals.

afterward a prominent member of the Government bought real estate for which as payment he gave nearly £10,000 of the first mortgage bonds of the Northern Railway.

Many other of the railways were so badly constructed that after the contractors had turned them over to the owning companies, great additional expenditures were required to put them even in the most passable shape. And this notwithstanding the fact that public subsidies often were enough to pay for one-half or more of the entire cost of construction.

An example of this fact was the case of the Cobourg and Peterboro Railway, the contractor for which was the ubiquitous Samuel Zimmerman. Although this road was only 30 miles long, the cost amounted to nearly $1,000,000, of which sum municipalities contributed $500,000. The road-bed was badly deficient, and the equipment not much better. With a celebration the road was finally opened for traffic, but hardly had the winter of 1853 set in when the railway's bridge, three miles long across Rice Lake, was crushed in and splintered by the ice. An examination revealed that the work had been scamped; the piles had not been sufficiently driven or properly stayed. Costly repair work had to be done before the road was tolerably fit for travel.[26]

Grafting was general; and one serious scandal after another now developing revealed that the railway promoters resorted to any means to secure funds from the public treasury.

The Great Southern Railway Corruption

By what methods railway contracts, municipal loans and the control of railways were often secured was evidenced in the disclosures, in 1857, concerning the Great Southern Railway.

The Great Southern Railway project was a scheme to form

[26] Trout's *The Railways of Canada,* a short and laudatory work, published in 1871, pp. 117-118.

a railway running from the Niagara River to the Detroit and St. Clair rivers. It was to traverse the rich agricultural belt of southern Ontario. This railway, as planned, was to be an amalgamation of two railroads, one chartered to run in the west of Ontario, the other in the eastern section.

The eastern part of this ambitious project was the Woodstock and Lake Erie Railway, chartered in 1848 to be completed within ten years. Originally Hincks was one of its promoters, but he later withdrew. So notorious was the general rascality that attended this railway's progress, or rather lack of progress, that in 1857 a Select Committee of the Legislative Assembly was appointed to investigate the whole Great Southern scheme.

This committee reported, on May 20, 1857, these facts: That in 1852, Samuel Zimmerman made a bargain with the railway's directors to supply two-thirds of the funds with which to construct and operate the road. In exchange, he was to get one-third in bonds, the same amount in stock and the same in cash from the Company.

A $50,000 Bribe for a Contract

How did Zimmerman manage to get this contract? The Select Legislative Committee reported that " for his influence and exertions in obtaining the contract for Zimmerman and Company, Henry de Blaquiere, one of the directors, is distinctly proved to have received a bribe of no less a sum than $50,000 under this contract in which the said De Blaquiere admits he was a secret partner to the extent of one-half of the profits." [27]

The directors of the Woodstock and Lake Erie Railway is-

[27] The full report and testimony are published in *Journals of the Legislative Assembly, Province of Canada*, 1857, Appendices to the 15th Vol., Appendix No. 6.

sued assurances that the £250,000 of the railway's stock had all been paid up. They engaged two agents, one of whom was a clergyman, to carry these tidings to the various municipalities along the line, and prevail upon those municipalities to invest in the railway in the form of loan subsidies. The people of those municipalities were gravely assured that there could be no possible failure to pay back the municipal loans; the Company, they were told, was backed by men of undoubted good faith. The municipalities in question were further assured that the loans asked for would reach only one-half of the cost of construction.

Fraud and Bribery

The exchequers of various municipalities were opened up, and out came loans to the Woodstock and Lake Erie Railway totaling £145,000 ($725,000). As a matter of fact, the Select Committee reported, the representations so made by the Company's agents were all false and fraudulent. Little of the stock had been paid up; and after they obtained the municipal loans, the Company's directors, without letting the municipalities know the fact, changed the contract from a cash to a credit basis.

The Township of Windham was one of the municipalities induced to give a loan of $100,000. How came it that this obscure, rustic place was so extremely generous? The Reeve (or Mayor) of Windham was ostentatiously doubtful of the ability of so small a community to stand so large a loan. After the loan had been voted, it became his duty, the Select Committee reported, "to hand over to the Railway Company, under certain conditions, the necessary papers to enable them to obtain Government debentures, under the by-law.

"To do this, the Reeve appeared to have what he called 'scruples.' . . . Means were soon found to remove them. A subcontractor was sent to him with an envelope containing $500

which was quietly handed to him. The ' scruples ' were removed, and twenty minutes after, the necessary papers were
in the hands of the Secretary of the Company; subsequently
the messenger carried the Reeve another envelope containing
an additional $500, one hundred of which he deducted for his
own services for negotiating the transaction, and the balance
of which he handed to the Reeve as payment in full for the
removal of his scruples." [28]

Plunder on Construction Work

The Woodstock and Lake Erie Company's directors now
made some appearance of construction work to distract attention from their frauds. In 1854 the contractors suspended
work. Up to this time the subcontractors had received £87,-
000 (whether English or Provincial currency is not stated),
yet they had done only about £32,000 worth of work. [29] Some
of the directors boldly grafted large sums. They caused the
railway to be surveyed over much of their own land which
they had bought cheap or got for nothing, and they now made
the municipalities pay them heavily for it. For a worn-out
brick yard the Company paid £5,000. [30]

Something had to be done in Parliament and speedily, or
else the charter would be automatically forfeited by the time
limit expiring. A bill was lobbied through, granting an extension of time.

Mr. Buchanan Gives a $100,000 Bribe

It was at this point that a rich Hamilton merchant of wide
commercial interests, namely, Isaac Buchanan, came forward.

[28] *Journals of the Legislative Assembly,* etc., 1857, Appendix No. 6
to the 15th Vol. (The pages of this document are not numbered.)
[29] *Ibid.*
[30] *Ibid.*

Buchanan was a noted politician, serving for a time as member of the Canadian Parliament and as President of the Executive Council. Presently he announced that he had control of the Woodstock and Lake Erie Railway. The Select Legislative Committee described the mode he used in getting control.

" It simply consisted," that Committee reported, " in the giving of a direct bribe of $100,000 to obtain the removal of three of the Directors, and the substitution in their stead of three of his own nominees, he having previously succeeded in securing without purchase the remaining four to accede to and aid him in carrying out his plans for the transference of the charter to a rival company." [31]

For a while there was " a life and death struggle " between Buchanan and Zimmerman, and litigation a plenty, but they united their interests, and after Zimmerman's death the interests of both were represented by the new board of directors consisting of such " high social lights " as Buchanan, Thomas G. Ridout, James C. Street and others.

More Bribery

Buchanan now had the eastern line for the projected Great Southern Railway. He at once set about getting the western. There was a chartered railway called the Amherstburg and St. Thomas Railway promoted by members of Parliament in 1852. The value of its charter consisted in supplying an extension of the Woodstock and Lake Erie Railway westward.

According to Buchanan's story before the Select Committee, a group of American capitalists of the New York Central Railway and the Michigan Central had sought to get control of a southern railway through Ontario, and that if they were successful, they would seriously compete with the Great Western Railway in which he, Buchanan, was " heavily interested."

[31] *Ibid.*

Buchanan insisted that in his aim to thwart those American capitalists, he had the support of all of the Great Western Railway Company's directors except Brydges. On the other hand, it was alleged that Buchanan's sole object was to " hold up " the Great Western, and force it to buy the Great Southern project from himself at an exorbitant price.

How Buchanan acquired control of the Amherstburg and St. Thomas Railway scheme was described by the Select Legislative Committee.

Peculiarly Humiliating and Painful

" While devising means to this end," the Committee reported, " a Mr. Van Voorhis comes most opportunely to his [Buchanan's] relief with a suggestion made by Mr. Hodge that for a consideration the coveted object could be obtained. Mr. Buchanan, after a little prudent consideration, determined as to the sum to be offered, and the proposition of Mr. Buchanan [sic] being reduced to writing, Mr. Buchanan accepts. The negotiations being concluded, Mr. De Blaquiere, who up to this point appears only in the background, steps in, receives $100,000, and then with his two brother directors withdraws and allows Mr. Buchanan and his two nominees to take their places; Mr. Van Voorhis as the negotiator between the two parties receiving for his services an undertaking that he shall have a preference contract of 35 miles of road. Whether or not others shared in the profits of this shameless transaction, your Committee have not been able certainly to ascertain." [32]

The next move was to get a Bill passed by Parliament amalgamating the Woodstock and Lake Erie Railway and the Amherstburg and St. Thomas Railway

" . . . That gross wrong," the Select Committee concluded

[32] *Ibid.* The testimony upon which the committee based its findings was extremely specific and voluminous.

its report, " has been practiced by parties officially and in otherwise in connection with the said Company, is fully established,
and that those concerned in the perpetration of such wrong
are individuals who have been hitherto occupying high and
honorable positions in society and public stations, is a circumstance of a peculiarly humiliating and painful character."

But the Select Committee's report did not reveal all the
prevailing corruption.   More was disclosed in the evidence itself and in the Parliamentary debates.   One member of Parliament, it appeared, stood out for a considerable bribe in connection with Great Southern Railway charter matters, nor was
he the only member.implicated in the disclosures.[33]

The Great Western Eulogizes Itself

Buchanan had testified, as we have seen, that his motive was
to get for the Great Western Railway the control of the Southern Railroad from the Niagara to the Detroit River.   The
Great Western Railway Company, he said, having done its
best to prevent the passage of the charter, had wanted to get
control of the competitive line to obviate the necessity of double
tracking its own line.   The Great Western Railway Company
repudiated this alleged object, and more than intimated that
a " hold-up " was attempted upon it.

With a great air of virtue, the directors of the Great Western Railway now came forward with a jibe at their projected
competitor, the Great Southern Railway.

They reported in 1857 that " during the last twelve months

[33] The president of the Amherstburg and St. Thomas Railway
Company in 1857 was Arthur Rankin, a member of the Parliament
of the Province of Canada, and the Company's vice-president was G.
Macbeth, another member of Parliament.   Rankin made a claim for
£25,000 from Zimmerman's estate for certain services rendered, presumably by him (Rankin) as a member of the Railway Committee of
the House.— See, *Journals of the Legislative Assembly*, 1857, Appendices to 15th Vol., Appendix No. 6.

considerable discussion has arisen in regard to the projected Southern Line through Canada, which last summer [was] attempted to be forced upon this Company. In the last session of the Provincial Legislature many disgraceful disclosures were made as to the past history of that scheme arising out of the rival claims of certain parties to the control of the line.

"These disclosures showing an extent of bribery and dishonesty which have rarely been paralleled in the history *of any joint stock undertaking* . . . cannot fail to increase the satisfaction of the shareholders that this Company was preserved from any connection with the scheme." [34]

When this report was made the Great Western Railway was headed partly by British capitalists and partly by Canadian politicians: Robert Gill of England was its president; John Young of Hamilton, Ont., its vice-president, and its two secretaries were British and Canadian.

For the time, the Great Southern Railway scheme had to be suspended; the operations of its promoters caused such a wide scandal that legislators discreetly refrained from sanctioning further powers. But it was subsequently revived as the Canada Southern Railway, and became an accomplished fact. The control was later acquired by the Vanderbilts, the American railway magnates owning the New York Central Railway, the Michigan Central and other lines. The Canada Southern Railway later was owned and controlled by the Vanderbilts, J. P. Morgan, William Rockefeller and other American magnates.

It is a noteworthy fact that at the very time Buchanan was doing his bribery, Commodore Cornelius Vanderbilt, the founder of the great Vanderbilt fortune, was amassing his original millions by a huge system of commercial blackmail on competing steamship lines, the exact facts as to which (citing official documents and court records), are related specifically in the *History of the Great American Fortunes.*

[34] Trout's *Railways of Canada,* 1871, pp. 88-89.

Some More Unpleasant Disclosures

But the foregoing were by no means the only railway scandals developing.

Reports and charges, exceedingly embarrassing to certain government functionaries, were current in 1858; and a Select Standing Committee of Public Accounts was ordered to investigate.

The chairman of this committee was A. T. Galt. This gentleman had been, as we have seen, the Canadian executive of the British American Land Company, the affairs of which he had converted into "a highly profitable state." He had been a prime owner of the St. Lawrence and Atlantic Railway, which, as we have seen, became part of the Grand Trunk Railway system. He was, also, as previously noted, a promoter of the Grand Trunk Railway of Canada, and a Grand Trunk contractor. Another member of the Committee was Hon. William Cayley, member of Parliament. As Inspector-General (Finance Minister), one of Cayley's functions was to borrow money for the Provincial debts.

Examined on June 8, 1858, Cayley reluctantly gave this testimony: That he had advanced £10,000 of Government money to the Cobourg and Peterboro Railway Company; that he was not a stockholder, but that at one time — in 1856 — he held bonds in the railway, and that the loan to the Company was under negotiation two or three months previously. The president and lessee of this railway, Cayley testified, was D'Arcy Boulton, with whom he was connected by marriage. (Boulton, it may be interpolated, had been Mayor of Cobourg in 1853, and later, as a member of Parliament had put an Act through that body chartering the building of this railway; he later became president of the Midland Railway.) The interrogator was curious to know whether Boulton, as lessee of the Cobourg and Peterboro Railway, had paid the rent in depreciated bonds, and whether Cayley had supplied him with the bonds? Cayley admitted that he had sold some bonds — between £4,000 and £5,000 worth of them — to Boulton, for which Boulton had paid him chiefly in land; Boulton's uncle was the Hon. Peter Robinson, Commissioner of Crown Lands.

More transactions were then uncovered. Cayley testified that out of the sums that the Grand Trunk Railway had received from the Government under the specific Act of 1856, that Railway Company had advanced large sums to other railway companies having no legal connection with it, and apparently separate roads. To the Port Hope and Lindsay Railway (later the Midland Railway), £13,000 had been advanced, and similar large advances were made to other railways, yet Cayley's published accounts contained no reference to these transactions in which public funds were freely used.[35]

In a written statement handed in to the Committee, on June 10, 1858, Cayley stated that the advances made by him to certain railway companies were sanctioned by an Order-in-Council which provided that the securities given in exchange were to be reported and passed upon by Solicitor-General Smith of Upper Canada, acting for the Government. Questioning brought out the fact that at that identical time Smith received a fee of £100 of railway company funds for professional serv-

---

[35] *Appendix to the 16th Vol., Journals of the Legislative Assembly of Canada,* 1858, Vol. XVI, No. 4, p. H., etc. Bank funds were likewise profusely used by the railway promoters. T. G. Ridout, Cashier of the Bank of Upper Canada, testified that that bank had advanced, on the recommendation and authority of the Government, nearly £60,000 to the promoters of the Cobourg and Peterboro Railway and the Ottawa and Prescott Railway. If, said Ridout, these two companies should fail to give the Grand Trunk Railway Company satisfactory security for the repayment of the money, the bank would have a fair claim against the Government.

Some years later the Bank of Upper Canada failed in a large crash. Its funds had been absorbed to an immense extent by advances to "land speculators, politicians, adventurers and men of that gentlemanly type who, though in business, scorn to soil their fingers with its details."

ices.[36] Cayley gave much other illuminating testimony, not the least interesting of which was his statement that the president of the Grand Trunk Railway Company was his colleague, the Receiver-General of the Province.[37]

It was in this very year, and only two months after giving this testimony, that Cayley was influential in having the Bank of Canada, a private institution, incorporated by Act of Parliament, and he himself headed the list of incorporators.

Funds Lifted Out of the Public Treasury

Perhaps, however, the most incisive testimony was that, on June 14, 1858, of Auditor-General John Langton: —

Q. 379. "Was £16,083, 6s., 8d., drawn directly from the public chest in the year 1857, and lent to the Cobourg and Peterboro Railway Company?"

A. "It was."

Q. 380. "Had Parliament given any authority for applying the Provincial money in such a manner?"

A. "Not that I am aware of."

Q. 385. "Was £160,000 drawn directly from the public chest in the year 1857, and lent to the Grand Trunk Railway Company?"

A. "It was."

Q. 386. "Had Parliament given any authority for applying the Provincial money in such a manner?"

A. "I am not aware that it had."

Q. 387. "Was the money restored to the chest in 1857?"

A. "No." [38]

[36] *Ibid.*, Questions Nos. 333 and 334.
[37] *Ibid.*, Question No. 342. Cayley was, and became still more so, a prominent corporation capitalist. Twenty years later we find him a director of the Dominion Telegraph Company of which Swinyard was Managing Director.
[38] *Ibid.* That such instructive facts were brought out was due to

It was, however, later returned, Langton stated, as also was that advanced to the Cobourg and Peterboro Railway Company — restorations no doubt opportunely stimulated by the investigating committee's inquisition.

Loans Turn Out To Be Mostly Worthless

Among divers other findings, the Select Standing Committee of Public Accounts reported that of £35,538 thus loaned to incorporated companies, little or none would ever be recovered, as the security was worthless. The Quebec Turnpike Trust was in possession of £33,882 of public money and had never paid one shilling of interest. The Province of Canada had paid £88,274 on bonds of the Ontario, Simcoe and Huron Railway, without adequate security. The Great Western Railway Company, although in receipt of large revenues, had paid no interest to the Government on advances,— and so the findings ran on, telling in official terminology of the methods by which the public funds had been indiscriminately placed at the disposal of certain railways and other favored companies. All of these corporations, it need hardly be said, were promoted, largely owned and directed by prominent Canadian politicians.

The fact was also established that £500,000 of Government debentures had been sold in England at 99¼ when, at the same time, the quotation prices of the stock exchange for those bonds were 105 to 107. This transaction caused a large loss to the Province of Canada. The additional fact was brought out that a certain Parliamentary supporter of the Government sold to the Government £20,000 of Hamilton debenture bonds at 97¼, although in the market their quotation was only 80; by this operation the Government favorite pocketed a profit of $17,500.

unsparing and persistent questioning by George Brown, a member of the Committee.

A Defeated Resolution

Now came a much-commented upon action on the part of a majority of the Public Accounts Committee. At a meeting on March 22, 1859, one of its members, Foley, offered a resolution condemning the practice on the part of Government functionaries of overriding the law by granting to individuals, on various pretenses, large sums of money, not only unauthorized by law but in direct contravention of law. This resolution was promptly consigned to limbo by a vote of 6 to 3. One of those voting against it was A. T. Galt.[39]

Without mentioning this circumstance of the resolution, Dent, however, inadvertently gives the explanation. "It had come to light," he narrates, "that in the year 1859, a sum of $100,000 had been advanced from the public chest by Mr. Galt, then Minister of Finance in the Cartier-Macdonald Government,[40] to redeem bonds given by the City of Montreal to the St. Lawrence and Atlantic Railway Company. By an arrangement entered into after their issue, these bonds had been made redeemable by the Grand Trunk, to which Company the Provincial advance had really been made; and this had been done without the sanction or knowledge of Parliament." [41]

[39] See *Appendix to 17th Vol., Journals of the Legislative Assembly, Prov. of Canada,* Vol. 17, No. 2, Appendix No. 5.

[40] Says Pope: "The Hon. Mr. Ross, Speaker of the Legislative Council and a member of the Government, had been solicitor for the railway, and was a shareholder in the road, as was Mr. Hincks. Nor was the Grand Trunk without influence on the left of the Speaker. Mr. Holton was largely interested, as was Mr. Galt. Indeed, that gentleman was supposed by some members of the Opposition to be so closely identified with the railway, that when, in 1858, Mr. Cartier announced the personnel of his Ministry, W. L. Mackenzie . . . shouted, at mention of Mr. Galt's name, 'Grand Trunk Jobber!' . . ." Joseph Pope's *Sir John Macdonald, Prime Minister of Canada,* Vol. I, pp. 110–111. Galt was, in fact (as we have seen) a member of the contracting firm of Gzowski and Company, which constructed the Grand Trunk's line from Toronto to Sarnia.

[41] Dent's *The Last Forty Years: Canada Since the Union of 1841,*

As we have seen, A. T. Galt was a chief promoter of the St. Lawrence and Atlantic Railway and the Grand Trunk Railway of Canada. He was also, as previously narrated, a member of a Grand Trunk Railway Construction Company. And it may be said here that he also was concerned in other enterprises. He was an original promoter, in 1855, of the Eastern Townships Bank. He greatly assisted in founding the textile mills at Sherbrooke. He became, in 1869, a leading promoter of the Sherbrooke, Eastern Townships and Kennebec Railway, chartered in that year.[42] Subsequently, he became a proprietor of the coal lands at Lethbridge, Alberta, converting them from public property into his personal property, and becoming at once a coal magnate of the first rank. Galt also became president of the Canada Guarantee Company — a large corporation.[43]

The disclosures already made regarding the methods of the Grand Trunk and other railroad promoters were serious enough. But very soon came another embarrassing scandal.

Mail Subsidies and Ministries

On August 29, 1863, the Montreal *Gazette* published a story to the effect that an attempt had been made by Prime Minister John Sandfield Macdonald, aided by several of his colleagues, to bribe the heads of the Grand Trunk Railway in Canada to employ the Company's influence on behalf of the ministerial party in the general elections of that year. The day following the announcement of the alleged plot, the Hon. James Ferrier and C. J. Brydges published letters corroborating several points

Vol. II, p. 438. Dent proceeds to tell how on June 14, 1864, Parliament passed a resolution (by a vote of 60 to 58) censuring this transaction, although fixing upon Galt only a culpable negligence in keeping the Provincial Accounts. The passage of this resolution caused the resignation of the Ministry.

[42] See *Statutes of the Province of Quebec*, 1869, pp. 242–243.
[43] See *Monetary Times*, Feb. 15, 1878, p. 967.

of the alleged revelations, and agreeing on the story that on the evening of the day preceding the nomination of the Hon. John Young, the ministerial candidate opposing the Hon. Thomas D'Arcy McGee, Macdonald arranged to meet Ferrier at his lodgings in Montreal to discuss the long-pending settlement of the Grand Trunk claim for carriage of the Canadian mails. Ferrier claimed that Macdonald distinctly promised that he would make the rate $150 per mile, provided the Grand Trunk would throw the weight of its influence in the then pending elections on the side of the Government. Ferrier's telegrams to Brydges, the general manager of the railway, bore out his statement of the proposal made by Premier Macdonald.

Ferrier and Brydges both professed that they had replied to Macdonald that they would not depart from their "policy of absolute neutrality in politics," and they complained of the Government's broken promises. It was claimed that because the officials of the railway would not throw their influence in favor of the Government in the elections that the administration had adopted an Order-in-Council making the postal subsidy to the Grand Trunk Railway, $100 instead of the $150 promised. Friends of the Government claimed, however, that the Grand Trunk was a party to a conspiracy with the Opposition for the overthrow of the Administration. On the day following the publication of the alleged scandal, the discussion of the matter occupied the whole attention of the House during both afternoon and evening sessions.

Grand Trunk's Mail Subsidy

The investigation following this particular scandal dealt with the methods by which the Grand Trunk directors, after already getting a large mail subsidy, sought to hold up the Government for an extraordinarily larger sum; at the time that this effort was made, these directors, in fact, themselves largely composed the very personnel of the Government Ministers and Parliamentary leaders at one and the same time.

The facts came out in 1864, after a new Administration had come in, when Postmaster-General Oliver Mowatt reported in response to an order from Parliament: —

That shortly after assuming control of the Atlantic and St. Lawrence Railway, the directors of the Grand Trunk Railway, on August 17, 1853, passed a resolution greatly increasing their charge for carrying mails from about $25 a mile to $110 a mile per annum.

" When this resolution was passed," Mowatt's report proceeded, " it appears from the Minute made at the time, that the following directors were present: — The Honorable John Ross in the Chair; Hon. James Morris, Hon. F. Hincks, Hon. M. Cameron, Hon. Peter McGill, E. F. Whitmore, Esq., W. H. Ponton, Esq., Col. Tache and Captain Rhodes.[44]   The Honorable James Morris had been Postmaster-General until the 16th of August, 1853, and the Honorable M. Cameron became Postmaster-General and held the office on the 17th of August, the very day of the meeting. The verbal intimation which the Postmaster-General received, by thus being present, seems to have been the only one given him. No trace of any written communication has been found in any of the public departments, nor so far as appears, among the records of the Company."

An Agreement of Which There Was No Evidence

Postmaster-General Mowatt, in his terse, dry way pointed out the nature of the process. Here were some leading chiefs of the Government, one of whom succeeded another as Post-

[44] As has already been noted, Ross, Morris, Hincks, Cameron and McGill were all at various times personally interested as stockholders in the Grand Trunk Railway or in various corporations the charters of which they had promoted through Parliament.

master-General (the very official having jurisdiction over mail subsidies). They met as directors, government or other, of the Grand Trunk Railway, and resolved that they " were willing " to accept $110 a mile. Then they solemnly dispersed and immediately pretended to resume their separate functions as Cabinet Ministers and legislators.

" The undersigned," went on Mowatt's report, " perceives that the Honorable Mr. Galt, when Finance Minister, speaks of $110 as ' the rate first agreed upon by the Government.' But the undersigned has failed to discover any evidence of any such agreement. However, the Company from the first, sent in their accounts at $110 a mile, and continued doing so until April, 1861."

The raid was considered much too audacious. Other Government officials raised a tempest. Sidney Smith, the Postmaster-General, in 1858, denounced the $110 rate demanded by the Grand Trunk and the $100 rate demanded by the Great Western Railway as grossly excessive, and a Committee of the Executive Council, June 18, 1858, recommended the payment of much less than half of the demanded sums as fully adequate.

The Grand Trunk's High Influence

" This report," Mowatt further proceeded, " was approved by his Excellency in Council, on the 18th of September, 1858. Hon. Mr. Cartier, solicitor for the Grand Trunk Company, was at this time the Canadian Premier, and the Hon. Mr. Ross, then president of the Company, was at the same time president of the Executive Council. Mr. Watkin, who afterward became president of the Company, in an official letter to the Provincial Secretary, of 29th Nov., 1862, states that Mr. Ross, at the time the Order-in-Council of 1858 was submitted, protested against the rate fixed therein as entirely inadequate, though he did not formally oppose the proposition, being (as Mr. Watkin curiously adds) 'unfortunately for the Grand Trunk Company, a member of the then Government.'"

But the Government " with all its Grand Trunk influences established " did allow a rate of $70 a mile, and this rate was continued after the overthrow, in 1862, of the Cartier Ministry. No great trouble would have resulted had not the Grand Trunk Railway Company, in 1862, " suddenly claimed an enormous amount "— in some cases $300 to $850 a mile. Mowatt incorporated in his report a copy of the Company's own prospectus showing the large number of Government officials on its list of directors and shareholders, and commented, " But it is a remarkable fact that while so enormous an amount is now claimed for postal services, and while this prospectus constitutes so important a part of the argument of the Company in support of the claim, postal services are not once alluded to in the prospectus as an item from which any part of the probable revenue was to be expected." [45]   Mowatt succeeded in having the rate fixed at $60 a mile; the Grand Trunk's claims were making such a decided scandal, that the pushers considered it prudent to drop their full demands.

Northern Railway Loans

It is now necessary to turn again to the Northern Railway, running from Toronto to Collingwood. We have already related the details of the jobbery at the inception of this railway in which Prime Minister Hincks and Mayor Bowes of Toronto were secret partners.

[45] For Postmaster-General Mowatt's full report see *Sess. Paper No. 28, Vol. III, 2nd Sess. of the 8th Parl. of the Province of Canada,* Sess. 1864. In a private letter to L. H. Holton, February 19, 1862, George Brown, editor of the Toronto *Globe,* and a member of Parliament, wrote that, " Mr. Brydges is regularly installed in the Grand Trunk. He is trying to accomplish an increased subsidy by private arrangement with the members." See *Life and Speeches of George Brown,* p. 198.

At the same time, in 1853-1854, when, in order to get railway legislation Prime Minister Hincks' approval first had to be obtained, further legislation was enacted by which the Government of the Province of Canada advanced to the Northern Railway Company £475,000 sterling, constituting a first lien upon the road. But the Company did not pay anything to the Government of either principal or interest. The Company then underwent a metamorphosis of reorganization. In 1859 an Order-in-Council was issued, confirmed by an Act in 1860, granting the bonded debt of the Company priority both in payment of interest and security over the Government lien, excepting about only £9,000 of mortgage bonds. By this arrangement the Government received the scanty comfort of also becoming possessor of a £50,000 second preference bond in part payment of interest then due on the Government lien.

As law now stood, the Company did not have to meet the payment on the £475,000 of the Government money until it had paid all of the charges on the £533,900 of its own outstanding bonds, the holders of which were now in possession of the road. Eight years passed; and then, in 1868, they were allowed to issue £150,000 sterling of more bonds, which also were allowed priority over the Government lien.

These bonds were then sold or distributed by the Company; and the practical effect of this astute arrangement was that, to enable the Company to obtain about £30,000 in cash, a permanent annual charge of £6,000 sterling was placed ahead of the Government lien.

Subtle Financial Transactions.

Then came still another financial twisting, when, in 1872, the Northern Railway leased the Northern Extension Railway — a lease confirmed by Act of Parliament. The involved manner in which this lease was arranged, made any payment on the Government lien still more remote.

" An examination of this lease," reported the Select Parliamentary Committee, " disclosed the fact that arrangements were made whereby the interest on debentures to be issued by the Northern Extension was to be paid by the Northern Railway, and charged ' in the nature of a rental upon the earnings of the line of railway of the lessees, and to be recognized in the working expenses thereof.' As it appears that £177,600 of debentures and improvement bonds were issued, the effect of this Act was to place the interest on this amount, being about £10,000 sterling per annum, ahead not only of the Government lien, but also of all of the Northern Railway preference bonds. . . ." [46]

Four years later the Northern Railway owners were allowed to extinguish their responsibility for the £475,000 Government lien upon terms so favorable to them that they themselves must have been astonished at their great success. These terms were the payment of £100,000 sterling, together with £2,000 sterling interest, and £13,500 sterling as arrears of interest on the second preference bonds — making £115,500 sterling in all. This settlement left the Government still owner of £50,000 sterling of second preference bonds, and also entitled to £50,000 sterling for third preference bonds and interest.[47]

The Prime Minister Gets a Testimonial

The self-evident loss to the Government was extensive. By what persuasive means were some of these various ends brought about? What were the specific influences brought to bear upon members of the Government? The nature of

[46] Report of Cyril Archibald, Chairman of the Select Committee, *Dom. House of Commons, Appendix to Journal,* etc., *Vol. XI,* 1877, *Appendix No.* 5, *Sess. Paper No.* 10, p. iv.
[47] *Ibid.*

some of those methods were revealed by the report of the Select Parliamentary Investigating Committee, in 1876-1877, which reported: —

That on November 12, 1869, Sir John Macdonald (Prime Minister of Canada from 1867-1873) made a draft for $500 on F. W. Cumberland, General Manager of the Northern Railway Company, which draft was accepted at maturity by Cumberland and paid out of the Northern Railway funds; that on November 18, 1869, another such draft drawn by Macdonald on Cumberland was similarly paid; and that the proceeds were used to defray the election expenses of Sir Francis Hincks, who at that very time was a member of the Canadian Government.

The Committee further reported that Cumberland, Hon. John Ross and Hon. John B. Robinson subscribed to a testimonial to Macdonald; that Cumberland and Ross each gave $1,000, and Robinson $500; and that on January 14, 1871, a check for $2,500 was paid to the Hon. D. L. Macpherson, treasurer of the fund, who called at the Company's office to get the check; and that this check originally entered as an asset on the Company's books was later changed "to municipal bonuses and Government subsidies." Macdonald and Macpherson denied that they knew that the Company contributed to the testimonial.

The Committee itemized further sums that it classified as improperly paid out of the Northern Railway Company's funds — sums that defrayed the election expenses of certain stated politicians, one of whom was Robinson, president of the Northern Railway Company. These sums were entered on the Company's books as follows: One-third to "Contingencies," one-third to "Parliamentary Expenses," and one-third to "Legal Expenses." The committee reported various other findings, one of which was that money had been paid out for stock in a certain Toronto newspaper, at or about presumably the very time that Robinson had so engineered matters as to get $200,000 from the City of Toronto.[48]

The Corrupt System Described

" Corruption taints the majority of railway enterprises from their inception to completion," wrote David Mills, a member of the Dominion Parliament, and later Dominion Minister of the Interior. " Charters are sought, not infrequently, for the purposes of speculation. Sometimes they are used to blackmail existing railway lines. However much a railroad is needed, a charter is seldom obtained without difficulty, and stock is bestowed for Parliamentary support. The names of well-known railway men are sought to give credit to the projected enterprise, a number of shares are tendered them for their ' eminent services,' and they are seldom declined.

" When a railway scheme is finally launched, it finds a large number of friends — engineers and professional contractors, the owners of rolling mills, and the builders of cars and locomotives. The getters of land grants, and the traders in railway stocks, all come to its aid, and it may be, experience its bounty. These constitute the grand army of a private railway enterprise.

" Besides these, there is a numerous band of camp followers, who expect in a variety of ways ' to reap where they have not sown,' but about whose special services nothing need be said. It is this numerous host of allies and followers which ' can kill or keep alive ' a railway project, and because they have this power, must be paid, that add to the cost of every rival railway undertaking." In his article Mills but stated a further well-known fact when he wrote: " In order to pay in-

[48] *Ibid.,* p. v, etc. In the Committee's estimation, the impropriety of these contributions to members of the Government, etc., arose from the fact that the funds thus given were applicable to the payment of the Government lien.

terest upon bonds or dividends upon stocks, a road is allowed
to deteriorate. Then come accidents, in which scores of passengers are mangled or scalded." [49]

[49] *Railway Reform — The Canadian Pacific Railway,* by David Mills,
M. P., in the *Canadian Monthly and National Review,* Nov., 1872, pp.
438–439.

CHAPTER XII

CONTEST FOR THE PACIFIC RAILWAY

When the Hudson's Bay Company formally relinquished, in consideration of a payment of $1,500,000 and a reservation of one-twentieth of the area surrendered, its claim upon the vast territory from the Red River to the Rocky Mountains, railway projectors at once saw an opportunity to transfer into their private possession much of this coveted region.

Land Grants and Subsidies Assured

The first move to this end was not long in coming. On April 11, 1871, Sir George E. Cartier moved in the Dominion House of Commons that the House go into Committee on a resolution that a Pacific Railway be constructed by private enterprise and that it be given liberal public aid in grants of land, money and other modes of subsidy. Galt supported Cartier's motion, which was adopted.[1] Cartier was then solicitor for the Grand Trunk Railway, and Galt, as we have seen, had been not only a leading promoter of that railway, but only two years previously had, in association with Charles J. Brydges and others, secured a charter for the Sherbrooke, Eastern Townships and Kennebec Railway.[2] The head, real or titular, of the particular Company now seeking the Pacific Railway charter and grants was Senator David L. Macpherson

[1] *Parliamentary Debates, Dom. House of Commons,* 1871, Vol. II, p. 1028.
[2] *Statutes of Canada,* 1869, pp. 242–243.

who, as we have previously noted, was a member of the contracting firm of Gzowski and Company which had constructed the Grand Trunk Railway west of Toronto, and which was so large an owner of the stock of one of the Grand Trunk's chief subsidiary lines. The Grand Trunk Railway was now controlled by an English board of directors headed by Thomas Baring, Lord Wolverton and others, and by a Canadian board consisting of Brydges, James Ferrier and William Molson.

It was evident that the Grand Trunk capitalists intended getting hold, if they possibly could, of this immensely valuable projected Pacific Railway charter and subsidies. But they quickly discovered that the rush for so great a prize was not to be uncontested. Another company of capitalists came forward in hot competition.

Sir Hugh Allan's Company

This competitive group was headed by Sir Hugh Allan of Montreal. Allan was one of the most conspicuous men of capital of his time; and as the founder of one of the largest and at present most powerful Canadian fortunes, his career deserves more than a passing notice. Sir Hugh Montague Allan, son of Sir Hugh Allan, today is a dominating factor on the board of directors of nineteen of Canada's large corporations.

A merchant, contractor and shipbuilder, Sir Hugh Allan founded the Montreal Steamship Company, or Allan Line, the ships of which plied to Europe. It was in about the year 1853, Morgan says, that through the influence of John Ross, Cartier, L. T. Drummond and other politicians in power that Allan obtained ship-building and mail-carrying contracts from the Canadian Government.[3] From these long-continuing mail subsidies, Sir Hugh Allan gathered in enormous profits. A

[3] *Biographies of Celebrated Canadians* (Edit. of 1862), p. 673.

contract that he secured from Postmaster-General Campbell in 1869 provided for the payment to him of £54,500 a year as mail subsidy.[4] The great sums thus paid to Allan were later — on April 18, 1873 — the occasion of a severe opposition on the part of Holton in the Dominion House of Commons.

Montreal Warehouse Transaction

By means of his political connections Sir Hugh Allan obtained other privileges and properties. He was president of the Montreal Warehouse Company, one of the transactions of which was exposed in the Dominion House of Commons.

According to a statement there made by Mr. Holton on April 1, 1871, the Government, in 1865, had bought from private parties a tract of land adjoining the Lachine Canal basin in Montreal. This purchase was made on the recommendation of Allan for the ostensible purpose of increasing the wharfage and shed accommodation at the place. After the Confederation of the Provinces and the formation of the Dominion Government, the Montreal Warehousing Company applied to the Government for the purchase of a lot. On the advice of the officials of the Public Works Department, the Government refused to sell it. But, on July 19, 1870, when the Minister of Public Works was absent, the Minister of Militia acting for him reported to the Council in favor of granting the lease of this lot to the Montreal Warehousing Company for the term of 21 years at an annual rental of $700. This ridiculously small sum represented less than the simple interest on one-half the cost of the land.

When Holton moved that the Government take immediate steps to resume possession of the land for public uses, as conditionally provided for by a clause in the lease, Hector Lange-

[4] *Sessional Papers, Dom. Parl.*, 1869, Vol. II, No. 5, Sess. Paper No. 34, p. 4.

vin, Minister of Public Works, defended the transaction. In the course of his explanation, Langevin ironically described a similar transaction by which accuser Holton, along with Hooker and John Young, had themselves benefited when, in 1851, they had bought Lachine Canal basin lots at public auction from the Government. Young had not only purchased lots from the Government, but Holton and Hooker had also sold him for £4,000 the lots which they had bought, " making a very handsome profit by the transaction."

"A Very Nice Transaction"

" Were you then opposed to the Government selling this land? " Langevin in effect asked Holton. " The action of the Government at that time," Langevin taunted, " met the approval of the honorable gentleman, and was a very nice transaction for him." Which it was, Holton admitted, but asserted that he had opposed the Government sale, and only when it was held had he stepped forward in his character, not as a member of Parliament, but " as a merchant doing business in Montreal. I invested in them as a good speculation." The John Young here referred to was the eminent John Young who at the very time that the foregoing transaction was accomplished was a member of the Hincks Government; Young was also a pushful railway promoter. Mr. Mackenzie bluntly declared of the Montreal Warehousing Company's lease that " the whole matter could only be regarded as a ' job.' " Holton's motion was lost.[5]

Very shrewd was Sir Hugh Allan considered in thus getting this valuable land for a mere pittance of a rental. While securing such governmental favors, Allan was reaping extraordinary profits from the promotion of many interests. His

[5] *Parliamentary Debates, Fourth Session,* 1871, Vol. II, pp. 44 and 766–770.

steamship line yielded large revenues. If the proved disclosures that were subsequently made as to the methods of the Allan Line are to be regarded as evidence of its previous methods, then it is fair to assume that those methods were by no means new when the Montreal *Witness* newspaper arraigned the Allan Line for the filth, overcrowding, discomfort and incivility to the herds of steerage passengers whose sufferings were coined into profits. This particular fact is one of court record.

The Allan Line sued the Montreal *Witness* for $50,000 damages for alleged libel; and when this case came to trial in 1883, less than a year after Sir Hugh Allan's death, the jury, after hearing all of the evidence during a trial of eight days, returned a verdict in favor of the Montreal *Witness* on all counts. This verdict was considered all the more conclusive inasmuch as the Allan Line had spent large sums in getting evidence taken by a Commission.[6] Severe comments were generally made upon this Company which, while drawing large subsidies from the Dominion Government, was thus indirectly proved guilty of flagrant mistreatment of the most helpless class of its passengers crowded under the most pitiful, inhuman conditions down in the steerage.

Squeezing of Laborers

There was no official investigation previous to 1887 of the treatment of its workers by the Allan Line; but it is not unreasonable to assume that the practices then reported by the " Royal Commission on the Relations of Capital and Labor " had not been suddenly introduced. The testimony revealed the most oppressive exploitation of its workers by the Allan Line; many of the longshoremen were often compelled to work 30 to 35 hours at a stretch for the wretched wages of

[6] See *Monetary Times*, Nov. 2, 1883, p. 491.

20 cents an hour, and they had to submit to the meanest ex-actions, besides.[7]

"The Allan Line," reported the Commission, "retains one per cent. of the wages of its employes, and with this amount so retained insures them in the Citizens' Insurance Company, which, in case of death, pays $500 to the heirs of the victim, or $5 a week in case of inability to work resulting from acci-dent. . . . We find that the longshoremen of the Allan Line pay a premium . . . equivalent to an annual premium of $9.12 for a protection of ten hours a day during 365 days. An accident insurance company of Montreal would give the same indemnity . . . upon a premium of $8.75, payable per quarter, and the policy which it would give covers not only accidents happening during the ten hours of the work but all the acci-dents that could happen during the twenty-four hours of the day.

"The insurance system put in force by the Allan Line is, then, onerous for the insured workmen; moreover, it has the double effect of being compulsory, and of being completely beyond the control of those interested, who are not in posses-sion of any document establishing their claim." [8]

The president of the Citizens' Insurance Company which thus mulcted the workers of the Allan Line was Sir Hugh Allan, and he remained so till his death,[9] when his holdings went to his family. Longshoremen employed by the Allan Line testified that no man could get employment from the Allan Company unless he consented to this insurance scheme.[10]

[7] *Report of Royal Commission on the Relations of Labor and Capital,* 1889, Que. Evidence, Part I, pp. 176–184.

[8] *Ibid.,* pp. 20–21. (Appendix C.) The premium of $8.75 referred to by the Commission was unquestionably an *annual* premium, payable per quarter; the Commission's meaning on this point while not clearly ex-pressed, is evident enough.

[9] See *Monetary Times,* Dec. 15, 1882, p. 657, giving a list of corpora-tions of which Allan was president or vice-president.

[10] *Report of Royal Commission on the Relations of Labor and Capital,* 1889, Que. Evidence, Part I, p. 176.

Sir Hugh Allan, Foremost Capitalist

Multifarious were Sir Hugh Allan's financial and industrial interests. He was president of the Merchants' Bank for which he secured the charter in 1864, and he was or became president of 15 more corporations and vice-president of six corporations. These corporations comprised telegraph, navigation, coal and iron, tobacco, cotton manufacturing, sewing machine, cattle, rolling mills, paper, car, elevator, coal and other companies. He was the first president of the Quebec, Montreal, Ottawa and Occidental Railroad, originally projected as the Northern Colonization Railroad.

An aggressive type of capitalist, Sir Hugh Allan lived in his " handsome residence of Ravenscraig," and knighted " as some have supposed because he entertained, splendidly, some members of the Royal Family." A contemporary writer further wrote of him, " Rigid as a martinet, and a stickler for economy and system in business matters, Sir Hugh Allan still could find time to lecture in church."

The prize of the Canadian Pacific franchise was one of magnitude. There they lay, immense domains of public land all ready to be secured under color of law, and there was the public treasury easy of access as experience had proved. So far as the Canadian Parliament went, a majority of its members could be favorably swayed. But what of the Canadian people? Some strong argument was necessary for the influencing of them to the point where they would agree that the donation of tens of millions of acres of land and tens of millions of dollars was a patriotic and indispensable act.

" Give Generously and Patriotically "

The railway promoters had their argument ready. They pointed to the " distinguished liberality " of the United States

Government and the State Legislatures in giving bountiful subsidies in lands and cash to railway promoters. Was the Canadian Government to be less patriotic?

In making this plea, the Canadian railway promoters omitted mentioning two facts.

One fact was that compared to those of the United States, the population and resources of Canada were poor and meager. The second fact was that virtually every· subsidy and other railroad legislation in the United States had been obtained by bribery.

Bribery in the United States

Thus, for example, the projectors of the La Crosse and Milwaukee Railway corrupted Wisconsin legislators and influential politicians, State officials and certain editors with bribes totaling $800,000 in order to create favorable agitation and consideration for an Act giving to that railway company a land grant of about 1,000,000 acres, valued then at nearly $18,000,-000.[11]

A special committee of Congress was appointed in 1857 to investigate charges of corruption in connection with an Act giving enormous land grants in Iowa, Minnesota and other States to the Des Moines Navigation and Railroad Company; the committee recommended the expulsion of four members of Congress, reporting that one of them, Orasmus B. Matteson, was a leader of a corrupt combination and had received for disbursement a corruption fund of $100,000 and " other valuable considerations." [12]

The Union Pacific Railway Company obtained, in 1864, the

[11] *Report of the Joint Select Committee Appointed to Investigate into Alleged Frauds and Corruption*, etc., *Appendices to Wisconsin Senate and Assembly Journals*, 1858.
[12] *Reports of Committees, House of Representatives, Thirty-fourth Congress, Third Session*, 1856–1857, Report No. 243, Vol. III.

passage of an Act giving it a land grant of 12,000,000 acres, and also a loan of $27,213,000 in Government bonds. A special committee of Congress reported after investigation, in 1873, that the promoters of the Union Pacific Railway had expended a corruption fund of $436,000 to get the Act of 1864 passed, and that another corruption fund of $126,000 had been used to get a supplemental Act passed in 1871.[13]

In the year 1868 Jay Gould and his associate directors of the Erie Railway spent at least $1,000,000 in corrupting the New York Legislature, and Cornelius Vanderbilt, of the New York Central Railroad, had spent a large amount for the same purposes.[14]

These are but a few instances of the frequency with which bribery had been employed in the United States.

American Capitalists League with Allan

Associated with Sir Hugh Allan in the Canadian Pacific Railway scheme were a choice group of American capitalists — George W. McMullen, W. B. Ogden, George W. Cass, W. G. Fargo, the banking firm of Winslow, Lanier and Company, Jay Cooke and others.

Some of these American capitalists such as Fargo were heads of express companies; others were railway promoters or officials. Scott, for instance, controlled the Pennsylvania Railroad, and became the chief promoter of the Texas Pacific Railway project which was accompanied, in 1876, by such a wide corruption of Congress. Heading one aggressive group of railway capitalists in the United States, Scott was opposed by another group headed by Collis P. Huntington, the Central and the Southern Pacific railways magnate. These two groups

---

[13] *Reports of Committees, Credit Mobilier Reports, Forty-second Congress, Third Session, 1872–1873,* Doc. No. 78, p. xvii.
[14] See *History of the Great American Fortunes,* Vol. II, pp. 310–317, giving the official facts.

furiously contested for the division of land-grant and other spoils in southwestern United States. Each side introduced its Bills in Congress, and each effectively, systematically set out to corrupt Congress. Both groups used great sums of money to attain their ends.[15]

He Tries to Unite Competing Interests

The folly of two companies competing for the Canadian Pacific charter and subsidies was evident to the discerning Sir Hugh Allan. Why not amalgamate all conflicting interests, join in sharing the proceeds, and thus remove all antagonisms and cross-purposes? This was Allan's plan, and he tried hard to bring it about. At the same time he sought by negotiation to provide for every interest or group that in any way presented themselves as obstacles to the consummation of his own ends.

". . . A party in the interest of the Hudson's Bay Company," Allan wrote to McMullen, on December 29, 1871, " consisting of Donald A. Smith, D. McInnes, G. Laidlaw, G. [eorge] Stephen, Daniel Torrence (of New York), and one or two others have given notice in the *Official Gazette* that they will apply for a charter to make a railroad from Pembina to Fort Garry. That is the only one that affects us. . . ." Allan wrote further that, " I think we are sure of Cartier's opposition." Cartier, that powerful politician and Cabinet member of Macdonald's Ministry, was (as we have seen), solicitor for the Grand Trunk Railway. Allan wrote that Brydges, of the

---

[15] Huntington wrote freely to Colton, an associate railway capitalist, of the specific sums used; these letters later came to light in a lawsuit. "It is impossible," reported the Pacific Railway Commission after an extended investigation (Vol. I, p. 121 of its Report), " to read the evidence of C. P. Huntington and Leland Stanford and the Colton letters without reaching the conclusion that very large sums of money have been improperly used in connection with legislation." For full details as to this corruption see the chapter " The Pacific Quartet " in Vol. III, *History of the Great American Fortunes,* and pp. 572–573 *History of the Supreme Court of the United States.*

Grand Trunk, was using all his influence with Cartier to thwart the scheme.

Seeks to Buy Over Competitors

Allan's next letter revealed the methods he had in mind of seeking to win Brydges over. On January 24, 1872, Allan wrote to Charles M. Smith and McMullen saying that his (Allan's) subscription of $1,450,000 to the stock of the proposed Canadian Pacific Railway Company " includes the sum of $200,000 furnished jointly by you and myself, to be transferred in whole or in part to Mr. C. J. Brydges on condition of his joining the organization and giving it the benefit of his assistance and influence. . . ." [16]

Brydges, however, kept on making trouble, as was shown by a letter written by Allan, from Montreal, February 23, 1872.

On the next day, February 24, 1872, Allan wrote to Charles M. Smith of Chicago, " Since writing to you yesterday, I have seen Mr. D. L. Macpherson of Toronto, who is a member of the Dominion Senate, and rather an important person to gain over to our side. He has been applied to by our opponents, and uses that as a lever by which to obtain better terms from us. He insists on getting $250,000 of stock, and threatens opposition if he does not get it. You will remember, he is one of those I proposed as Directors. I will do the best I can, but I think that McMullen, you and myself will have to give up some of our stock to conciliate these parties." [17]

A Proposed Allotment of Stock

Four days later, Sir Hugh Allan wrote again to Charles M. Smith: " It seems pretty certain that in addition to money

[16] See Enclosure No. 3 (Appendix) in *Report of the Royal Commission, Pacific Railway, With Despatches,* 1873, p. 72.
[17] *Ibid.,* p. 73.

payments the following stock will have to be distributed: —
D. L. Macpherson, $100,000; A. B. Foster, $100,000; Donald
A. Smith, $100,000; C. J. Brydges, $100,000; J. J. C. Abbott,
$50,000; D. McInnes, $50,000; John Shedden, $50,000; A. Al-
lan, $50,000; C. S. Gzowski, $50,000; George Brown,
$50,000; A. S. Hincks, $50,000; H. Nathan, $50,000; T. Mc-
Greevy, $50,000; — total $850,000. Please say if this is
agreeable to you? I do not think we can do with less,
and may have to give more. I do not think we will require
more than $100,000 in cash, but I am not sure as yet. Who
am I to draw on for money when it is wanted, and what proof
of payment will be required? You are aware I cannot get
receipts. Our Legislature meets on the 11th of April, and
I am already deep in preparation for the game. Every day
brings up some new difficulty to be encountered, but I hope
to meet them all successfully. Write to me immediately.

" P. S.— I think you will have to *go it blind in the matter of
money — cash payments. I have already paid $8,500, and
have not a voucher and cannot get one.*" [18]

Adroit a business man as was Allan he did not know the
danger of committing his surreptitious moves to writing. No
doubt he did not harbor the remotest suspicion that before long
these very tell-tale letters would become public property. He
kept writing with the greatest freedom.

[18] Enclosure No. 3 (Appendix), *Report of the Royal Commission,
Pacific Railway*, etc., 1873, pp. 73 and 194. Italics in the original.
When these letters became public, George Brown, editor and proprietor of the Toronto *Globe* denied circumstantially that Allan, in
proposing to set aside $50,000 stock for him, acted with his (Brown's)
authority or knowledge. "I have never in my life," Brown stated,
"had the slightest interest, directly or indirectly, in any contract
or work of any kind dependent on public aid, and the Pacific Railway
contract was certainly the last enterprise I could, under any circumstances, have been induced to touch." There is no reason to doubt
the truth of Brown's statement. It is probable that the $50,000 of
stock was thus proposed to be given to Brown in the remote hope —
although an abortive one — of trying to buy off the opposition of
Brown's newspaper — the Toronto *Globe*.

Sir Hugh Allan's Secret Methods

On July 1, 1872, Allan wrote to an American capitalist in New York (name not revealed) that the cry " No Yankee dictation " had forced the unwilling and ostensible dropping of every American name from the scheme. In this letter Allan accused Cartier (then Dominion Minister of Militia and Defense, and at the same time salaried solicitor for the Grand Trunk Railway), of preventing the building of an opposition line from Montreal to Ottawa, " and the same reason made him [Cartier] desirous of giving the contract for the Canadian Pacific into the hands of parties connected with the Grand Trunk Railway, and to this end he fanned the flame of opposition to us." Allan added that Cartier, the leader and chief of the French party, had control of 45 members of Parliament " who have followed Cartier and voted in a solid phalanx for all his measures." Inasmuch as the Government majority was generally less than 45, Allan said that it was important to win over this compact body of Cartier's followers, and that he had taken measures to that end. " As you may suppose," Allan concluded, " the matter has not reached this point without great expense — a large portion of it payable when the contract is obtained; but I think it will reach not less than $300,000."

What means did Sir Hugh Allan now take to strike back at Cartier?

Allan wrote further that, ". . . means must be taken to influence the public, and I employed several young French writers to write it up in their own newspapers. I subscribed a controlling influence in the stock, and proceeded to subsidize the newspapers themselves, both editors and proprietors. I went to the country through which the road would pass, and called on many of the inhabitants. I visited the priests and made friends of them, and I employed agents to go among the principal people and talk it up. I then began to hold public meetings, and attended to them myself, making frequent speeches in French to them, showing them where their true interest lay. The scheme at once became popular. I formed a Committee to influence the members of the Legislature. This succeeded so well that, in a short time, it had 27 out of 45 on whom I could rely, and the electors of the ward in this city, which Cartier himself represents, notified him that unless the contract for the Pacific Railway was given in the interests of Lower Canada, he need not present himself for re-election. He did not believe this, but when he came here and met his constituents he found, to his surprise, that their determination was unchanged. He then agreed to give the contract as required. . . ." [19]

"Now Wanted — $200,000 for Elections"

Sir Hugh Allan's various methods were successful in influencing Cartier, for we find Cartier writing this "private and confidential" letter to Allan, July 30, 1872:

"The friends of the Government will expect to be assisted with funds in the pending elections, and any amount which you or your Company shall advance for that purpose shall be recouped to you. A memorandum of immediate requirements is below." This memorandum read:

"NOW WANTED.

"Sir John A. Macdonald	$25,000
Hon. Mr. Langevin	15,000
Sir. G. E. C.	20,000
Sir J. A. (add.)	10,000
Hon. Mr. Langevin	100,000
Sir G. E. C.	30,000." [20]

[19] Enclosure No. 3, *Report of the Royal Commission, Pacific Railway*, etc., 1873, pp. 75-76.
[20] *Report of the Royal Commission, Pacific Railway*, etc., 1873, pp. 136-137 of Testimony.

On August 7, 1872, Allan wrote, " I have already paid away about $250,000, and will have to pay at least $50,000 before the end of the month. I don't know as even that will finish it, but hope so." [21]

An Attempted Fusion

The " great bribery scheme " engineered by Sir Hugh Allan had now reached the point where it was considered that the machinery of Government was "properly fixed." There remained the final necessity of attempting to unify the competing companies. On October 15, 1872, a Provisional Board of Directors for the Canada Pacific Railway Company was formed.

Heading this board was Sir Hugh Allan whose particular methods are aptly and with the fullest candor described in his own correspondence. The Hon. J. J. C. Abbott, M. P., was the second on the list; of Abbott a eulogist wrote, " Capitalists who are sensitive to their interests, elected him to the Directorship of the most important financial institutions, notably the Citizens' Insurance Company, Merchants' Bank, Bank of Montreal and Canadian Pacific Railway." This biographer further wrote of Abbott that, " Early in his career he had for clients the Molsons, Allans, Merchants' Bank and Molson's Bank, and, from its inception, the Canadian Pacific Railway," the solicitorship of which he later resigned. He refused, said this writer, appointment to a chief justiceship, possibly because the receipts of his office were many times a judge's salary.[22]

[21] Sir Richard Cartwright in his recently published *Reminiscences* wrote (p. 377, Appendix E): " It must always be borne in mind, in dealing with this matter, that a contribution of $200,000 or $300,000 for election purposes meant a vast deal more in the Canada of forty years ago than it would today. Looking at the difference in population, and still more in available wealth, it is no exaggeration to say that it would almost equal a contribution of two or three millions in hard cash now."

[22] As we have seen, Abbott was one of the incorporators of the Chaudiere Valley Railway Company, chartered in 1864.

Other members on the Provisional Board of Directors of the Canada Pacific Railway were Senators A. B. Foster, John Hamilton, David Christie and James Skead. The Hon. Donald A. Smith, representing a Manitoba constituency in the Dominion Parliament, was on the Provisional Board of Directors of the Canada Pacific Railway. So, too, on the board, were Hon. J. J. Ross, M. P. and Legislative Councillor; Hon. Chief Judge Coursol of Montreal; Henry Nathan, M. P. for Victoria, B. C.; Andrew Allan, brother of Sir Hugh; Hon. Louis Archambault, M. P. and Dominion Minister of Agriculture, and sundry other members of Parliament.[23]

That this was a formidable combination of men of political and other influence was fully recognized.

Fifty Million Acres and $30,000,000

But this scheme failed; the Interoceanic Railway Company refused to amalgamate, and Allan was driven to the necessity of organizing an entirely new company.

So long as the two big competing companies contesting for the transcontinental charter and subsidies had been unable to come to terms of amalgamation, neither could get anything from the Dominion Government. But the formation of the new company by Sir Hugh Allan settled the difficulty. On February 5, 1873, the charter of this Company was signed by the Governor-General. By the provisions of this charter, the Canadian Pacific Railway Company pledged itself to build the railway within ten years from July 20, 1871, in consideration of which it was to receive a land grant of 50,000,000 acres, and a subsidy of $30,000,000 payable from time to time in installments. The Company was allowed a capital of $10,000,000.

[23] *Report of the Royal Commission, Pacific Railway,* etc., Appendix, p. 38.

Charges of Bargaining and Bribery

After the session of Parliament opened, Lucius S. Huntington, in the House of Commons, rose on April 2, 1873, and in effect accused Premier Sir John A. Macdonald and the Government of having sold the charter for the Canadian Pacific Railway in return for a large sum of money to be used for election purposes. Huntington demanded an investigating committee; it may here be explained, by the way, that Huntington was not a stranger to railway charters; he, James Ferrier and other politicians and members of Parliament had been the incorporators of the Missisquoi and Black Rivers Railway Company, chartered in 1870,[24] and he, John Henry Pope, Charles J. Brydges and others had secured, in 1866, a charter for the Waterloo, Magog and Stanstead Railway Company.[25]

At first Premier Macdonald refused to appoint an investigating committee, but subsequently regarded it as expedient to comply. In this case the House of Commons adopted the unusual procedure of itself choosing the investigating committee.

This committee was droning along, without any effect, when suddenly Huntington published a series of telegrams and letters written by Sir Hugh Allan; from some of these we have already given extracts. " It has never been clearly explained," Sir Richard Cartwright wrote, " how and why Sir John allowed these very compromising letters of Sir Hugh Allan and others to fall into his enemies' hands when he could apparently have got possession of them by paying a comparatively small sum of money. He may have thought the offer was a trap. I do not know, and the reason remains more or less of a mystery, the more so as Sir John showed in other

[24] *Statutes of the Province of Quebec, 1870, pp. 118–119.*
[25] *Statutes of the Province of Canada, 1866, p. 514.*

ways that he was in a temper to stop at nothing if he could escape a hostile verdict." [26]

But who was it that supplied the incriminating McMullen correspondence? If the statements made in the Dominion House of Commons, on April 24, 1877, by Mr. Haggart, are to be credited, the informer who thus turned against Macdonald's Government, was the Hon. A. B. Foster. " It was a notorious fact," said Haggart, " that the information used to turn out the late Government was furnished by the Hon. A. B. Foster, and everybody expected that the honorable gentleman would receive his reward for same. And he did. The manner in which the contracts for the Georgian Bay Branch and the Canada Central Railway were let showed it." Haggart described the affair as a " disgraceful transaction." [27]

The publication of Allan's correspondence made a widespread stir and uncommon sensation except, as Governor-General Lord Dufferin cynically wrote, in that " section of society within politics, whose feeling may be stimulated by other considerations." [28]

A Royal Commission was now appointed to investigate.

The Evidence and Disclosures

According to McMullen's statement, the only members of the Government with whom he and the other promoters dealt were Macdonald and Finance Minister Sir Francis Hincks;

[26] *Reminiscences,* p. 105.

[27] *Debates in the House of Commons,* 1877, Vol. III, pp. 1700 and 1789-1790. In 1871 Foster had bought the rights of a Mr. Bolckow in the Brockville and Ottawa Railway and the Canada Central Railway, and he also purchased large quantities of rails. He was to pay $2,000,000 in installments, but could not meet his obligations, and suffered financial reverses in 1877. At the instance of competitive American contractors he was imprisoned for a trivial debt of a few dollars. He died shortly afterward.

[28] Dispatch of August 18, 1873.

that Hincks visited New York in the early part of August, 1871, and at interviews with two prominent railway bankers, had advised them and their associates to cease negotiations with C. W. Smith and himself (McMullen), and to open them directly with Sir Hugh Allan. McMullen further stated that Hincks later told him (McMullen) of Cartier's Grand Trunk jealousy of Allan. Large levies of funds, McMullen said, were levied on the American capitalists by the promoters.[29] Daniel Y. McMullen, a brother and partner of George W. McMullen, gave corroborative testimony.

Sir John A. Macdonald was called as a witness; as we have previously noted, Macdonald had, nearly twenty years before, been an incorporator of various companies, and he had been connected with the Trust and Loan Company of Upper Canada which " owes much of its success to his exertions." Later, he became president of the Manufacturers' Life Assurance Company.

Macdonald's own evidence showed that he had personally bargained in the charter traffic with Sir Hugh Allan, and that he had received funds from Allan for use in election purposes.

Premier Macdonald testified that the Government had asked Donald Smith to be a member of the Canada Pacific Board; Smith was " the representative man of the Hudson's Bay Company in Canada " and the " Government thought it would be a great advantage to get the assistance and influence of that powerful corporation in England, if the Company had to go to that market to borrow. . . ." But when the Government, Premier Macdonald's testimony continued, came to the conclusion to exclude members of Parliament, Smith was excluded, " and upon Smith's recommendation, Mr. McDermott,

[29] *Report of the Royal Commission, Pacific Railway*, etc., 1873. Enclosure No. 5, Appendix, pp. 85–90. Sir George E. Cartier died before this investigation was held; therefore his side of the story cannot be given.

a wealthy merchant in Winnipeg, was appointed in Smith's place." [30]

Prime Minister Macdonald's explanation was not well received. The testimony showed that the construction work was to be undertaken by a company composed of the identical men promoting the railway project, and thus from the profits of the construction work were to recoup themselves for their previous outlays. [31]

Allan Admits Expending $350,000

Summoned as a witness by the Royal Commission, Allan himself produced the letter in which Sir George E. Cartier had asked him for various sums of money for use by the Government in the pending elections. (We have already given the text of this letter.) "As the letter now appears," Allan testified, "the memorandum is for $110,000, but at the time it was written the first three items amounting to $60,000 only were mentioned. Sir George said, however, that they could talk of that afterwards. Accordingly, I paid over the first three sums of money to the gentlemen indicated. Afterwards Sir George requested me to send a further amount to Sir John A. Macdonald of $10,000, and $10,000 to Mr. Langevin and $30,000 to the Central Committee of Elections, and the three sums last mentioned in the memorandum were then added to it by Sir George."

Later, more demands upon Allan were made, and soon Allan found that he had contributed $162,600, of which $85,-000 went to Sir George E. Cartier's Committee, $45,000 to

[30] *Ibid.*, p. 115 of Testimony.
[31] See *Ibid.*, Exhibit K. pp. 210–211 of Report. The construction contract was to be let to the Canada Land and Improvement Company. This contract was signed by Sir Hugh Allan, Donald A. Smith, George W. McMullen, Jay Cooke and Company, Thomas A. Scott and others. Of the total capital of $5,725,000, Allan, Smith and McMullen subscribed $4,500,000.

Sir John A. Macdonald's election expenses in Ontario, and $32,600 toward Langevin's electoral expenses in Quebec.

" I also find," Allan went on, " for the assistance of other friends of my own in connection with the elections, between $16,000 and $17,000.

" These sums, with the preliminary expenses on the Pacific and various railroads in which I was engaged, more or less directly connected with the Pacific enterprises, made up the amount of my advances to about $350,000." [32]

Sir Hugh Allan also testified that Sir Francis Hincks, Dominion Minister of Finance, asked him to get his (Hincks') son in the Montreal Warehousing Company's offices; of this Company, as we have seen, Allan was president. Hincks' son failed to get the appointment. Allan further testified that " my property invested in various ways connected with the country in business of all kinds, amounts to about $6,000,-000," [33] an amount which, compared to the present purchasing power of money, equals perhaps $60,000,000. Allan's income was reported at $500,000 to $600,000 a year; expressed in terms of the then greater purchasing power of money, it was an annual income that today would perhaps be equal to $5,000,000 or $6,000,000.

The Large Bank Graft

It may be added that railway charter trafficking was not the only kind carried on; the banks, also, did not lack their share of " Government encouragement." A. T. Galt, Dominion Finance Minister in 1867, was a big bank stockholder; Sir John Rose who succeeded him was a partner in a large international banking firm, and Sir Francis Hincks, who suc-

[32] *Report of the Royal Commission, Pacific Railway*, etc., 1873, p. 137.
[33] *Ibid.*, p. 143.

ceeded Rose as Minister of Finance,[34] was not only a bank
stockholder and director, but became president of the Consolidated Bank of Montreal which failed so disastrously in
1879 with an assortment of $1,420,000 in bad and doubtful
debts.[35]

It appeared, according to statements made in the Dominion
Parliament by Mr. (later Sir) Charles Tupper, Sir Richard
Cartwright and Mr. Blake that in the years immediately preceding 1873, the Bank of Ontario received an average of $360,-
000 a year of public Government money deposited without having to pay interest, thus giving that bank a present of $30,000
a year; that $1,100,000 was deposited in the Montreal City and
District Savings Bank of which Finance Minister Hincks was
a Director or President, and that of this $1,100,000 of Govern-
ment or public deposits, only $400,000 drew interest. Mr.
Blake said that these deposits of the people's money " were
spread over thirty-seven different institutions, and of course,
members of Parliament were likely to be shareholders in the
larger and more stable institutions." Sir Richard Cartwright
(Minister of Finance 1873-1878), stated that the amount of
Government money on deposit on December 31, 1871, was

[34] There were four successive Ministers of Finance under the Macdonald Administration from 1867 to 1873. Hincks occupied that post
from October, 1869, to February, 1873, and was succeeded by Sir
Samuel Leonard Tilley.

[35] This bank was the result of the merger of two banks — a Montreal and a Toronto bank. It crashed in 1879 owing fully $3,000,000.
Just before the failure Sir Francis Hincks at a stormy meeting of
the stockholders tried to reassure them. "This bank," then commented the *Monetary Times,* "has the advantage of being governed
by a President whose qualifications are never better displayed than in
making a speech under difficult circumstances. 'Many a time and oft'
Sir Francis Hincks has confronted opposing forces in Parliament and
he has a perfect mastery of the art of putting things in such a light as
to disarm opposition."— *Monetary Times,* June 13, 1879, p. 1534. Sir
Francis Hincks was convicted on the technical charge of being a party
to the making of false returns to the Government, but the general
supposition was that he had been used by parties who managed to
escape the consequences.

nearly $8,000,000, of which $4,300,000 bore no interest; the Bank of Montreal, it seems, was one of the banks profiting heavily.[36]

Donald A. Smith Turns Against Macdonald

The railway disclosures made it evident that Premier Macdonald had to retire, but if he had been able to obtain a favorable vote from Parliament itself, it was possible that Governor-General Lord Dufferin might have allowed him to choose his successor. "Finally," wrote Sir Richard Cartwright, "after some hesitation and after the debate had gone on for many days, Mr. Laird . . . declared his intention of voting with the Opposition. This, which was followed by a similar pronouncement from Mr. Donald Smith (now Lord Strathcona), put an end to all doubt as to how the vote would go, and Sir John, without more ado, tendered his resignation."[37] Out, therefore, went Prime Minister Sir John A. Macdonald and the whole of his Government, and in came a Ministry headed by Alexander Mackenzie.

Mr. Smith's Change of Front

Why, however, did Mr. Donald A. Smith change so suddenly from being an ardent supporter of Macdonald's administration to an opponent whose decisive vote at this critical juncture, added to a few other adverse votes, caused the resignation of Macdonald's Ministry? We have seen from Macdonald's own testimony how the Prime Minister recommended Mr. Smith for a place on the Board of Directors of the Canada Pacific Railway.

This was, indeed, a most vital question. It was but a few

---

[36] *Debates in the House of Commons, Third Session, Third Parliament,* pp. 919–923.
[37] *Reminiscences,* p. 118.

years later that Sir Charles Tupper, in the House of Commons, was so uncharitable as to accuse Mr. Smith in categorical fashion of certain distinct and supposedly palpable motives in thus turning against his political chief and patron, Macdonald. " Mr. Smith was a representative of the Hudson's Bay Company," announced Tupper [who had, in 1872 and 1873 occupied the posts of Minister of Inland Revenue and Minister of Customs under Macdonald], and he [Smith] had been pressing a claim on his right honorable friend [Macdonald] for public money; Sir John had held back, and Mr. Smith came to the conclusion that it would be just as well to jump the fence if there was to be a change of Government. But Mr. Smith was a canny man; he held back and sat on the fence and watched the course, certainly not in the interests of his country, because he did not want to jump too soon and find he had jumped into a ditch. But when he came to the conclusion that the Government was going out, he made the bolt, and I have no doubt that he has had a great deal of reason since for congratulating himself on having jumped as he did." [38]

An Uproar in Parliament

In the violent, extremely unparliamentary scene that occurred next day — a scene famous in the annals of the Dominion Parliament — various members more than intimated that after the honorable Mr. Donald A. Smith's sudden flop, and after the new Government took office, extensive contracts and corporate powers and proprietary possessions somehow came into the ownership of Mr. Smith and associates. When Smith said that he had received or desired no more from Mackenzie's than from Macdonald's Government, Tupper asked him point blank whether he (Smith) had not, in 1873,

[38] *Debates in the House of Commons, Dom. Parl.*, 1878, Vol. V, p. 2560.

telegraphed to Ottawa that he would be there to support the Government, and that he then knew all about the Canadian Pacific Railroad affair. Smith denied that he sent the telegram.

Whereupon there was a wild uproar. Mr. Smith charged Sir John A. Macdonald with having made certain statements in a private conversation. Macdonald accused Smith of stating a falsehood. Mr. Rochester got up and asked Smith " how much the other side offered him? "

At this, members suddenly became bereft of decorum, and shouted and gesticulated excitedly. Tupper called Smith's conduct a cowardly abuse, and charged him with detailing " what he knows to be falsehood." Excitement now multiplied; some members shouted " Order! "; others exploded into asking running questions. Tupper asserted that Smith had begged him to implore the leader of the Government to make him (Smith) a member of the Privy Council of Canada and was refused, which allegation Smith denied. Here there was more disorder, and still more so when Tupper repeatedly called Smith a coward, a " Mean, treacherous coward! " [39] A message from the Governor-General came in at that moment, and had the effect of diverting the diversion. According to Sir Richard Cartwright, nothing but the presence of the Sergeant-at-Arms and " a few stalwart keepers of the peace . . . prevented an absolute physical collision between the parties." Cartwright described Sir John Macdonald and Dr. Tupper as " absolutely beside themselves for the time being, while Mr. Smith was collected and composed." [40] Cartwright, it may be said, held a somewhat prejudiced and altogether opposing partisan view of Macdonald.

[39] *Ibid.*, p. 2564. The language here given is exactly that reported in Hansard.

[40] *Reminiscences*, p. 187. The scene as reported in Hansard, Cartwright further wrote, " but faintly represents what actually took place. The shouts and cries were so loud that but a part of what passed was heard and taken down by the reporters. . . ."—*Ibid.*, p. 388.

Of the charges made during this particular session we shall have more in detail to say in the next chapter. Whatever may have been the merits of the controversy as to why Donald A. Smith turned front, the fact remained that he and certain others chief of whom was George Stephen, future Lord Mount Stephen, became railway and land magnates of the first order under Mackenzie's Government, and during that period, by a series of laws, contracts and acquisitions, prepared the way for their subsequent construction, acquirement and ownership of the Canadian Pacific Railroad.

Sir Hugh Allan Gets Nothing

All of Sir Hugh Allan's bargainings and schemings were finally in vain; the charter granted to him and associates never received the sanction of Parliament and never became of effect. But seven years later — in 1880 — a company headed by George Stephen, with Donald A. Smith interested in the background, put through the actual measures practically giving them the Canadian Pacific Railway virtually free of cost and with a land grant of 25,000,000 acres.

CHAPTER XIII

ERA OF RAILWAY MAGNATES

After the disclosures of the methods used to get the Canadian Pacific Railway charter, money subsidies and land grants, an agitation set in to have the Government build the line, and parts of it were begun under Government supervision. But as shown by a Government advertisement in 1876 calling for proposals from private companies for the construction of the railway, the scheme of Government construction, operation and ownership was not held too seriously.

By 1878 only a little more than 100 miles of track were laid, and this line was a detached, isolated section running from Thunder Bay to Tetu Lake. There was also the Pembina branch over which the trains of the St. Paul and Pacific Railway entered Emerson; as to both the Pembina branch and the St. Paul and Pacific line we shall give further details in this chapter. The great project of a transcontinental railway system still remained a project. With the recent revelations fresh and sharp in the public mind, the subject was a sensitive one to the politicians both in and out of power.

The Intercolonial Railway

In the eastern part of Canada the construction of a railway to the seacoast at Halifax had also been provided for in the Confederation agreement, but this railway was early made a publicly-owned and publicly-operated system.

Some portions had been purchased by the New Brunswick

244

Government from private contractors and extended under public control; other parts had been independently constructed by the Nova Scotia Government. After the formation of the Dominion of Canada in 1867, the Dominion Government took control of these railways, and constructed connections and extensions. On November 9, 1872, all of these Government railways were consolidated under the name of the Intercolonial Railway. These formerly separate railways were the Nova Scotia Railway, 145 miles; the Intercolonial Railway, 118 miles; and the European and North American Railway, 108 miles. The Government railway thus now comprised 375 miles running from Halifax to St. John with some branches.

The next move was to connect the Intercolonial Railway with the Province of Quebec. In 1874 the Government had a line of 86 miles constructed between Riviere du Loup and St. Flavie. Another section of 290 miles between Ste. Flavie and Moncton was finished by 1876. The line of the Intercolonial Railway now extended from Riviere du Loup to Halifax. From the Grand Trunk Railway Company a line of 126 miles running from Riviere du Loup to Hadlow was bought in 1879, and with the subsequent acquirement or construction of various railway sections and by securing running rights over other sections, the Intercolonial Railway system extended from Montreal to Halifax, and to St. John and the Sydneys in Nova Scotia.

Conflicting Principles

While, therefore, in one great stretch of Canada the principle of public railway ownership was definitely established, the construction and ownership of railways in other great sections were turned over to individual capitalists who were allowed vast gratuities of money subsidies and land grants, and in other ways were given the fullest license to accumulate enormous private fortunes and corporate power speedily.

In the United States such an inconsistent, anomalous policy was unknown; there all of the railway charters were given to private companies and all of the railways were privately owned and operated; private ownership and operation and Government ownership and operation did not exist side by side as they did in Canada.

If, however, the Canadian Pacific Railway project, as originally planned, was allowed practically to lie dormant for the time, other projects were consummated. Although these projects and transactions were small compared to the Pacific railway scheme, their outgrowing powers and the profits derived were of much ultimate consequence. The chief beneficiaries of these transactions were some of the very men who developed into great railway, land-owning, bank and mine magnates, men who today stand out illustriously as among the most exemplary and foremost multimillionaire capitalists of Canada and of the United States.

Red River Line Scandal

One of these transactions was a certain contract given by the Canadian Government to the Red River Transportation Company. This corporation was an outgrowth of the activities of Donald A. Smith, under whom, as Chief Officer of the Hudson's Bay Company, the use of steamers upon the lakes and rivers of the North West Territories was first projected in 1871.

The circumstances of this contract and of another contract led to some extremely vigorous talk in the Dominion House of Commons in 1877 and 1878. Sir Charles Tupper, strong in his aptitude for delving into financial transactions, had critical remarks to make of a certain payment by the Dominion Government of $223,884 to the Red River Transportation

Company for conveying rails from Duluth to St. Boniface, near Fort Garry. The contract, he charged, had not been given by public tender, and the rates charged were enormous. A few days later — on April 24, 1877 — Tupper said that Mr. John Christian Schultz, M. P., who represented Manitoba, had informed him that Donald A. Smith held a third interest in the Red River Transportation Company.[1] It may here be repeated that Schultz later became Lieutenant-Governor of Manitoba.

Schultz arose to amplify Tupper's comments. He read certain correspondence of the Red River Transportation Company (of which N. W. Kittson was General Manager), and analyzing the payments by the Government, asserted that they were exorbitant. The fact that the Government had paid some hundreds of thousands of dollars to this line, he said, made easy the explanation why that Company could divide 80 per cent. on its stock among its shareholders.

Charges as to Its Contract

" But how came about this enormous waste of the public money?" Schultz inquired. " How was it that, when an opposition steamboat line was known to be in operation on the Red River, tenders were not asked for? And why was it that the enormous price . . . originally promised should have been extended . . . ?

" The honorable member for Selkirk [Donald A. Smith] said he had nothing to do with the Kittson line; but certain it was that rumor gave him the credit of owning indirectly a large quantity of its stock. Certain it was that Mr. Kittson merged the agency of the Hudson's Bay Company into the management of the Kittson line, which was commenced mainly

[1] *Debates in the House of Commons, Dom. Parl., 1877*, Vol. III, pp. 1689 and 1772.

with the boats of the Hudson's Bay Company. Of course, it was not at all likely that the name of the honorable member for Selkirk [Smith] appeared on the stock books of the Kittson Company, for that would vitiate the right of the company receiving bonded goods; yet there were other ways of holding stock than the open one of having names in full in the stock books of the company.

" If," Schultz pertinently asked, " no one deeply interested in the success of this line vouched for Mr. J. J. Hill, who so deftly manipulated the contract, how was it that the Premier chose to jump at the offer of a stray American, who came along with his offer to carry rails at twice the price the transportation was worth, and at least one-third more than it would have cost the Government had tenders been asked for from the rival line on the Red River and others? "

Here it may be parenthetically remarked that this charge made by Schultz was subsequently confirmed by the testimony before the Royal Commission on the Canadian Pacific Railway.

Toussaint Trudeau, Deputy Minister of Railways and Canals, testified before that Commission that on April 16, 1875, Fuller and Milne, steamboat competitors of the Red River Transportation Company, had previously made a much better offer for the transportation of rails than had Kittson, but that James J. Hill had appeared in Ottawa, and after an interview with the Minister, the contract had been hurriedly given (without competition being invited) to Kittson. In its " Conclusions," the Royal Commission on the Canadian Pacific Railway reported that the rates offered by Fuller and Milne would, had their tender been accepted, have meant a very considering saving to the Government; that the direct difference between the whole quantity at Kittson's rates and those of Fuller and Milne was about $44,000 American currency; and that even although it was getting exorbitant prices, the Red River Transportation Company did not fully carry out its contract.[2]

Mr. Schultz's Statements

We shall now return to the debate in the House of Commons, on April 24, 1877. Concluding his remarks as to Red River Transportation Company transaction, Schultz said that he firmly believed that Donald A. Smith was precisely what Tupper had stated — a participator in the profits of the Red River Transportation Company. When the Speaker called Schultz to order saying that Donald A. Smith had positively denied being a shareholder in the Company, or participating in its profits, Schultz reiterated his statement, saying that he based his belief mainly on public documents, and especially on letters that he read. Schultz declared that J. J. Hill had had a very strong backing in his dealings with the Government.[3]

The J. J. Hill here referred to was James J. Hill, that great present-day railway magnate of the United States. A Canadian, he had gone to Minnesota to seek his fortune; and of some of his methods in accumulating his enormous wealth, we shall have more to say presently.

The matter of the Red River Transportation Company did not end with this day's enlivening proceedings. It came up again in the House of Commons on April 4, 1878, when in the course of a vitriolic debate, Schultz resumed his heated attack upon Donald A. Smith and his methods. After Smith had given a long defense of the Red River Transportation Company, Schultz described at length what he termed its greed, and told how settlers going to Manitoba were " huddled like sheep and treated like hogs on the lower decks of those very

[2] See *Report of the Royal Commission on the Canadian Pacific Railway*, Vol. II, p. 969, and Vol. III, pp. 276–284.

[3] *Debates in the House of Commons*, etc., 1877, Vol. III, pp. 1800–1801.

steamers." It was a notorious monopoly, he said, and paid big dividends; its freight charges were a gross imposition.[4]

But was Donald A. Smith connected with the Red River Transportation Company which profited so highly from Government contracts? One of his eulogists, Alexander Begg, wrote assertively that "although his name does not appear, he was a powerful factor in building up the steamboat facilities on the Red River. . . ."[5]

St. Paul and Pacific Railway

There was, however, another transaction which caused a much greater stir in and out of Parliament. This was the acquisition by Donald A. Smith and associates of the St. Paul and Pacific Railway, and the later leasing to it by the Canadian Government of the Pembina branch of the projected Canadian Pacific Railway.

The early history of the St. Paul and Pacific Railway was full of scandals.

Its original promoter was Russell Sage, a Troy, New York, grocery merchant. After he and his partners had successfully concocted a certain swindle, Sage as successfully cheated his own partners out of the proceeds of that swindle.[6]

The City of Troy had built a railroad called the Troy and Schenectady Railway. Sage was a leading member of the Troy Common Council and one of Troy's directors of that railway. He manipulated matters so that the City of Troy was persuaded into selling the road, and it was his own vote that decided it. Sold for $200,000, the Troy and Schenectady Railway was promptly bought in by a syndicate, headed by Sage,

---

[4] *Ibid.*, p. 1685.
[5] *History of the Northwest,* Vol. III, p. 100.
[6] The specific details are related in the *History of the Great American Fortunes,* Vol. III, pp. 14-16, citing the records of the Supreme Court of the United States.

paying only $50,000 in cash. It was subsequently sold by Sage and partners for $900,000 to the New York Central Railroad syndicate. Sage then had himself elected and re-elected to Congress in 1853 and 1854, and was busy during the years when Acts directly or indirectly giving immense land grants to railways were lobbied or bribed through that body.[7]

Its Original Plundering by Sage

One of these railways was the Minnesota and Pacific Railway. Robbed into insolvency by the plundering of construction companies composed of the identical men who promoted the railway, it was foreclosed, and was bought in by the very men who had looted it.

In order to cover their lootings by legal artifices, and thus prevent defrauded creditors from recovering, they caused an Act to be passed by the Minnesota Legislature reorganizing the railroad into two divisions, one called the St. Paul and Pacific, and the other the First Division of the St. Paul and Pacific Railway Company. At the head of the group controlling both of these apparently separate roads was Russell Sage. In exchange for mortgages on the line and on its land grant, Dutch capitalists were wheedled into advancing $13,-380,000 for the completion of the line, and thus avert the forfeiture of its land grant, as threatened by the Minnesota Legislature. Great parts of the sums advanced by capitalists in Holland were fraudulently diverted by the promoters,[8] and the entire road in 1875 went into bankruptcy.[9]

[7] See full details in Chapters I and II, Vol. III of the *History of the Great American Fortunes*, giving the facts from official documents.

[8] These fraudulent methods are described in Dillon's (U. S.) *Circuit Court Reports*, Vol. V, pp. 451–459 and 519–536 in which Judge Dillon states the facts.

[9] This necessarily is merely an outline of the looting of this railway by Sage and associates. The full narrative, citing from the facts as set forth in the United States court records, is given in Chapter II, Vol. III of the *History of the Great American Fortunes*.

Farley Is Appointed Receiver

Judge Dillon in the United States Circuit Court appointed one Jesse P. Farley receiver. James J. Hill now stepped in. He discerned the opportunity of getting for almost nothing at a forced sale a railway of 500 miles with a land grant of more than 2,500,000 acres.

According to Farley's repeated statements in subsequent Court proceedings, Hill and Norman W. Kittson entered into a conspiracy with him (Farley) to betray the United States Courts, and that at the same time John S. Kennedy, of New York City, the representative of the Dutch bondholders, conspired with him to betray those bond-holders. Hill denied these allegations, but Farley asserted and reasserted them in many court proceedings.[10] Farley was an ignorant man who had seen some railroad experience in Iowa; that he was recommended to the Court as receiver by Kennedy is definitely stated in the Court decisions.[11]

The Receiver's Collusion

If Farley's sworn statements may be believed, he was to mismanage the affairs of the railway so that the price of the bonds would be reduced, and he was to inform Hill and Kittson of every move that he made. At the right time Hill and Kittson were to come forward, and get control of the railway. Neither Hill nor Kittson had the necessary money to do this, but according to Farley they were to give a two-fifths or 40-per cent. interest to anyone supplying the funds. Farley

[10] See Farley vs. St. Paul, Minneapolis and Manitoba Railroad Company, *Federal Reporter*, Vol. XIV, pp. 114-118; *United States Reports*, Vol. CXX, pp. 303-318; Farley vs. Hill, *Federal Reporter*, Vol. XXXIX, pp. 531-532; Farley vs. Norman W. Kittson et. al., *Minnesota Reports*, Vol. XXVII, pp. 102-107.
[11] *Federal Reporter*, Vol. XXIX, p. 516.

asserted that this agreement further provided that a three-fifths or 60-per cent. interest was to be reserved for himself and for Hill and Kittson,— one-fifth for each of the trio.[12]

In view of threatened forfeiture of the St. Paul and Pacific Railway's franchises and land grants, the urgent, immediate consideration was to construct the extensions at once. But from where were the necessary funds to come?

Enter Donald A. Smith and George Stephen

This contingency was soon provided for. Kittson brought in two fellow Canadians. One was Donald A. Smith, connected like himself with the Hudson's Bay Company; the other was George Stephen, President of the Bank of Montreal.

Hill and his associates now bought in the whole of the $28,-000,000 of the St. Paul and Pacific Railway bonds at an absurdly low price. In some cases only three per cent. of their value was paid; in other cases from 13¼ to 75 per cent. of their par value. Hill and his partners, however, were not required to pay in immediate cash. The bonds were chiefly acquired on the understanding that they were not to be paid for until the railway was finally reorganized.

The funds in hand were spent in a hasty effort to construct the extensions, and so forestall the forfeiture law. " Under these circumstances," the Court record states, " the receiver at the instance of Mr. George Stephen and other large bond-holders (James J. Hill, Donald A. Smith and Norman W. Kittson) hurried to Court, and got an order on April 18, 1878, to get authority to issue debentures to complete the extensions." [13] Under the authority of the Court, Farley, from

[12] Farley vs. Norman W. Kittson et. al., *Minnesota Reports,* Vol. XXVII, p. 103.
[13] John S. Kennedy et. al. vs. The St. Paul and Pacific Railway Company, et. al., Dillon's *Circuit Court Reports,* 1879–1880, Vol. V, p. 527.

the funds advanced by the Hill-Stephen syndicate, caused 125 miles of railway to be constructed at an aggregate cost of $1,016,300. This extension gave an unbroken connection between the city of St. Paul, Minnesota, and the railway system in Manitoba.

The next step was to get from the Canadian Government a lease to the St. Paul and Pacific Railway Company of the Pembina branch of the Canadian Pacific Railway, the construction of which had been done at Canada's expense. On March 7, 1878, a dispatch had been published in the Toronto *Globe* stating that the St. Paul *Pioneer Press* had editorially asserted that the purchasers of the St. Paul and Pacific Railway bonds were Hill, Kittson, Smith and Stephen. The editorial further affirmed that they had effected a lease, on favorable terms, of the Pembina branch, and warning " antagonistic parties " not to waste valuable time in trying to get that branch, the lease of which, it was averred, was thus already secured.

An Exciting Day in Parliament

On April 4, 1878, Schultz inquired in the Dominion House of Commons whether any such arrangement had been made. Premier Mackenzie replied negatively. If, said Schultz, the Premier's statement was true, then Hill and associates must have been " using the grossest falsehoods for the purpose of preventing the Northern Pacific and other railroads from asking that connection with our line which they [Hill, etc.] were seeking for themselves." [14]   Referring to Hill and Smith, Mackenzie Bowell said that care should be taken as to the placing of such power " in the hands of the same parties who have exacted enormous freight rates from the people of the North-

[14] *Debates in the House of Commons,* etc., 1878, Vol. IV, pp. 355 and 1680.

west — rates so enormous that they almost doubled the cost of goods taken into that country." [15]

In fact, Bowell more than implied that Donald A. Smith was using his position in Parliament for the personal benefit of himself and associates. If, Bowell said, the dispatch from St. Paul was true, then "we have the extraordinary spectacle in the House of the champion of this proposed lease using his power and influence as a very humble and obedient supporter of the Government to secure to himself and his partners the advantage of a lease. Either it was true, or it was not true." Bowell declared that he was inclined to infer its truth from the fact that Smith had not denied a charge of this kind made twice in the House.[16]

More Attacks on Mr. Smith

Sir John A. Macdonald accused Smith of more warmly and strongly advocating the lease Bill, "which is in his own interest and which will put money in his own pocket," than the Minister who introduced it. Macdonald termed it a fraudulent measure.[17] More opposition came from another House member, Mr. White. "There seems," said White, "to be a party in the House — a very prominent party — who cares more for the Hudson's Bay Company, the Montreal Bank and private matters than for the interests of the people of Manitoba. . . . No one will believe that the honorable member for Selkirk [Smith] cares as much for the interests of the country generally as he does for his own pocket. . . ." [18]

When during this debate Smith made a defense of his actions, Schultz said in reply that he (Schultz) " would content

[15] *Ibid.*, p. 1681. Mackenzie Bowell was later Dominion Minister of Customs and Minister of Trade and Commerce.
[16] *Ibid.*, p. 1689.
[17] *Ibid.*, pp. 1690–1691.
[18] *Ibid.*, p. 1692.

himself simply with commending to that honorable gentleman [Smith] the story of a gentleman in New York, who, when wishing to state directly his opinion of the veracity of a person he believed to be a consummate liar, said of him, ' That all he could say was if he should meet him going down Broadway with Annanias and Sapphira he should take all three to belong to the same family.' " [19]

When, on May 9, 1878, Premier Mackenzie served notice for adjournment, and denounced the Senate's action in throwing out the Pembina Branch Bill, Sir John A. Macdonald scored Mackenzie and commended the Senate's action " which would put a stop to their [the Government's] bargain with the honorable member for Selkirk to make him a rich man and to pay him for his servile support. . . . The circumstances of an honorable gentleman [Smith] getting up and advocating a proposal in which he was interested was suspicious." [20]

Lease of the Pembina Branch

The Mackenzie Government, however, did make a lease with George Stephen, on August 3, 1878, granting exclusive running powers for ten years over the Pembina branch, extending from Pembina to Winnipeg, to the St. Paul and Pacific Railway (or as it was later termed, the St. Paul, Minneapolis and Manitoba Railway).

But Mackenzie's Government was soon put out of power; and its successor, taking advantage of a certain clause, gave a contract to Upper and Company to equip and operate part of the road. A queer transaction now developed. One of the partners of that firm sold out to a Mr. Willis who, according to rumor, was in fact an employe and agent of the St. Paul and Pacific Railway coterie.

[19] *Ibid.,* p. 1686.
[20] *Ibid.,* Vol. V, pp. 2556–2557.

Various complications now set in of too involved a nature to describe here. It was complained that the St. Paul and Pacific Railway Company formed a compact for a uniform tariff of rates, and that in defiance of its agreement with the Canadian Government, the St. Paul and Pacific Railroad Company was interchanging traffic with the steamboats of the Red River Transportation Company, thus lessening the chances of Upper and Company making their undertaking pay.[21] The sequel was that Upper and Company came to an understanding by which the St. Paul and Pacific obtained running rights.

Hill, Smith, Stephen and Company Get the Railroad

On April 11, 1879, a final order of foreclosure was decreed, and on June 14, 1879, the St. Paul and Pacific Railway was sold to Hill and associates composing what was called the St. Paul, Minneapolis and Manitoba Railroad Company, which Hill and associates had organized a month before the sale for the express purpose of buying the St. Paul and Pacific Railway under foreclosure. The total sum for which the road was sold was $6,780,000, and they were allowed to turn in receiver's debentures and bonds in payment.

Farley later testified that this railroad thus sold for $6,780,-000 was then worth, at the very least, $15,000,000. In fact, in the suit in 1880 of Wetmore vs. the St. Paul and Pacific Railroad Company, to set aside the sale, Judge Miller, in the United States Circuit Court, estimated the 565 miles of railroad and the land grant of 2,586,606 acres to be worth $20,-000,000 or more.[22]

Hill and associates not only owned the St. Paul and Pacific bonds, but they apportioned the stock among themselves. Hill and Kittson each received 57,646 shares of stock, and the

[21] *Monetary Times,* May 9, 1879.
[22] Dillon's *Circuit Court Reports,* 1879–1880,, Vol. V, p. 531.

other members of the syndicate their share.[23] From a part of the land grant alone, aside from the railroad property itself, Hill and associates at once obtained more than twice the sum that they had paid for the whole property. Immediately after the foreclosure sale, they sold the greater part of the land grant for $13,068,887.

There now remains a large and vital question. How and where did Hill, Kittson, Smith and Stephen get the funds with which they consummated the St. Paul and Pacific Railway transaction?

A Troublous Bank of Montreal Meeting

In 1879, financial circles in Montreal were excited by the report that many millions of dollars had been taken out of the Bank of Montreal, without the consent or knowledge of the directors, and put into the St. Paul and Pacific Railway. The meeting of the bank's shareholders, on June 4, 1879, was a stormy one. The official stenographic published report of that meeting contained this paragraph:

" Mr. John McDonald said that he coincided to what had been said in regard to bank losses. . . . There never was such a melancholy statement offered to the shareholders as this one. The advances to directors towered far beyond a million dollars. He would like to see men at the head of the institution who would not require such accommodation. (Applause.) It had been rumored outside that some of the directors were largely interested in a road in the West, and required a large amount on that account."

Similar comments were made by other shareholders. Donald A. Smith, who had become a Bank of Montreal director in 1873, denied that the railway referred to was indebted to the bank. General Manager Richard B. Angus said regard-

[23] *United States Reports,* Vol. CXX, p. 308.

ing the Directors' loans that " it would not be judicious at any time to give even a detailed statement of those accounts." [24]

Pointed Questions

Commenting on this meeting, the *Monetary Times* said editorially, June 13, 1879: ". . . The recent meeting of the Bank of Montreal presented a remarkable contrast to what has been customary on those occasions for many years back. . . . Some rather pointed questions were put with reference to certain large advances said to have been made by the Bank for railway purposes which, however, were only met by the statement that although the advances were large, undoubted security was held for them. This is not an uncommon phase with bankers when inconvenient questions are put by inquisitive stockholders, and it might have been well to be a little more precise. Certain advances to directors of the Bank were also the subject of criticism. These were met by the somewhat bluff statement that if these advances were required to be paid off, the Bank could have its money in a short time. This answer, though it amounted to very little, appeared to have the desired effect, and no further questions on the subject were asked. With regard to certain large accounts, the information was given that the Bank had only four in which the advances exceed $400,000; but by how much these accounts exceed this sum was not informed. . . ."

Alleged Source of $8,000,000

Much mystery was maintained as to precisely what had happened. But a few years later John Charlton represented

[24] See Toronto *Globe* and other newspapers of June 5th, 1879. Lord Strathcona and Mount Royal is still one of the largest shareholders in the Bank of Montreal; he holds 2,777 shares.— See, *List of Shareholders in the Chartered Banks of Canada* (published by the Dom. Gov't.), p. 48.

the case thus in the Dominion House of Commons when describing the composition and antecedents of the personnel of the chief owners of the Canadian Pacific Railway Company:

"A member of this Company was once President of the Bank of Montreal — a responsible position. When in that position he [Stephen] took $8,000,000 from the chest of the Bank of Montreal without the consent or knowledge of the directors of that bank,— at least he is reported to have done so. He is reported to have invested it in the St. Paul and Minneapolis Railway. Now, supposing this gentleman when he removed the money from the bank, and invested it, had lost the money, he would have been a defaulter to the extent of $8,000,000; but I hold that although the investment was successful, though he was enabled to return the money, morally his conduct was just as reprehensible as if he had lost every cent. I say he had no business to take $8,000,000 belonging to a corporation of which he was president, without the knowledge of the directors, and use that money in any speculation whatever."

Charlton might have added, by way of contrast, that, in 1876, one Barber, a clerk of the Bank of Montreal under President George Stephen, had been sentenced to five years in the penitentiary for embezzling funds with which to speculate in stocks.

" He is reported," Charlton went on, still referring to George Stephen, " to have invested that money, as I have said, in the St. Paul and Minneapolis Railway, and through collusion with the Receiver of that road, it is said he procured a report as to the condition of its affairs which was sent to Holland, where the stock was held, which report induced the Dutch bondholders and stockholders to part with their interest in the road at less than it was worth, thus enabling them to buy the road at less than its value. And having used the Receiver as his tool, he forgot the old adage, that there should be honor among thieves. He is charged with having forgotten to give the Receiver his share of the plunder, and the Receiver is said to have brought suit in the United States Court at St. Paul. The Court refused to entertain the suit on the ground that it would not degrade itself by giving a decision as to how plunder should be divided among different members of a gang. . . ." [25]   Charlton omitted to add that Richard B. Angus, General Manager of the Bank of Montreal, had resigned in 1879 to take charge of the financial management of the St. Paul, Minneapolis and Manitoba Railway. At the same time, Donald A. Smith ceased to be governor of the Hudson's Bay Company, and Charles J. Brydges became Land Commissioner of that Company. [26]

Farley Sues for His Share

In truth, Receiver Farley did bring suit against Kittson, Hill and associates, in the Minnesota Supreme Court, and did claim one-fifth of the capital stock of the railroad and one-fifth of all other securities and property acquired by that syndicate, which claim he based upon his assertion that they

[25] *Debates, House of Commons, Dom. Parl.,* 1884, Vol. I, pp. 390–391.

[26] We have repeatedly referred to Brydges' railroad career. A word more as to his bank activities. He was president of the Mechanics' Bank which suspended in 1879 with only $2,500 actual cash on hand to meet a circulation of $168,000 payable on demand! " Well knowing," commented the *Monetary Times,* January 6, 1879, " what slender resources were at its command for meeting liabilities, the managers have pushed its notes into circulation by the most improper methods. . . . The bank had several agencies in the country districts of Lower Canada, and almost the sole business of these agencies was to force the notes of the Mechanics' Bank upon the unsuspecting people of the locality. Not content with paying out the bills of the bank over the counter in the ordinary way, its agents would visit hotels, board steamboats and employ other persons to do the same thing, solely to gather in the bills of other institutions and exchange them for bills of the defunct bank. . . . It is notorious that many banks, generally the smaller ones in the Province of Quebec, are pursuing precisely the same tactics to get out their bills. . . ."

had got the property by reason of his collusion. But Judge Gil-
fillan, in the absence of the production of any written agreement, decided that Farley had not proved his case.[27]

Likewise, Farley sued the St. Paul, Minneapolis and Manitoba Railroad Company in the United States Circuit Court.
The attorneys for the railway had an effective plea ready.
They urged that the case be non-suited on the ground that
a court official — which the Receiver was — who had betrayed his trust had no standing in court. To rid themselves
of Farley's claims they admitted his contention of collusion!
Here was fine candor! In this plea Judges Treat and Nelson, in 1882, concurred, saying in part:

"Courts will not and ought not be made the agencies
whereby frauds are in any respect recognized or aided. They
will not unravel a tangled web of fraud for the benefit of anyone enmeshed therein through whose agency the web was
woven. Especially must that be a rule where a trusted officer
of a court, whose position is both advisory and judiciary,
seeks its assistance to compel alleged confederates to share
with him the spoils acquired through his concealments and
deceits, which he admits were deemed by his confederates
and his confederates necessary to their success through his
betrayal of his trust."[28]

Then followed other parts of the Court's decision practically confirming Farley's statements that he had entered into
a conspiracy of collusion with Hill, Kittson and their partners, on the one hand, and Kennedy, on the other. "T'
plaintiff," continued the decision, "conceived a scheme to
wreck the vast railroad interests which it was his duty to protect. Through a betrayal of his trust under such circumstances, according to his version of the facts, these vast

---

[27] *Minnesota Reports,* Vol. XXVII, pp. 102–107.
[28] *Federal Reporter,* Vol. XIV, pp. 114–118.

railroad properties have been secured, and a profit realized of $15,000,000 or more." [29]

Farley Loses; the Rest Become Multimillionaires.

Farley carried his suit twice to the Supreme Court of the United States, but after thirteen years of litigation the final decision was adverse to him on the ground that he had not proved his claim.[30]

But what of the men whom Farley alleged conspired with him, or who were alleged to have profited by his betrayal of duty? It is almost superfluous to describe their rapid ascent. The capitalization of this particular railroad was gradually run up to $210,000,000. Hill became the great multimillionaire railway autocrat of the north-west United States. Kennedy became a multimillionaire; when he died, in 1909, his fortune was estimated at from $30,000,000 to $60,000,000, according to the estimates put upon the value of his enormous pile of railway stock. George Stephen, as we shall see, was, before many years, created a Sir, and then raised to the peerage as Lord Mount Stephen. Donald A. Smith, in 1886, was created a Knight Commander of the Most Distinguished Order of St. Michael and St. George, and subsequently Lord Strathcona and Mount Royal.

[29] *Ibid.*, p. 117.
[30] See *United States Reports,* Vol. CXX, pp. 303–318 and *Ibid.,* Vol. CL, pp. 572–577.

CHAPTER XIV

PROGRESS OF THE RAILWAY LORDS

Flushed with their success in acquiring the St. Paul and Pacific Railway, five of the men concerned or interested in that transaction soon reached out to get, and did get, an even immensely richer prize. This was the contract for constructing the Canadian Pacific Railway and the proprietorship of that railroad.

These five men were George Stephen, James J. Hill, John S. Kennedy, Richard B. Angus, together with Donald A. Smith, who, although his name did not appear in the contract, was an active directing figure in the group. Compacted with them in the contract were Donald McIntyre of Montreal and two banking firms, that of Morton, Rose and Company of New York and London and the house of Kohn, Reinach and Company of Paris, France.

Macdonald Returns to Power

Out of power had gone the Government headed by Mackenzie, and back to Premiership had come Sir John A. Macdonald, in October, 1878. Only a few years previously the great Canadian Railway charter scandal had dislodged Macdonald from his high power, and made his administration a by-word. It had not seemed possible that he could ever resume the office of Prime Minister. The forces that put him back were, to a large extent, economic forces.

True, Macdonald was an astute politician who was credited with `sagaciously knowing how to ally himself with the Roman Catholic hierarchy, on the one hand, and, on the other, with the Orangemen. But Sir Richard Cartwright points out the real forces chiefly exerting themselves to get Macdonald back in office. The manufacturers wanted high tariff duties; and as Macdonald was willing to give them all that they wanted, they raised a large campaign fund for him and his party, and having very considerable influence with the newspaper press they also swayed the opinions of the electorate. There was also, Cartwright asserted, an influential body of contractors who " resented being held fast to their engagements and longed exceedingly for a renewal of the régime under which comfortable repayment in the shape of liberal extras could always be reckoned on in return for a subscription to party funds at the right moment." [1]

Too much of a monotone of partisan bias colors Cartwright's positiveness; without doubt, his asseverations contain truth, yet not the whole truth; with equal accuracy Macdonald's supporters could have retorted and could have produced the proofs that under Mackenzie's administration certain contractors had grown rich.

Somber and cynical is the picture drawn by Sir Richard Cartwright of the state of public mind at that period. The general public, according to him, had " given up expecting anything like honor or honesty in politics from public men." [2]

Politics was, in fact, a business; the Canadian Parliament was crowded with men who were there to initiate, extend or conserve class or personal interests; of the 206 members of the Dominion House of Commons, in 1878, there were 56 merchants, 55 lawyers, 12 gentlemen of leisure, and an assortment of manufacturers, insurance company presidents, shipbuilding and lumber capitalists, contractors, and a few

[1] See Cartwright's *Reminiscences,* pp. 189–191.
[2] *Ibid.,* p. 256.

journalists, physicians and farmers.[3] The same ratio held true of successive Parliaments. Cartwright's error, however, consisted in regarding the exposures in 1873 as the first and original evidence of " official corruption and degradation." Those exposures were doubtless striking, but, as we have seen, they had been preceded by a series of different scandals each of which had, in its day, been impressive.

Canadian Pacific Railway Contract.

Apparently the Canadian Pacific Railway project was removed from being made an instrument of profit to contractors, for in 1880 the Dominion House of Commons had approved a resolution to construct that railway as a Government work. Suddenly, a few months later, the Macdónald Administration announced its intention of giving the contract for the entire scheme to a syndicate composed of George Stephen and Company. Donald A. Smith's name was absent in this contract. But his partners or close business associates were its principal beneficiaries. Mr. Smith at this juncture kept most diffidently in the background.

When the provisions of this contract were made public, the expressions of general astonishment were loud and great. When had any Company, excepting the Hudson's Bay Company, been invested with such extraordinary privileges and powers, immunities and rights? What group of men had ever received such vast subsidies in both money and land as were proposed in this all-empowering charter? Every reservation, qualification and limitation of powers contained in the original Act of 1874 were set aside by the provisions of this charter, and privileges and powers never originally contemplated were lavishly conferred upon a mere handful of alert promoters.

[3] *Monetary Times,* May 3, 1878, p. 1285.

A Gift of $62,000,000 and 25,000,000 Acres

By the terms of this munificent contract the Government obligated itself to complete certain unfinished parts of the railway, and to transfer to Stephen and partners for their own benefit more than 700 miles of railway the construction of which ultimately cost the Government $37,785,000. In these 700 odd miles was included the important and much-coveted Pembina branch, forming the connecting link of the St. Paul and Pacific Railway to Winnipeg. The contract apparently made a gift to the contractors of $25,000,000 but it actually involved a total contribution by the Canadian Government of more than $62,000,000 which sum was further augmented by necessary expenditures to extinguish the Indian title to lands granted to Stephen and associates. These additional outlays were equal, if capitalized, to $30,000,000 more.

And what was the entirety of this land grant? A huge domain of 25,000,000 acres of choice lands, valued even in that day before the great inrush of settlers began, at $79,500,-000 at the very least estimate.

Extraordinary Powers Given

These were far from being the only donations made in the contract. It was distinctly provided that in making the land grant only land fairly suitable for settlement was to be allotted the contractors. In other words, they were to have the pick of the finest lands, for the contract further specified that they were to have large powers of selection of the land.[4] They were also to control the land sales.

[4] The extraordinary powers and property conferred by these provisions may be better understood by comparing this land grant with the railway land grants in the United States. The grants in the United States consisted invariably of arbitrary alternate sections, which is to say that the railway companies had to take their chances on the

Then came other vast and expansive powers given in the contract. All property and the capital stock were to be exempted from taxation by the Dominion and Provincial governments and by the municipalities. This exemption was not a limited but a perpetual one. Likewise the land grant was to be exempted from taxation, until sold or occupied, for 20 years from the date of the grant. This was a privilege of itself worth great sums of money.

Further, the contract exempted from import duties a large part of the materials required to construct the railway. In certain directions it guaranteed the Company a monopoly of railroad construction and traffic for a period of 20 years. Another clause productive of great complaint was inserted. By this clause the Government bound itself not to reduce — or in other language, regulate — the Company's railway rates unless the Company made a net revenue exceeding 10 per cent. on the capital invested in the construction of the railway. This was a provision especially arousing distrust and apprehension; it was pointed out that by stock-juggling devices, the profits could always be nominally made to appear lower than 10 per cent., and thus perpetually furnish a legal justification for extorting high railway rates. This, it may be parenthetically said, is precisely what did happen.

The contract also provided for the payment of the money subsidies and land grants in amounts entirely disproportionate to the prairie section of the railway, the construction of which section was the easiest and most profitable, and which was intended by the contractors to be the earliest completed. Finally, the contract gave the fullest power forever to the company to build branch lines in various parts of the Domin-

quality of land that they were allotted. It might be good agricultural or timber land or poor, barren land. The Canadian Pacific Railway Company received alternate sections, also, but it had powers of selection such as railway companies in the United States did not have.

ion, and it incorporated various other important comprehensive powers and privileges.

Futile Opposition to the Charter

A competing company of Canadian capitalists offered terms much more favorable to the Government, and sought to get a contract for the Canadian Pacific Railway. But the allegation was made that its offer was not genuine. Its efforts were in vain. Amendment after amendment to the Stephen-Hill contract was introduced in the Dominion House of Commons by opponents. Specifying the immense powers and rights donated in the contract to a handful of men, they emphasized the fact that none of these powers had been contained in the original Act of 1874. They insisted that the direct gift of $25,000,000 and of 25,000,000 acres of land was not in the public interest and should not be legalized. The exemption of all of the Company's property and capital stock from taxation was condemned by them. They called attention to the fact that the clause in the original Act by which the Government had power to acquire the railway whenever it was considered advisable by the public interest, was stricken out in the contract.

Amendments offered by Sir Albert Smith, Sir Richard Cartwright, Wilfrid Laurier, David Mills and 19 other members of the House of Commons were all voted down.[5] The chief argument used by Macdonald and his majority was that to facilitate the colonization and settlement of the West, a transcontinental railway was necessary, and that no capitalists would construct it unless they were given the fullest aid and encouragement. A resolution in favor of the contract being given to George Stephen and associates was then carried, and on

[5] *Debates, House of Commons, Dom. Parl.*, Session 1880–1881, Vol. I, pp. 702–764.

February 17, 1881, a Bill incorporating the Canadian Pacific Railway Company was passed. Subsequently, it may here be said, that Company received a gift of 1,702,458 acres of more land grant for its Souris branches.

Now the way was wide open for George Stephen and partners to gather in fortunes of hundreds of millions of dollars, all within a few years. That they quickly availed themselves of the opportunities thus presented was soon evident.

Chinese Coolie Labor Imported

First, the contractors organized a construction company composed of themselves or dummies, thus ensuring themselves from the outset an enormous profit on construction and greatly increasing the cost.

At the same time they or the subcontractors imported gangs of Chinese coolies to do much of the work of construction in the West at the cheapest possible outlay. Robert Ward, a commission merchant, shipping agent and agent for railroad contractors, testified before the Royal Commission on Chinese Labor that " in 1882 my firm had between 5,000 and 6,000 Chinese consigned to them from Hong Kong. These men were under engagement to the contractors of the Canadian Pacific Railway, and arrived in ten different vessels . . ." [6] Andrew Onderdonk, a civil engineer and Canadian Pacific Railroad subcontractor, testified that he had employed as many as 6,000 Chinese at one time.[7] The Chinese, testified another witness, were slaves to all intents and purposes; they were exploited by the Chinese Companies who sold them in semi-servitude to the white contractors. The Chinese, he said, " were welcomed by the same class of individuals that

[6] *Report of the Royal Commission on Chinese Labor,* 1885, Sess. Paper No. 54 A, p. 84, *Sess. Papers, Dom. House of Commons,* Vol. XVIII, No. 11, 1885.
[7] *Ibid.,* p. 148.

now desire to perpetuate their stay — men that have no object beyond their own aggrandizement and greed, and who would worship Confucius rather than Christ if they were going to make money out of it." [8]

The habitations of the Chinese laborers were generally wretched hovels; they lived amid filth and neglect.[9] " I have never yet known an English or French gentleman from the old countries," testified David William Gordon, a contractor and builder and M. P., for Vancouver, " who would feed their dogs upon the food consumed by the ordinary Chinese laborer." [10]

Construction and Land Companies

Profits from construction work thus yielded great revenues. But the Canadian Pacific magnates or their associates organized other interconnected agencies from which they extracted additional great wealth.

One of these was the Canadian North West Land Company formed in 1882 to acquire 5,000,000 acres of the Canadian Pacific Railway land grant. The controlling spirits in this Company were Lord Elphinstone in England, and Donald A. Smith in Canada. One of the managing directors was Edmund B. Osler, the distinguished Canadian millionaire and knight of present times. By 1883, fully 1,500,000 acres had been conveyed by the Canadian Pacific Railway Company to the Canada North West Land Company, and of that amount 65,621 acres had already been sold at an average price of nearly $6 an acre. At the Company's annual meeting, in 1883, Osler spoke glowingly of the Company's prospects. He described the beginning of the overflow of the population of the United States, and asserted that the Canada North West Company had among the best, if not the best, lands in the North West. Mr. Osler's enthusiastic speech, as officially reported, continued:

[8] *Ibid.*, p. 132. [9] *Ibid.*, p. 87. [10] *Ibid.*, p. 134.

" The interests which this Company has in town and village sites along the road [the C. P. R.] is one which must come in time to be enormously valuable. . . . Every man who goes into that country as a farmer builds up a little village near his point of residence, and as the increase of population goes on, the interest we have in town and village sites will be of enormous value (Hear! hear!) . . . I believe that when you have half your land sold the value of the remaining half will be very much greater than the value of the whole estate today, no matter how valuable it may be. (Cheers.) . . ." [11]

This, however, was not all of the business justifying exuberant optimism.

The Canadian Pacific Railway Company had, as we have noted, agreed to sell 5,000,000 acres of land to the Canada North West Land Company. Later, the quantity purchased was reduced to 2,200,000 acres. The land company claimed exemption from municipal and school taxation on all lands that had not actually been selected by it and conveyed.

Of this asserted exemption the Manitoba Legislature, in 1888, complained, saying that although evading taxation the Canada North West Land Company was " exercising rights of ownership and control over said lands, in many instances leasing and selling the same and taking the profits thereof." The legislative resolution went on to say that the Company had refused to pay taxes on its lands, although those lands had increased in value, and although improvements had been paid for by the taxes collected on the adjoining lands of settlers and private owners. It was because of such evasion of taxation and claim of exemption, the resolution further said, that many municipalities throughout Manitoba had been obliged " to impose heavy burdens on the resident and individual landowners, and the settlement of the country has been

[11] Official advertised report of the annual meeting in the *Monetary Times,* July 20, 1883, pp. 69-72.

greatly retarded." The Government was called upon by the resolution to assist in a test case brought by one of the municipalities in Manitoba against the Canada North West Land Company.[12]

They Gather in More Millions

Accompanying these transactions were a series of other transactions by which members of the Canadian Pacific Railway Syndicate pocketed large profits. It was charged that by the initial manipulation of stocks which they sold to themselves at 25 cents on the dollar, they made a collective profit of $9,000,000 at the very start. Another method was by

[12] *Journals of the Legislative Assembly of Manitoba,* 1888, Vol. XIX, pp. 61–62. The present effects of that clause in the C. P. R. contract with the Government relieving the railway company from taxation for 20 years were recently set forth in an editorial in the *Grain Growers' Guide,* published at Winnipeg. The editorial (issue of September 24, 1913), said in part:

"What we want to call special attention to just now, however, is the heavy burden which is placed upon the people of the West by the clause in the C. P. R. contract which exempts the lands granted to the C. P. R. from taxation. This exemption was supposed to extend for 20 years, but, through the carelessness of the people's representatives and the cleverness of C. P. R. lawyers, it is still effective though the contract was made 32 years ago. The result is that in many rural municipalities and school districts there is very little land which can be assessed for taxes. The lack of schools and roads in such districts can easily be understood. In such districts either the few farmers whose land is assessable must be excessively taxed, or schools and roads must be done without. This condition is seen at its worst in the C. P. R. irrigation district, in Alberta, where the railway company secured both odd and even numbered sections. Lands owned by the C. P. R. or held by others under agreement of sale are not liable for taxes. Those which have been patented to purchasers are liable, but there is such a small area taxable that in the school districts of Irricana, Crowfoot and Goderich it has been found impossible to support the schools. Goderich and Crowfoot schools have consequently been closed, while at Irricana the school is being maintained by private subscriptions. The C. P. R. in the year ending on June 30 last, made a profit of over $46,000,000. Nevertheless, the children of farmers living on the prairies of Saskatchewan and Alberta are deprived of even a common school education because the C. P. R. through a legal quibble has escaped the obligation of paying taxes. . . ."

selling to themselves as heads of the Canadian Pacific various small railways which they either individually owned or effectively controlled.

The Grand Trunk Railway Company had extended its possessions by amalgamating in its system various lines such as the Great Western Railway, and later it absorbed the Northern Railway and the Hamilton and North Western Railway with which it had previously — in 1879 — arranged a pooling agreement. The Midland Railway of Canada passed into its possession; this line was an amalgamation of the Toronto and Nipissing Railway, the Whitby, Port Perry and Lindsay Railway, the Toronto and Ottawa Railway and two other railways with the Midland Railway. After a series of financial difficulties and strikes, in which its workers demanded long-due arrears of pay, the Midland Railway Company settled with its creditors for 22 cents on the dollar,[13] and passed into the control of George A. Cox, an insurance agent, who had been quietly buying its stock. Following the amalgamation with the five other railways, Cox, in 1881, became president of the Midland Railway of Canada, the 455 miles and $11,600,000 stock and bonds of which soon were acquired by the Grand Trunk.[14] It was greatly by reason of this transaction that Cox became a millionaire, enabling him to expand later into so notable a capitalist with a variety of large financial and industrial interests. The Grand Trunk Railway had fused other railways — the Grey and Bruce, the St. Lawrence and Ottawa, the Vermont Central and others. The great competitor of the Grand Trunk — the Canadian Pacific — now began the same process of amalgamation of small lines.

George Stephen, Edmund B. Osler and various associates had early begun to get control of different railways. In 1881

[13] *Monetary Times*, February 22, 1878, pp. 995–996.
[14] *Ibid.*, 1881. Robert Jaffray, another noted capitalist and a close partner of Cox in subsequent transactions, was associated with Cox in this amalgamation.

Osler was president of the Ontario and Quebec Railway, and George Stephen was one of the directors. George Stephen and Donald A. Smith were also directors of the Atlantic and North Western Railway Company, and Osler was vice president of the Toronto, Grey and Bruce Railway. In turn, these railways often absorbed other railways. The Atlantic and Western Railway, after becoming a branch of the Canadian Pacific, absorbed the Waterloo and Magog Railway the directors of which did not care to have the threat made by the Atlantic and Northeastern Railway of building a parallel line carried out.[15] Methods such as these were invariably effective.

To the forefront now came Donald A. Smith. Hill, Kennedy and McIntyre withdrew from the Canadian Pacific's board of directors in 1883, and Smith became a director. From thence for decades he was the most powerful figure in the executive committee of that railway company. George Stephen long remained president of the company, and subsequently Edmund B. Osler was elected a director.

Ask for $45,000,000 More Public Aid.

Only three years after they had obtained the money subsidy of $25,000,000 and the land grant of 25,000,000 acres for the main line, George Stephen and his Canadian Pacific Railway Syndicate had a Bill introduced in Parliament, in 1884, to give them sums, in the form of loans, totaling nearly $45,-000,000 more. These amounts they asked on the ground that they were essential to the completion of the railway.

Lively scenes in the House of Commons followed the pushing of this Bill. The fight really developed into a contest between the Canadian Pacific Railway forces and those of the

[15] *Monetary Times,* July 23, 1886, p. 90. The Atlantic and Western Railway ran from Smith's Falls to Lachine.

Grand Trunk Railway. M. M. Fleming accused the directors composing the Canadian Pacific Syndicate of buying up, in their private capacity, the shares and bonds of the Credit Valley Railway (running from Toronto to St. Thomas) at 30 and 35 cents on the dollar, and then arranging with their own company to value them at 100 cents on the dollar.[16] Yet, he said, the Credit Valley Railway had received $1,000,-000 in bonuses from Ontario municipalities for the specific purpose of providing competition. Mr. Fleming went on to say that the members of the Canadian Pacific Syndicate were absorbing for their private interests all of the feeders of the Grand Trunk that they could possibly secure.

Mr. Fleming further stated that of the $65,000,000 of stock issued by the Canadian Pacific Railway, $25,000,000 of it went into the hands of the original members of the syndicate, part of which sum they took as payment for construction work done by a construction company composed of themselves. Of that $25,000,000 of stock, $20,000,000 of it, said Fleming, was taken by these same men at 25 cents on the dollar, with the resulting profit of at least $9,000,000. At the time that they got the contract, Fleming asserted, they subscribed only $4,000,000; now they claimed to have spent $23,-563,564 on construction work, although the Minister of Railways placed the sum thus spent at $16,053,364.

" People will ask," continued Fleming, " where are the enormous sums the original contractors made? Where have these gentlemen put these enormous profits which they have made out of this transaction? And after they have made such great profits on the construction of the railway, why do they not advance out of their enormous fortunes sufficient to carry on the contract as rapidly as possible? "[17]

[16] *Debates, House of Commons, Dom. of Canada,* Session 1884, Vol. I, p. 318.
[17] *Ibid.,* p. 320.

$10,000,000 Profit From Construction

Mr. Lister declared that he believed that the Government was " in the palm of the hand of the managers of that Company." Mr. Orton and others speaking in favor of the Bill, asserted that because of the intrigues and influence of the Grand Trunk Railway Company in England, the Canadian Pacific had been unable to float a loan; therefore the Government should come to its aid.[18] Mr. Cameron said he believed that the Canadian Pacific Syndicate made $10,000,000 from their North American Construction Company, by means of which Company they had been able to contract with themselves, yet other sections of the railway were still to be completed.[19] Mr. Rykert denounced the opponents of the Bill, and declared that many of those members of the House that he named were beneficiaries of large colonization land-grant companies in the North West.[20] Among others that Rykert attacked was Mr. Jaffray of the Toronto *Globe,* which attack, as we shall see in a later chapter, was to cost Rykert dear.

Mr. Charlton asserted that the Canadian Pacific Syndicate had received $54,247,000 cash receipts from various sources; he declared that George Stephen and partners had watered the Company's stock and had organized a construction company to build the road; their manipulations, he said, were not honest. He then traced Stephen's antecedents, and described the St. Paul and Pacific Railway and the Bank of Montreal transactions, and said there were " rings within rings."

[18] *Ibid.,* p. 344, etc. This was by no means a new charge. In 1877 the Grand Trunk Railway Company was accused of having ruined the credit of the North Shore Railway Company in England and thus preventing it from selling bonds. It was also charged with having brought about the rejection by the rate payers of Toronto of a by-law granting $300,000 aid to the Toronto and Ottawa Railway which formed the western continuation of the North Shore Railway.— See *Monetary Times,* December 28, 1877, p. 755.

[19] *Debates, House of Commons,* etc., 1884, Vol. I, p. 359.

[20] *Ibid.,* p. 369.

An Endless Chain of Profits

" We know," Charlton went on, " that a construction company was formed for the purpose of vastly increasing the cost of the road, and putting the increased cost into the pockets of a ring of speculators. We know that the stock of the Company has been watered most scandalously, and that the result is that the people of this country will be called upon to pay 10 per cent. in perpetuity upon all of the water injected into that stock." [21]   Mr. Gillmor drew attention to the fact that Canada's population was only 4,000,000; the workingmen, said he, would have to pay the bill.   Mr. Blake declared that it was well known that the Canadian Pacific Railway " have thus far engaged in the construction of the least costly and most remunerative portions of their line; that the more costly and difficult and less profitable portions remain to be constructed; and that it is to enable them to construct the latter that they are now making application to Parliament for aid." [22]

[21] *Ibid.*, p. 391.   That these strictures were not idle talk is evidenced by the agrarian complaints and grievances now being made in western Canada.   A recent editorial in the *Grain Growers' Guide* presented this view:
" Certain Eastern newspapers and politicians are very fond of talking about the debt which the West owes to the East for its self-sacrifice in bearing the whole cost of building the C. P. R. into this country.   As a matter of fact, however, anyone who knows anything about Western conditions knows that the West is every day paying very dearly for the C. P. R. and for the bad bargain which Eastern politicians made to secure the construction of that road.   The 25,000,000 acres of land which the C. P. R. got in the original contract were all Western lands, and many a Western farmer will have to hand over half the proceeds of his crop this fall as an instalment on the purchase of some of the land that was thus given away by the Government.   Everybody knows, of course, that the Government has always allowed the C. P. R. to charge the people of the West from 66 to 100 per cent. higher rates for the carriage of freight and express parcels than it charges in the East for the same service."
[22] *Debates, House of Commons*, etc., 1884, Vol. I, p. 378.

Free Railroad Passes

A seething, truculent debate that was, each side taunting the other, and neither seriously denying the charges that each made. It could not be denied that members of both political parties were interested as promoters or stockholders in various railway charters and subsidies, and in colonization land companies, timber limits, coal lands, and contracts of different kinds all of which they had obtained, or were now securing, by means of their Parliamentary power and of Government concession. As to these ramifications of personal interests on the part of a considerable number of members of Parliament, pertinent details are set forth in the chapter following this.

Members of Parliament all, or nearly all, accepted free railroad passes. In a debate in the House of Commons subsequently, Lister asserted that, "As a matter of fact a very large number of the members of this House hold passes from the railway companies," and Mr. Amyot held that "free passes should be granted to all [members] so as not to be the means of corruption when Bills concerning certain railways come before the House. It is no use trying to deceive the public, for all the members are glad to have free passes. We do not go into politics in this Country because we are rich. We know very well that some members have given votes with reluctance — I do not say this year — because of the free passes which they had received or which were offered to them." [23]

An Alleged $100,000 Fund

It was almost at the very time that the Canadian Pacific Loan Aid Bill was before the House of Commons that certain

[23] *Debates, House of Commons, Dom. of Can.*, Session 1888, Vol. II, p. 1422.

allegations were forthcoming as to how the votes of certain members were secured in advance.

We have already traced the inception of the North Shore Railway, and narrated how it was alleged that the Grand Trunk Railway Company had, by ruining its credit in England, prevented the sale of its bonds. The Government of Quebec then came to the assistance of the North Shore Railway Company to which was given subsidies aggregating $13,000,000. Financial troubles caused its sale in 1882 for $8,000,000 to a syndicate headed by M. L. N. Senecal, who, at an enormous profit, sold it to the Grand Trunk. It was charged that Senecal gave to Sir Hector Langevin $100,000 together with other sums which were alleged to have been expended in favor of Conservative candidates for election to the House of Commons, in 1882. The circumstances of the sale of the North Shore Railway caused such a scandal that the Government of the Province of Quebec appointed Judge Routhier to investigate; he, however, announced that he would not inquire into the matter of the alleged $100,000 fund, as that inquiry would be beyond his jurisdiction.[24]

Stephen and Partners Get Nearly $45,000,000 Loan

The Bill to give the Canadian Pacific Railway Company an additional loan became a law; under this Bill, passed by the Dominion Parliament in 1884, that Company received a total of $44,880,912. So much money was the Company gathering in, that within two years it was able to pay back $29,880,912 of this loan.

As we have noted, the foremost argument used in granting the Canadian Pacific Railway contract and charter was that subsidies and a guarantee of monopoly were necessary to induce capitalists to invest money in " so vast and hazardous

[24] *Monetary Times,* Oct. 2, 1885, p. 376.

an enterprise," and "thus promote colonization and settlement." A resolution introduced in the Manitoba Legislature, in 1888, was full of wrath. It denounced the Canadian Pacific's monopoly. That monopoly and the ensuing extortions, it said, were the cause of the prevailing stagnation in business, and the despondency and discontent among the people. The monopoly, the resolution read further, "prevents many coming in the country which they know to be at the mercy of one corporation, and is causing many good citizens to leave it." [25]

Agitation was now carried on to get the Canadian Pacific to relinquish its monopoly — an agitation that was no doubt partly stimulated and accelerated by promoters of other projected railway lines.

An incident developed at this juncture when Premier Greenway and Attorney-General Martin of Manitoba went to Ottawa. Sir George Stephen voluntarily informed Greenway personally that no proposition having any reference to their errand had been made by the Canadian Government or by the Canadian Pacific Railway Company. Greenway wrote that he (Greenway) "was at a loss to understand such a statement, especially when being informed by the Right Hon. the Premier, immediately subsequent to the statement made by Sir George Stephen, that the Government of Canada had met the President of the Canadian Pacific Railway Company [Stephen] and that the matter was progressing favorably." [26]

A Gift of $15,000,000 More

As a "solatium" for its supposed relinquishment of a monopoly, which, according to Premier Greenway, never had any foundation so far as the old Province of Manitoba was con-

[25] *Journals, Legislative Assembly of Manitoba, and Sess. Papers 1 to 32*, Vol. XVIII, 1887.
[26] *Ibid.*, 1888, Vol. XIX, *Sess. Paper No. 4.*

cerned, the Canadian Pacific Railway Company received a guarantee from the Dominion Government of $15,000,000 in bonds. But the very next year a motion in the Manitoba Legislature complained that despite this settlement, the Canadian Pacific was continuing resistance to the construction of competing railways in Manitoba,[27] and nine years later another motion denounced the Canadian Pacific's elevator monopoly by which the grain product was controlled. This resolution was, however, amended so as to omit all reference to the Canadian Pacific Railway.[28]

By this time the Canadian Pacific Railway Company had received in Government assistance $18,720,000 more, so that, not counting the enormous value of its land grant estimated at hundreds of millions of dollars, it had obtained more than $206,000,000 in Government aid. This $206,000,000 included $65,000,000 of its capital stock guaranteed. Of its land grant, it relinquished 6,793,014 acres in consideration of the payment of $10,189,521. This direct aid of more than $206,000,000 in the form of Government cash subsidies, guarantees, loans and bonds, was, however, only a part of what the Canadian Pacific, or lines which it acquired, eventually received. More subsidies, land grants and hugely valuable coal mines all rapidly came into its proprietary possession.

27 *Ibid.*, 1889, Vol. XXI, p. 18 of *Journals.*
28 *Ibid.*, 1898, Vol. XXX, p. 30.

CHAPTER XV

EXTENSION OF RAILWAY POSSESSIONS

Immense as was the ramification of the properties already controlled and largely owned by Donald A. Smith, George Stephen and the remainder of the Canadian Pacific Railway group, their possessions were hugely augmented by the acquisition, either by purchase or lease, of other railways chartered during this period and endowed with great land grants and extensive money subsidies.

A Donation of 1,399,000 Acres

The Manitoba South Western Colonization Railway was one of these. By an Order-in-Council, the Dominion Government, in 1880, made a gift to this railway of 1,328,000 acres of valuable land. Computing this land as then worth at least $10,000,000, Edward Blake, in the Dominion House of Commons prodded Premier Macdonald about the transaction and denounced it.[1] The gift stood, and Manitoba added a loan of $900,000. The Manitoba South Western Colonization Railway ultimately received a total of 1,399,640 acres, and later passed under lease to the Canadian Pacific Railway Company.

Large Land Grant to the North West Central

Another of the richly-subsidized railways subsequently passing into the control of the Canadian Pacific group was the Great North West Central Railway. This was a line char-

[1] *Debates, House of Commons, Dom. Parl.*, Session 1880–1881, Vol. I, pp. 112–113.

tered in 1882 as the Souris and Rocky Mountain Railway; the Company made some appearance of constructing the road but evidently none to pay its workers; various remonstrative petitions went in to Parliament from its laborers asserting that they had not been paid for a whole year's labor. The principal promoter of the charter of this railway was a member of the House of Commons who, it was openly charged (as we shall see), had received a gratuity of $386,000 of Souris and Rocky Mountain Railway stock.

The successor of the Souris and Rocky Mountain Railway Company was the North West Central Railway Company empowered to take over the line and construct a railway of about 450 miles from Brandon to Battleford, in the Province of Saskatchewan. The Company had originally been allowed the privilege of purchasing land at the rate of $1.06 an acre to the extent of 6,400 acres for each mile of the railway. This was considered a rich enough gift. But the promoters did not see why they should pay anything when they could contrive to get the land as a gift.

They managed their plans with such success that, on July 29, 1885, an Order-in-Council was issued permitting them to take the land as a free grant, conditional upon the railway being built.

Still, the railway line remained on paper, which was as far as most of its construction went. An amendment to the original Act was now, in 1886, introduced by James Beaty, member for West Toronto, in Parliament sanctioning the giving of the land grant as a vested right to that company or any other company that might construct the road.

Charges of Corruption

Suddenly, certain interested members of the House of Commons were much perturbed over definite charges leaking into the newspapers that corruption had accompanied the gliding course of legislation dealing with the North West Central Railway Bill of 1884.

Members of Parliament were constrained to bestir them-selves to attempt explanations. No languor marked this day's proceedings.

D. B. Woodworth, a member from Nova Scotia, admitted that he had introduced and promoted the Bill of 1884. "I was not aware, Sir," he said with naïve candor, "nor am I yet aware but that it was the general custom of members of Parliament to be interested in railway charters if they pleased, just as if they were not members of Parliament; and believ-ing that, I went into this matter the same as though I were not a member of Parliament." [2]

Amplifying his statement, Woodworth averred that he had promoted the Bill at the instigation of Beaty. He wrote a letter to Beaty, he said, agreeing with Beaty "that after $50,-000 — if the road could be made to pay that — was divided among the directors, whatever franchises were left, we were mutually to be interested in." Woodworth said that Beaty never replied to this letter. Later Beaty (so explained Wood-worth), had a Bill drawn up, amending the original charter. "I looked at the Bill," Woodworth continued, "and found that all the guards, all the checks, ensuring payment to the workmen upon the road — the old Souris and Rocky Moun-tain Railway, of which this was a revival — had been left out." In the Railway Committee Woodworth objected to the Bill — so he now stated — and the Committee struck out the objectionable clauses. He and Beaty then and there quarreled. Notwithstanding Beaty's denial, Woodworth in-sisted that he and Beaty were jointly interested in the rail-way.[3]

[2] *Debates, House of Commons,* etc., Session, 1886, Vol. II, p. 974.
[3] *Ibid.,* p. 975.

A Demand for $675,000

The members of the House were still more keenly interested when Woodworth went on: "I stated to the [Railway] Committee that I had a letter that the member for West Toronto [Beaty] had demanded as his share of the profit in building that road from a contractor whom he wished to undertake the work, the modest sum of $675,000. I read that letter. At a subsequent meeting I read a letter from another man, whose name I forget now, saying that he heard the member for West Toronto demand that as the modest sum for what he called 'the boy.'

"There was not an honest attempt to build one foot of this road," Woodworth continued. "There was not an honest attempt to put a theodolite on the road, to take a measurement, to take a level; to do anything, to go out there even, as I understand, to put a foot on the road, but merely to hawk [the charter of] the road. . . . I say this was a charter selling and nothing else." Woodworth then submitted a copy of an agreement signed by James Beaty, as president of the North West Central Railway Company, to award a contract to build a part of the railway.[4]

Influences at Work in Parliament

Mr. Mitchell, a member of the House Railway Committee, then said that although the foregoing facts were brought out before the Committee "there were some influences" which prevented a forfeiture of the charter and which granted an extension of time to the railway's promoters.[5] Edward Blake arose and said that the North West Central Railway Company was "converted largely into a directorate of politicians and members of Parliament."[6]

---

[4] *Ibid.*, p. 976.   [5] *Ibid.*, p. 979.   [6] *Ibid.*

Beaty now had his say. He denied any specific arrangement with Woodworth, and asserted that he had got in touch with American capitalists who wanted to build the road.

One Member Gets $386,000 in Stock

Severe denunciation of the whole scheme then came from John Charlton, another member of the House of Commons. He said that "it was an astonishing fact that the Government of Canada, after all of the revelations that have been made in regard to the transaction now under the consideration of the House, should insist upon granting this charter. . . . We have in this case a member of this House in the possession of $386,000 worth of capital stock which he admits . . . has not cost him a cent. . . .

"Now, we have a statute which imposes a fine of $2,000 on every member of the House for every day he sits in the House while he has a contract with the Government." Charlton further declared that a "system of contract brokerage was going on," and said that the member who got the $386,000 of capital stock did it for the purpose of controlling the company, "and putting into his pocket all of the bonuses granted and gain made out of it." [7]

More caustic and specific was Hon. J. F. Lister's denunciation. " . . . We find," he said, "the honorable member for West Toronto and his friends on the directorate are not railway builders at all. Most of them, I believe, are lawyers practicing in the City of Toronto. They never did anything about railways. . . . It is a monstrous thing that members of Parliament, sitting here representing the people, are permitted to traffic in railway charters. It is a scandal, a burning disgrace."

[7] *Ibid.*, p. 982.

An Alleged $100,000 for a Minister

Lister then read affidavits made by D. McConachie of Hamilton, and E. A. C. Pew of Welland. McConachie deposed that in September, 1885, he saw Beaty for the purpose of negotiating for the contract to build the North West Central Railway, and proposed to deposit the sum of $125,000 in the Canadian Bank of Commerce. Beaty,— so McConachie attested,— repeated the expression, "But you see there is nothing in it for the boy." The affidavit stated further that Beaty said that Hon. Thomas White, Minister of the Interior, was his friend, "and that it would be desirable to give the Hon. Thomas White, the Minister of the Interior, the sum of $100,-000. . . . And said James Beaty justified said payment to the honorable Minister of the Interior upon the grounds that said Minister had renewed the land grants in the matter voluntarily and without waiting for Parliament to meet."

The affidavit further stated that Beaty additionally declared during this interview that after the payment of the $100,000 to White, and after other members of the House of Commons associated with Beaty were " shared with," his (Beaty's) portion of the $675,000 would be small, " considering his personal time given and means spent in furthering the project." [8]

Pew's affidavit made similar statements, particularly as regarded Beaty's declaration that it would be desirable to give $100,000 to Minister of the Interior White.[9]

A Day of Recrimination

Defending himself, White asserted that the character of the men making these affidavits was such that their statements

[8] *Debates, House of Commons, Dom. Parl.*, Session 1886, Vol. II, pp. 995 and 1709.
[9] *Ibid.*

were not to be taken seriously. White said that Pew was well known by his association with the Manitoba and South Western Railway and his conduct in connection with that project, revelations as to which had been made in the courts; he was not a man, White alleged, whose statement could be depended upon.[10]

The debate at this point became exceedingly bitter, members of the House interjecting derogatory, sharp remarks, and some of them seeking to divert attention from the charges made against them by making charges against other members. " I know," said White, at one stage of the proceedings, " that presidents of important railway corporations in England have announced the opinions they had from counsel in Canada, members of Parliament, and even declared the amount,— $2,-000,— which they paid for the opinion." [11]

The satirical Dr. George Landerkin, called " the Wit of the House," here projected himself into the acrimonious debate. He specified four members of the House of Commons who were associated with Beaty in railroad projects in Manitoba. " Well," he commented, " it is a gratifying thing to the people of Manitoba to find that there are such benevolent members in this House who are prepared to sacrifice their comforts to construct railways for the people of Manitoba, and who receive 6,400 acres of land per mile, when the construction of it, perhaps, is not worth more than 640."

Long List of Parliamentary Railway Promoters

Citing from the *Parliamentary Companion,* Landerkin said that Mackenzie Bowell, member for North Hastings and Dominion Minister of Customs, was president of the North Hastings Railway which received a Dominion Government subsidy of $10,500. Mr. Bowell rose to explain, saying that

[10] *Ibid.,* p. 995.   [11] *Ibid.,* p. 997.

he *had been* president of the Belleville and North Hastings Railway before it had passed into the hands of the Grand Trunk Railway. Bowell asserted that the Grand Trunk Railway Company did not accept the subsidy money.[12]

Reading further from the *Parliamentary Companion*, Landerkin said that Mr. Bryson, member of the House for Pontiac, was a director of the Pontiac and Pacific Junction Railway. Bryson later denied this, but Landerkin replied that he was quoting the *Parliamentary Companion*, which contained autobiographies presumably written by the members of the House themselves. But Bryson did not deny Mr. Lister's statement subsequently that he (Bryson) was a stockholder in the Long Sault Railway, bonused to the extent of $25,600, nor did he deny that he was interested in the Gatineau Railway.[13]

Landerkin further declared that Mr. Wood, member of the House for Westmoreland, was president of the Caraquet Railway, which received a Government subsidy of $76,800 in a single year.[14] Wood did not deny this statement. "I see," Landerkin dryly went on, "that the Secretary of State, the member for Terrebonne, is also director of a railway, and I presume that he will look after the interests of that railway." "He is getting a pretty good slice of it," added Mr. Mitchell, another House member.[15]

As Landerkin went on to make statement after statement it became increasingly evident to the other House members that he had his facts well in hand.

---

[12] *Debates, House of Commons*, etc., Session 1886, Vol. II, pp. 999–1000. Both Landerkin and Bowell later became associated with capitalist enterprises; Landerkin as president of the Canada Mutual Mining and Developing Company, and Bowell as president of the Hasting Loan and Investment Company.

[13] *Ibid.*, p. 1061.

[14] *Ibid.*, p. 999. For further details as to the scandals relating to this project see later in this work.

[15] *Ibid.*, p. 999.

The Roll Call Proceeds

Proceeding with his bill of particulars, Landerkin said that Mr. Colby, member of the House of Commons for Stanstead, was a director of the Massawippi Railway; Colby did not deny the statement.[16] Landerkin declared that R. N. Hall, member of the House for Sherbrooke, was president of the Massawippi Railway, and a director of the Quebec Central Railway which extracted $211,200 from Parliament in 1884; Hall made no denial.[17] Of Mr. Hay, member of the House for Center Toronto, Landerkin said that he was a director of the Credit Valley Railway. " Ten years ago," ejaculated Hay.[18]

Still reading from the *Parliamentary Companion*, Landerkin said that Mr. Ives, member of the House for Richmond and Wolfe, and son-in-law of John Henry Pope, Minister of Railways, was a director of the International Railway which in a single year had received $170,000 of Government subsidies. Ives admitted that he was a solicitor for that railway, but denied any further interest.[19] Another member of the House, Landerkin stated, was a director of the Kingston and Pembroke Railway which received a Government subsidy of $48,000; this particular member of Parliament was the representative of Frontenac.[20]

[16] *Ibid.*, p. 1000. This railway ran from Magog to Coaticook; the Government of Quebec contributed a subsidy of $80,000.

[17] *Ibid.* The Quebec Central Railway received in bonuses a total of $533,301.30 from the Dominion Government, $1,076,123.14 from the Quebec Government, and $103,000 from municipalities. Part of it was originally chartered as the Levis and Kennebec Railway.

[18] *Ibid.* The Credit Valley Railway received a bonus of $531,000 from the Government of Ontario, and $1,085,000 bonuses from municipalities.

[19] *Debates, House of Commons,* etc., Session 1886, Vol. II, p. 1077.

[20] *Ibid.*, p. 1000. But the $48,000 subsidy from the Dominion Government was only a part of the total received by the Kingston and Pembroke Railway; the Province of Ontario gave it a bonus of $456,493, and municipalities gave it the sum of $509,320. This railway, 104 miles long, affiliated for some time with the Canadian Pacific Railway, is now leased and operated by the Canadian Pacific.

Continuing, Landerkin said that Mr. Mackintosh, member of the House for Ottawa, was president of the Ottawa Colonization Company, and of the Gatineau Railway, which latter, Landerkin said, received $320,000 Government subsidy. Mackintosh denied that he had ever got a dollar. " It may all be spent by this time," retorted Landerkin breezily.[21] Landerkin doubtless here referred to the Ottawa Valley and Gatineau Railway, which railway company received $319,982 Quebec Government subsidy.

The Minister of Railways, Too

" I come now," went on Landerkin, " to the honorable member for Compton, the Minister of Railways [John Henry Pope]. He is president of the International Railway, which runs from Montreal through the State of Maine." This railway company had received a total in 15 years of $2,250,000 in Government subsidies.[22]

Landerkin proceeded to state that Mr. Wallace, member for West York, was president of the York Farmers' Colonization Company, and that Mr. White, member of the House for North Renfrew, was a director of the Pontiac and Pacific Junction Railway which, Landerkin said, secured $272,000 in Government subsidy. "He is pretty solid," commented Landerkin descriptively, "and when the division bell rings he is on hand." [23]

" An Empire Bartered Away "

Next day came more revelations of how members of Parliament and their associates obtained from the Government gifts of railway charters and subsidies, great pasture land

[21] *Debates, House of Commons,* Session, 1886, Vol. II, p. 1000.
[22] *Ibid.*
[23] *Ibid.*

leases at one cent an acre, valuable coal land leases, colonization grants of vast areas of public land at half price, and
extensive timber limits.

"Members of Parliament," said Charlton, "brothers of
members of Parliament, nephews of members of Parliament
— the faithful and deserving of every kind, every station and
every degree, have been the recipients of these favors at the
hands of Government; and hundreds, I had almost said thousands of limits, have been granted to the faithful without
competition. In secret an empire has been bartered away."
Charlton described these elements as "plunderers gathered to
the prey." [24]

More Hon. Members Placed

Aggressively J. F. Lister arose with his bill of particulars.
He said that Dalton McCarthy, member for North Simcoe,
was one of the incorporators of the Northern and Pacific
Junction Railway Company; that with McCarthy were associated Senator Frank Smith and Senator James Turner upon
the list of shareholders of that Company. "They appear to
hold 1,820 out of 2,000 shares. It is reported that they will
make at least $500,000 out of a railway which is heavily sub-
sidized by the Government." [25] These facts were not denied
by any of those named.

"I find," Lister went on, "that the International Railway
Company has upon its stock list the Hon. E. T. Brooks, the
Hon. John Henry Pope, Minister of Railways, the Hon. M.
H. Cochrane, and my honorable friend Mr. Ives. These
gentlemen are the stockholders of this road. I find that
another road, bonused to a very considerable extent, and in
which Mr. Pope is interested, received at one time $175,000
of the people's money. . . . I find that the road [railway] has

[24] *Debates, House of Commons,* etc., 1886, Vol. II, p. 1032.
[25] *Ibid.,* p. 1060.

been further bonused to the extent of $2,550,000 for the construction of a road from Montreal to the road in which Mr. Pope is interested, and will form a link of the new road. I say it is a disgrace to the country that a Minister of Railways, owning the International Road, which he had owned for nine or ten years, which this country owed nothing to, should come to this House and ask this Parliament to give him the enormous sum of $146,000 for placing iron upon the road owned by him and built years before, and which there was no reason in the wide world for assisting by bonus or anything else. . . ." [26]

" I go further," said Lister, " and I find that the Pontiac and Pacific Junction Railway from Aylmer to Pembroke was bonused to the extent of $270,000. This road is owned by the Secretary of State. He is a stockholder and the real owner of the road, and it is owned by Senator Ogilvie and the honorable member for North Renfrew (Mr. White). These are the stockholders in the road. Does anyone tell me that, under these circumstances, it is a small thing for three honorable members of this House, one of them a Minister of the Crown, to come to Parliament and ask this Parliament to give them $270,000? It is a monstrous and disgraceful thing that any member of Parliament should be a corporator in a railway seeking aid from this Government. . . ." [27]

These were exceedingly strong and specific statements to make with such positiveness but they were allowed to pass unchallenged, no one venturing to question any part of them or to dispute the accuracy of the whole.

[26] *Ibid.*, p. 1060. We have previously noted that John Henry Pope was one of the original promoters of the Eastern Townships Bank, chartered in 1853, the St. Francis Valley and Kennebec Railway chartered in 1869, and of the Waterloo and Magog Railway which last named line was sold to the Canadian Pacific Railway in 1886. See further particulars as to Pope in the next chapter.

[27] *Debates, House of Commons,* etc., 1886, p. 1060. The Government of the Province of Quebec voted the Pontiac and Pacific Junction Railway Company $600,000 in subsidies, of which $426,000 had been paid by 1911 on the construction of 71 of the projected 95 miles.

Further List of Parliamentary Stockholders.

In monotonous succession, Lister proceeded to detail the connection of various other members of Parliament with railway projects and lines.

Mr. Mackintosh, Mr. Bryson and Mr. Alonzo Wright were the stockholders of the Gatineau Railway which had received a Government bonus of $160,000.

The Hon. J. A. Chapleau (Dominion Secretary of State), J. J. C. Abbott, and Joseph Tasse, member for Ottawa, were the incorporators of the Montreal and Western Railway which had secured a Government bonus of $160,000. This railway was an 88-mile affair and was later bought by the Canadian Pacific Railway Company.

Lister went on to point out that Mr. Temple, member for York was " deeply interested " in the Miramachi Railway to which was voted a Government bonus of $128,000; Temple denied this, but Lister said he had such facts as satisfied him.

Mr. Landry, member for Kent, was, Lister stated, a stockholder in the St. Louis and Richibucto Railway, which fact Landry did not deny.

Mr. Burns, member for Gloucester, was deep in the Caraquet Railway, a charge that could not be denied; we shall later describe the scandal developing from the operations of this particular railway's projectors.

Mr. Bergin, member for Cornwall, and Mr. White, member for Renfrew, were stockholders in the Ontario and Pacific Railway which, Lister said, had obtained a Government bonus of $262,400. Not denied.

White, Tasse, and Mackintosh were stockholders in the Ottawa, Waddington and Northern Transportation Company which received a Government bonus of $166,000 voted by Parliament in 1885. Not denied.

Mr. Wood, member for Westmoreland, represented the New

Brunswick and Prince Edward Island Railway, the recipient of a Government bonus of $113,400, which connection was not denied. This railway also received $99,708.90 from the New Brunswick Government.

Mr. Montplaisir, member for Champlain, did not deny the charge that he was a stockholder in the Montreal and Champlain Railway, which, Lister said, had obtained a Government bonus of $300,000.

One after another Lister continued to detail the railway connections and interests of still other members of Parliament.[28]

The Bill Goes Through.

All of these exposures, however, were futile. Parliament made the land grant to the North West Central Railway Company. Three years later, its successor, the Great North West Central Railway Company was incorporated by an Order-in-Council, and on the same day — July 22, 1889 — another Order-in-Council gave the land grant of 320,000 acres to this company. The condition was that the entire line was to be built by 1892, but further Orders-in-Council, in 1889 and 1891, extended the time. Not until December, 1891, were the first 50 miles of the railway completed.[29] The total mileage by 1911 was only 112 miles.

The ownership of the stock of the Great North West Central Railway was acquired by the Canadian Pacific group in 1898, and is now a part, by perpetual lease, of the Canadian Pacific Railway. The Great North West Central land grant has been of great value; of the original grant of 320,000 acres, about 220,000 acres were sold by 1911, and the remaining 100,000 acres were held at the average price of $18.73

[28] Lister's full remarks on the subject appear in *Debates, House of Commons,* etc., 1886, Vol. II, pp. 1060–1077.
[29] *Sessional Paper No. 9,* 1892, pp. lxiv and lxv, *Sessional Papers, Dom. Parl.,* Vol. XXV, 1892.

an acre — a total price for the 100,000 acres of nearly $1,900,-
000. The Great North West Central Railway, with its extensive land grant, was indeed a fine prize.

Manitoba and North Western Railway Gets 1,501,376 Acres

At about the same period that the North West Central Railway was chartered, endowed and subsidized, another railway
— the Manitoba and North Western — was chartered with
a gift of a land grant of 1,501,376 acres. This line was run
from Portage-la-Prarie to Lanigan.

A financial arrangement was then devised to get the cash
to construct the road. The promoters prevailed upon the
Manitoba Government to advance them large loans of funds
upon the security of the very lands that had been granted by
the Dominion Government!

By an agreement of November 15, 1885, the Manitoba and
North Western Railway Company bound itself to pay 10
cents an acre survey fees on the lands to be turned over to
the Manitoba Government as security for the issues of rail-
road-aid Provincial bonds. Twelve years later the Manitoba
officials, we find, reported that up to that date the railway
Company had paid nothing under this agreement.[30] In 1899,
many serious scandals developed as to the management of
Manitoba's provincial finances, especially in regard to the ways
in which railway companies obtained public funds.

The Procuring of Public Funds

A Royal Commission was appointed to do some investigating.

This Commission reported that frequently " railway deben-

[30] *Journals, Legislative Assembly of Manitoba,* 1897, Vol. XXXIX,
Sessional Paper No. 10, p. 35.

tures for large amounts were guaranteed and handed over to agents of the contractors without the authority of an Order-in-Council."

It appeared from the report of this Commission that the Government of the Province of Manitoba had loaned Provincial bonds to the value of $787,426.67 to the Manitoba and North Western Railway Company, the Province taking as security one acre of the Company's land grant for each dollar advanced, the Company agreeing to pay five per cent. interest a year. From year to year the company defaulted in the payment of interest until the accumulated arrears amounted to $366,439.07, not counting the compounding of interest. The Manitoba and North Western Railway Company now owed $1,158,784.34 to the Province, for which debt Manitoba held as security 702,560 acres of the land grant.

Publicly Paid for but Privately Owned

These, however, were not the only funds that the Manitoba and North Western Railway Company obtained. From municipalities it received a donation of $215,600.

In public funds it had therefore obtained $1,374,384.34. The promoters owned the railway, but the money invested was public money. By laws passed in 1900, the Province of Manitoba relinquished all claims upon 160,000 acres of the 702,560 acres of the Company's land grant which it held as security, and in lieu of all its claims for principal and interest, the Province agreed to keep 542,560 acres in fee simple. This arrangement left the Province of Manitoba responsible for the payment of about $39,500 interest a year for ten years, and the principal of $787,426.67 due in 1910.[31] The case now stood thus:

[31] *Report of Royal Commission, Journals of the Legislative Assembly of Manitoba,* 1900, Vol. XXXII, *Sess. Paper No.* 21, pp. 393-448.

The Dominion Government had presented the Manitoba and North Western Railway Company with 1,501,376 acres of land.

The Company had then obtained $787,426.67 in funds from bonds issued by the Government of Manitoba, the Province taking 702,560 acres of the land grant as security.

By 1900 the Company owed the Province $1,158,784.34 and was confronted with a total of about $395,000 interest up to 1910 when the bonds matured — a full total of more than $1,553,784.34.

Meantime the Company also received a clear gift from municipalities in subsidies of $215,600.

The Government of the Province of Manitoba returned 160,000 acres of land to the Company, and in exchange for 542,560 acres assumed the full debt, principal and interest.

The Company, therefore, had received — all points considered — a total of more than $2,000,000 in public funds to build a prairie railroad of 379 miles, and the Company was still absolute owner of 958,816 acres of its authorized land grant. Public funds built the railway, and legislative authority presented it to a clique of promoters, who now owned not only the railway but a vast area of valuable land besides. The capitalization of the road was gradually run up to $12,361,-967.

The lease of the Manitoba and North Western Railway was acquired by the Canadian Pacific Railway.

Protesting against the granting of huge railway subsidies, A. H. Gillmor said in the Dominion House of Commons, on April 30, 1889, that " it has come to be the case now that no man can speak of economy or make reference to the taxpayers of this Dominion without being considered childish or imbecile to give a thought to the men who are toiling with all these burdens on their backs." [32]

[32] *Debates, House of Commons,* etc., 1889, Vol. II, pp. 1677–1678.

G. E. Casey, another member of the House of Commons, summarized the situation in this language: ". . . My honorable friends who have wasted a good deal of time arguing this question, seem to forget that the gentlemen who sit opposite are merely the political department of the Canadian Pacific Railway. It is really the Canadian Pacific Railway which governs. This is a conclusive proof that these honorable gentlemen are mere trustees for that railway of the political power of the country, as other gentlemen may be trustees for their bonds or land grant. It is a waste of time to argue with them as to whether they should obey the orders of their masters or not. They must carry out the behests of the Company." [33]

[33] *Ibid.*, p. 1683.

CHAPTER XVI

APPROPRIATION OF COAL, TIMBER AND OTHER LANDS

That coal deposits lay in British Columbia had been long known, and near Nanaimo coal had been mined since 1852. But it was not until Professor Richardson of the Dominion Geological Survey reported on the enormous extent and value of the coal fields radiating about 200 square miles from Nanaimo, that a certain group of capitalists decided that the time was ripe to transfer the ownership of a considerable, if not all, of this area to themselves.

This group was composed of Robert Dunsmuir, his son, James Dunsmuir, of Vancouver, John Bryden and three members of the renowned " Pacific Quartet," to wit, Charles Crocker, Leland Stanford and Collis P. Huntington of California. Robert Dunsmuir was a British Columbia capitalist and politician, becoming a leading member of the Government of that Province. Crocker, Stanford and Huntington were the three chief promoters and beneficiaries of the Southern Pacific and other railway projects in the United States; of the extensive bribery there that accompanied the passage of legislation consummated by them, we have already given some particulars.[1]

Such was the group that at once set about getting, and did get from the Dominion and the British Columbia governments laws granting a charter for the Esquimault and Nanaimo Rail-

[1] And many more examples are specifically related in Vol. III, of the *History of the Great American Fortunes.*

way together with subsidies of 1,900,000 acres of land, and $750,000 cash. These donations were authorized for a line of only 78 miles, running from Victoria to Wellington.

This happened in 1884. One member of the House of Commons, D. W. Gordon, of Vancouver, demanded of Premier Sir John A. Macdonald certain explanations. Had the Government published advertisements either in Canada or Great Britain inviting tenders for the construction of the Esquimault and Nanaimo Railway? If so, had the attention of the capitalists been called to the area of land subsidy to be given, or to the reported value of the coal deposits extending from Nanaimo to Seymour's Narrows? And why had the system of alternative sections in aid of railways been departed from in the contract entered into by the Government with Messrs. Dunsmuir, Huntington and associates?

Premier Macdonald Explains

Premier John A. Macdonald dismissed the questions with this brief reply which we give literally:

" No advertisement has been published by the Government or any department thereof inviting tenders for construction of the Esquimault and Nanaimo Railway. We are not aware whether any advertisements were published by the British Columbia Government, under the authority of the Legislature, or otherwise, for this purpose, nor whether they have called the attention of capitalists to the quantity of land to be given in aid of said railway." [2]

[2] *Debates, House of Commons,* 1884, Vol. I, p. 85. It may be said here, as illustrating Premier Macdonald's associations, that he became president of the Manufacturers' Life Assurance Company, a fact which, on March 12, 1889, led Lister to say in the House of Commons that " it was a dangerous precedent that the First Minister of the Government should allow his name to be used by any commercial corporation." Macdonald replied that the board of directors of that Company " for wealth, respectability and standing were not second to

It was asserted during this debate that so far as the coal lands that they were then mining were concerned, the Dunsmuir family had received Crown grants previous to the granting of the lands to the Esquimault and Nanaimo Railway.

Certain members of the House of Commons denounced the whole scheme as one giving to a small clique the monopoly of the coal deposits of Vancouver Island. But opposition was useless. The advocates of the promoters could plead long-established precedent, as for instance, the transfer by the Nova Scotia Government, in 1868, of one square mile calculated to contain 10,000,000 tons of coal, as a subsidy to the Glasgow and Cape Breton Coal and Railway Company. That subsidy, however, was not a gift in perpetuity, but was given in the form of a 78-year lease, the Company to pay the Government of Nova Scotia a royalty of eight cents per ton. The subsidy to the Esquimault and Nanaimo Railway Company was a gift without reservations.

The chief Government member vouching for the Esquimault and Nanaimo Railway Bill seems to have been Minister of Railways John Henry Pope who, as we have seen, had been a personal beneficiary of railway and other charters. He gave the most solemn assurances that the Bill was a good one. It was to Pope that Mr. Mitchell, a member of the House of Commons, referred a few years later " as the brains of the Administration. . . . No one has done more in directing the policy of the country — I will not even except the Premier — than the honorable Minister of Railways. There are few men who can sit here with a solid countenance, and answer to all attacks and questions that ' there ain't nothing to it ' better than my honorable friend." [3]

those of any Company in Canada; and in saying this I do not include myself. My standing is political, not financial."— *Debates, House of Commons,* etc., Session 1889, Vol. I, p. 592.
[3] *Debates, House of Commons,* etc., Session 1888, Vol. II, p. 1689.

Dunsmuir & Co., Are Successful

The Esquimault and Nanaimo Railway Bill was shoved through Parliament. Two years later — in April, 1886 — discussion over its great gratuities was renewed when a Bill was introduced in Parliament allowing a deviation of its line.

One member after another of the House of Commons poured forth vehement remarks.

E. C. Baker, member for Victoria, declared that the Dunsmuirs owned three-fifths, and the California stockholders two-fifths, of the Esquimault and Nanaimo Railway Company's stock. "This," he said with an air of authority, "I know from Mr. Dunsmuir himself, so that the control of the company is in the hands of Messrs. Dunsmuir and Son entirely." The purpose of this statement was to give assurance that Canadian capitalists controlled the project. Mr. Gordon, of Vancouver Island, said he opposed the original Bill because it gave an immense grant of coal lands on Vancouver Island to a monopoly. Sir Richard Cartwright expressed the same views.[4]

John Charlton charged that the Southern Pacific coterie had reached out its hands to plunder British Columbia; "they have secured a grant of $750,000 cash from the Dominion Government, and exceedingly valuable land grants from British Columbia, besides the control of almost the entire coal interest of Vancouver Island."[5]

Get Lands Worth Hundreds of Millions

The matter of these great grants to the Dunsmuirs and associates rankled long in the minds of those opposing the subsidy. When, on May 9, 1890, a debate over the Souris coal

[4] *Debates, House of Commons;* etc., 1886, Vol. I, p. 517.
[5] *Ibid.*

fields was on in the House of Commons, Mr. Mitchell of New Brunswick and other members of Parliament recurred to the subject. Mitchell estimated that the territory given to the Dunsmuirs and partners was worth $100,000,000 or $200,000,000.

It was the only coal mine of any extent, John Charlton said, on the Pacific Coast of Canada. " It is a disgrace," he commented, " that such a contract should have been made. Every man regrets it today. That coal mine is alone worth hundreds of millions of dollars — its value no man can calculate; and it is a disgrace that the Dunsmuir transaction was passed on just as little information as we are asked to pass these votes tonight." [6] On July 30, 1891, Charlton styled the grant as " a huge job, a swindle on the people," and asserted that Minister of Railways John Henry Pope had sponsored the original Bill.[7]

Again, less than a year later, Charlton, in the House of Commons, made another caustic denunciation. The Government, he said, was engaged in the business of promoting private speculation. He intimated strongly that in the great majority of cases these charters and subsidies had been characterized by graft on the part of somebody or a collection of somebodys. Already, he went on, 42,000,000 acres of land in Canada had been granted. He denounced the giving of the coal lands on Vancouver Island as " a bold swindle."

" There was," he said, " a little line of railway — I passed over it since — along the sea coast from Victoria to Nanaimo, a distance of 70 miles, the construction of which was scarcely necessary; and to promote the construction of that railway nearly all of the coal lands of the Island of Vancouver were

[6] *Debates, House of Commons,* etc., Session 1890, Vol. II, pp. 4691–4692.

[7] *Ibid.,* Session, 1891, Vol. II, p. 3150. When the original Esquimault and Nanaimo Railway Bill was introduced, Charlton stated, Pope said it was " all right," and it was rushed through. We have already given Pope's record as a railway promoter.

granted to a syndicate, the greater proportion of the capital being held in San Francisco by the Southern Pacific Railway magnates. I pointed out this fact at the time but the lobby influences here, the backing here, were too strong; the grant was made, the coal lands have gone; and the other day we were informed, in discussing the militia estimates, that the reason coal was so high when purchased in Vancouver Island, was that there was a monopoly, and we ourselves created that monopoly by the grant of the Nanaimo Railway Company." [8]

Employ Chinese Coolie Labor

At the time that the Dunsmuirs obtained these land grants and money subsidies, one of the arguments used in favor of the grants was that the development of the mining and other resources would give employment to labor. Subsequently it turned out that the labor employed was largely Chinese coolie labor.

Robert Dunsmuir admitted, in 1885, that he employed from 700 to 800 whites and Chinese in his Wellington coal mines, and that the Chinese did the manual work.[9]

The Chinese laborers existed in conditions of squalor, and worked for half or nearly half the wages that the whites did. Samuel M. Robins, Superintendent of the Vancouver Coal Mining and Land Company, testified that during the strike of the white workers, " we accepted the Chinese as a weapon to settle the strike." [10]   In his testimony, David William Gordon, M. P. for Vancouver, described how the Chinese Companies had the coolies under their control by a system of semi-servi-

---

[8] *Ibid.*, Session 1892, Vol. I, pp. 2271–2272.
[9] *Report of the Royal Commission on Chinese Immigration*, 1885, Dom. Sessional Papers, Vol. XVIII, No. 2, 1885, Sess. Paper No. 54 A, p. 127.
[10] *Ibid.*, p. 118. White laborers received about $2 a day wages, and Chinese $1 to $1.25 a day.

tude.[11]   It was estimated that there were 18,000 Chinese laborers then in British Columbia.

The Knights of Labor, L. A. No. 3017 of Nanaimo, handed
in to the Royal Commission a memorial declaring that the
Chinese laborer was without ties or family, and "was able
not only to live but to grow rich on wages far below the lowest
minimum on which we can possibly exist. They are thus
fitted to become all too dangerous competitors in the labor
market, while their docile servility, the natural outcome of
centuries of grinding poverty and humble submission to a
most oppressive system of government, renders them doubly
dangerous as the willing tools whereby grasping and tyrannical employers grind down all labor to the lowest living
point. . . . The Chinese live, generally, in wretched hovels,
dark, ill-ventilated, filthy and unwholesome, and crowded together in such numbers as must utterly preclude all ideas of
comfort, morality or even decency. . . ."

"A Princely Fortune Accumulated"

The memorial proceeded: "All of the immensely valuable coal mines contained within the vast railway reserve have
been handed over to one company, the principal shareholder
in which commenced but a few years ago without a dollar.
. . . So large have been the profits, that he has accumulated
a princely fortune, and has become all powerful in the Province, his influence pervading every part of our Provincial
Government, overshadowing our Provincial legislature, and
threatening its very existence."[12]

This referred to Robert Dunsmuir. The memorial estimated that at Dunsmuir's Wellington Colleries there were
about 450 Chinese to 300 or 350 whites. "Of the former quite
a number are still employed digging coal in spite of Mr. Duns-

[11] *Ibid.,* p. 135.   [12] *Ibid.,* p. 157.

muir's assurance that they would not be so employed. In the other colleries only one-fourth the total number employed are Chinese." [13]

Appalling tragedies frequently happened in the mines, causing great loss of life. A Labor Meeting, held at Harmony Hall, Victoria, B. C., February 15, 1888, called upon the Government to make enquiries " to prevent, if possible, terrible coal mining accidents, two of which during the past year have startled and horrified the Province." [14]

It was also resolved, as the opinion of this meeting, that not another acre of public land should henceforth be deeded to railways or for any other purpose except on the basis of 160 acres to each actual settler, which land, however, should not be alienated forever from public ownership. Also the national ownership of railways, telegraphs, etc., was demanded, and legislation was called for dealing with the Chinese evil. Manhood suffrage was demanded as " the true basis of liberty," and a demand made that the profits derived from machinery should be participated in by employes; " the capital utilized in manufactories should never receive more than legal interest." [15]

Multimillionaires and Political Rulers

Rapidly the Dunsmuirs bloomed into multimillionaires.

James Dunsmuir succeeded his father as president and chief

[13] *Ibid.*, p. 158. A part of the Knights of Labor memorial was a section reading, they "should have had the chance at least of becoming employers of labor," etc., etc.

[14] *Report of the Royal Commission on the Relations of Capital and Labor*, 1889, p. 131.

[15] *Ibid.* Other parts of these resolutions are of singular interest. Labor organizations were declared to be the direct and necessary result of bad land laws and the enormous power of capital uncontrolled by the Government; arbitration was held to be "the only reasonable mode of obtaining justice" in strikes which "were injurious"; that if capital, so called, was driven from the country by hostile legislation, it "was only an imaginary loss, as it is a mere medium of exchange, and can easily be created by legislation."

stockholder of the Union and the Wellington colliery companies and of the Esquimault and Nanaimo Railway Company. In 1900, he became Premier of British Columbia, and in 1906-1909, Lieutenant-Governor of that Province. In 1908 he was elected a director of the Canadian Pacific Railway Company. He personally owned, it was then reckoned, 40,000 acres of the most valuable land; the wealth of the Dunsmuir family has been placed at from $30,000,000 to $40,000,000. In 1910-1911 the mines operated by the Wellington Colliery Company were taken over by a new combination, the Canadian Collieries (Dunsmuir), Limited, headed by Sir William Mackenzie as president, and with a capital of $15,000,000. These mines now produce nearly 800,000 tons of coal a year.

During the same period in which the Nanaimo coal deposits were given away, a vast aggregation of other resources were presented by the Dominion Government to various individuals, many of whom were members of Parliament. In 1882 and 1886 resolutions condemning these practices were offered in the Dominion House of Commons. These resolutions were defeated. Although it was well known in the financial and political world that many members of Parliament were promoters of various coal, land-colonization and timber land companies, it was not until 1890 and 1891 that many of the facts were brought out formally in Parliament.

Rykert's Land Transaction

In 1890 the Toronto *Globe* exposed the land activities of John C. Rykert, an influential member of the Dominion House of Commons.

According to the published correspondence, Rykert had used his " extraordinary influence " with the Department of the Interior to get for John C. Adams the Cypress Hills timber limit in the North West Territories, Adams paying the Government $500 in full for the grant. The grant was made to Adams by an Order-in-Council on April 17, 1882. At about the same time, Adams signed an agreement in which document Adams, without the slightest circumlocution, stated that inasmuch as Rykert had secured the timber grant for him, he (Adams) contracted to give Rykert's wife, Nannie Marie Rykert, one-half of the proceeds of the grant.

Later, Adams sold the timber limit to Louis Sands of Michigan for $200,000; and, on January 16, 1883, Rykert received $74,200 — $35,000 in cash and $39,200 in notes — as his share of the purchase money.

But the Canadian Pacific Railway Company altered its claims of survey, and claimed the Cypress Hills timber limit as lying within one of the sections of its land grant. A hot contest then set in at Ottawa; and according to the published letters written by Adams and Rykert, Hugh J. Macdonald, son of Premier Sir John A. Macdonald, and J. Stewart Tupper, son of Sir Charles Tupper (Dominion Minister of Railways and Canals in 1879-1885), represented Adams in a legal capacity. Subsequently the Canadian Pacific Railway sold its claim to Sands at $2.25 an acre.

These charges came before the House of Commons, particularly as there were passages in Rykert's letters to Adams calling for explanation from some of the members. One of these private letters read: " I find difficulties surrounding us in every way in reference to the limit, and I find that the Canadian Pacific Railway have certain [Cabinet] Ministers working for them. I am afraid it will cost us each six or seven thousand dollars to get this matter made right. I have five or six at work for me, and have agreed to pay them well if they succeed. . . ." [16]   One of the names mentioned in these letters was that of Mackenzie Bowell, then Dominion Minister

[16] *Debates, House of Commons*, etc., Session 1890, Vol. I, p. 571.

of Customs. Bowell denied that he had in any way been concerned. D. McCarthy, another House member whose name was mentioned in the correspondence, denied that he had any interest, directly or indirectly. Sir John A. Macdonald admitted that his son and Sir Charles Tupper's son were the solicitors employed by Adams, but said that he believed that his son was acting honestly.[17]

On March 10, 1890, a letter from Stewart J. Tupper was read in the House of Commons making a denial of the statement that he ever acted for Rykert, Adams or Sands in Ottawa. Hugh J. Macdonald also denied that he had ever received a dollar from Rykert, Adams, Sands or anyone else excepting his share of the legal fee of $100 which his firm received. When these denials were made, Rykert produced a letter, dated February 21, 1890, from his partner, J. H. Ingersoll, who went to Minneapolis to there interview J. B. McArthur, a lawyer whose firm represented Sands. This letter read in part: ". . . He [McArthur] thinks that Mr. Stewart Tupper was in Ottawa at the time, but remembers quite well that Mr. H. J. Macdonald was about to start for Ottawa in reference to a Bill then before the House regarding the Manitoba and North Western Railway Company. . . ." Rykert insisted that he was correct in saying that young Macdonald and Tupper went to Ottawa.

" A Mountain Range of Well-Developed Rascality "

In introducing a motion that Rykert's conduct was " discreditable, corrupt and scandalous " Sir Richard Cartwright, in the debate the next day, said that he was not disposed to regard Rykert as the only sinner. " Every practical man knows perfectly well," Cartwright went on, " that in most cases of the kind which are coming before us, the facts are

17 *Ibid.*, p. 576.

apt, as a rule, to be exceedingly well covered. It is probable
that in not one case in ten, or one case in fifty, can we obtain
full and complete evidence detailed, as it is here, of all of the
ways and modes by which members of Parliament can exercise their influence for their own personal gain. . . . In fact,
Mr. Speaker, unless the thieves fall out, unless there is a quarrel
over the division of the plunder, unless these things come before a court of law and are subjected to the ruthless cross-
examination of counsel of both sides, it is the rarest thing
in the world to obtain absolute and complete proof such as
we have now recorded in our Votes and Proceedings. Here
such an accident has occurred. Here there was a quarrel over
the division of the spoils." Cartwright concluded by saying
that Rykert was only a peak but there was " a mountain range
of undiscovered, but well-developed rascality." [18]

Rykert got up and made sneering references to Cartwright's
remarks, saying that it was Cartwright who had charged the
Minister of Public Works with having received presents from
contractors, and that he had charged John Henry Pope,
formerly Minister of Railways, with having put in his pocket
$166,000.[19]

Industrious Members of Parliament

Denouncing the consecutive giving away of timber limits,
John Charlton added to the debate. He said that 25,300
square miles covering 16,192,000 acres in the North West,
had been granted to a horde of about 550 camp followers,
not one or 20 of whom were lumbermen at all. " I found [in
1886] on examining the records of the Department of the Interior, that there had been 850 square miles of timber lands
granted, upon the personal application of members of this
House and the Senate, to 17 different members of those bod-

[18] *Debates, House of Commons,* etc., Session 1890, Vol. I, p. 1718.
[19] *Ibid.,* p. 1738.

ies." Here Charlton gave the list of names of these members, and also a list of members that had secured timber limits for their relatives or friends. Tisdale, a House member, arose and accused Charlton of himself profiting to the extent of $100,000 from a timber limit. Charlton replied that he had bought the limit at a private sale from a man who had bought it at public auction.[20]

On May 2, 1890, Rykert resigned from Parliament.[21]

In 1891 another resolution condemning the practice of the Government in making these grants was introduced. Speaking at length on it, Charlton said that for 13 years the administration of the Dominion Government "had been characterized by favoritism, nepotism, jobbery, waste of public resources, corrupt practices, and by practices calculated to debase and debauch Parliament and to lower the moral tone of the community." His arraignment was a partisan one, but so far as the facts he gave were concerned, they contained the truth.

Predatory Schemes Described

First, Charlton said, there was the colonization scheme by which favored applicants received from the Government grants of land in blocks of townships at one-half the price at which those lands were sold to settlers. "These grants were made upon easy terms of payment, holding out to the speculator embarking in the scheme the prospect of great wealth in the securing of these grants under the colonization plan at a nominal price of $1 an acre."

There was another scheme, Charlton related, "by which speculators were enabled to secure mineral and coal land leases at a mere nominal price by private application."

Also there was the pasture land abuse. The only restriction in this case was that each pasture land grant should not

[20] *Ibid.*, p. 1769.   [21] *Ibid.*, p. 4355.

exceed 50,000 acres. The Government granted leases of millions of acres, at one cent an acre, to speculators, "far in advance of the wants of settlers."

Still further, Charlton went on, there were the grants of timber lands; he told how a tract of nearly 100,000 square miles, north and northwest of Lake Superior, was in dispute between the Government of Ontario and the Dominion of Canada; and how the Dominion Government proceeded to parcel a very large portion of that disputed territory, to which it had no title, among political favorites. "We now know of other influences,[22] Sir, that were at work besides these, and we can understand how strong was the position in which the Government intrenched itself through contract brokerage, through pasture land leases, through coal land leases, and through all these plans adopted by an unscrupulous Government to strengthen itself and to secure an additional support from the class who could wield an influence in the country.[23]

How the Coal Lands Went

"Let us," Charlton specified, "first take up the subject of coal leases. Up to February, 1883, four hundred and forty-nine applications had been received for coal leases; and I shall give a list of the members of this House who made private applications for coal leases which were placed in the hands of the Minister of the Interior and acted upon by him without competition being invited. These leases, when granted, were granted to those parties as favors; they were corrupt influences which gave the parties an unjust advantage over the public at large." Charlton then enumerated the names of benefiting members of Parliament, and continued:

"Thirteen applications by men who were, or have since

[22] This reference was doubtless to the Rykert scandal.
[23] *Debates, House of Commons,* etc., Session, 1891, Vol. II, p. 3430.

become members of this House. There were also two applications by Sir A. T. Galt who is reaping a fortune today from the coal leases granted to him,[24] and two by Hon. John Norquay [sometime Premier of Manitoba]. Here were 13 members of Parliament placed in a position, through favors granted to them by the Government, to seriously interfere with the independent exercise of their functions as members of this House." [25]

Land Jobbing Operations

Charlton then dealt with the colonization grants made on easy terms of payment at $1 an acre, and gave the names of 23 members of Parliament who thus benefited. Among them were Robert Hay, M. H. Gault, James Beaty, George Guillet and others more or less well known. " A total," Charlton summarized, " of 132 townships applied for by 23 members of Parliament; and of these applications at least 20 were speculative, made not with the intention of settling the land, but as a matter of speculation with the view of selling the grant to second parties.[26]

" Then," Charlton went on, " we come to the pasture leases under which, I think, over 2,000,000 acres of land were granted privately and without competition at one cent an acre rental per annum, and with no restriction except that the good boy who stood in with the Government should be limited to 50,000 acres. . . . Not in one-seventh of these cases was any stock placed on the ranches.[27]

" Then we come to the most important feature of these abuses, that is, the granting of timber limits. Up to February,

[24] The Galt mines were at Lethbridge, Alberta. Sir A. T. Galt's son, E. T. Galt, first was manager, in 1881-1890, of the North West Coal and Navigation Company, and in 1890 became managing director of the Alberta Railway and Coal Company.
[25] *Debates, House of Commons,* etc., 1891, Vol. II, p. 3431.
[26] *Ibid.,* p. 3431.
[27] *Ibid.,* pp. 3431-3432.

1885—returns have not been brought down to a later period —over 550 Orders-in-Council had been granted for timber limits of 50 square miles each, covering an area of over 23,000 square miles of timber territory; and the bonuses received [by the Government] for them were practically nil." [28]

Charlton proceeded to give a long list of names of members of Parliament applying for and receiving timber limits of 50 square miles each in 1884-1885. Senator A. W. Ogilvie was one of these members.[29] "Now," Charlton enumerated, "here are 23 members of Parliament — either then or now members of the House — besides three ex-members, William Elliott, Oscar Fulton and David Blain — 26 members of Parliament in all who have received timber limits from this Government on private applications, without being required to compete with others, and paying therefor the nominal rental of $5 per square mile." The Government, Charlton urged, should have advertised those timber lands, and sold them at auction to the highest bidder, "but, in place of this, these limits were placed in the hands of these members of Parliament, not one of whom intended to develop them, but only to hold them for speculation, and to sell them afterwards for large bonuses to persons who wished to buy them."

In addition to these members of Parliament, Charlton said that there were others who applied unsuccessfully for limits which, it turned out, had already been given away. Still other members secured timber grants for their relatives or friends.

Fifty-Seven Busy Legislators

"We have in these applications made by members of this House on behalf of their friends," Charlton continued with

[28] *Debates, House of Commons*, etc., Session 1891, Vol. II, p. 3432.
[29] Ogilvie lived in Montreal and was the head of grain and flour mills. He was a director or trustee of a number of private corporations, and president of the Western Loan and Trust Company.

vexatious mathematical precision, " a total of 79 applications presented by 34 members of Parliament, and covering 3,900 square miles, besides a total of 1,150 miles granted to members for themselves, making a grand total of 5,050 square miles of timber limits granted to members of Parliament on their applications, and we have 57 members applying either for themselves or friends."

Most of these grants, Charlton said, had been hawked about for sale just as railway charters had been. Among the list of the "deserving" who secured timber grants, Charlton specified, were Sir A. T. Galt, J. H. Beaty of Toronto, A. F. Drummond of Montreal, O. W. Bailey, son-in-law of the late Minister of Railways and Canals, and scores of others.[30]

A virulent debate now set in.

In the debate the fact was brought out that Honoré Robillard, member of the House of Commons for Ottawa, owned a one-half interest in a 79-mile timber limit license which he had been instrumental in getting. This timber grant was on the Indian Reserve; the Dominion Government had sold it to Robillard for $316. Of this sum the 100 Indians received 31 cents each! Subsequently the firm of Francis Brothers, to whom Robillard sold the timber grant, gathered in $55,000 cash, and that silent acquisitive member pocketed $15,000 as his share. In a single year the firm of Francis Brothers cut $8,250 of timber, and after two years of lumbering its valuable timber, the timber limit was considered of such value that $60,000 was paid by another firm for what remained of it.[31]

Another member of the House, N. C. Wallace, mentioned as interested in land companies, dryly retorted, by way of defense, that "when I first went into the colonization business I had for my guide the honorable member for East York

---

[30] *Debates, House of Commons*, etc., Session 1891, Vol. II, p. 3434.
[31] *Ibid.*, pp. 3469 and 3478.

[former Premier Mackenzie], who was among the first to incorporate a company for colonization purposes in the North West, of which he was a member and president. The application was made on the 10th of January, 1882. Alexander Mackenzie was the president, and one of the five promoters. Robert Jaffray, the president of the *Globe* Company, was one of the other promoters, and the Company was called the British Canadian Colonization Company, Limited. . . . Our charter, that of the York Farmer's Colonization Company, was copied exactly from the charter of the Company incorporated by the Hon. Alexander Mackenzie, the present member for East York and the late leader of the Liberal party and then a member of the House of Commons. . . ." [32]

Still another member, Watson, asserted that 100 colonization companies had monopolized large tracts of land in Manitoba and the North West for a number of years.[33]

[32] *Debates, House of Commons,* etc., 1891, Vol. II, p. 3481.
[33] *Ibid.,* p. 3506. In his *Reminiscences* Sir Richard Cartwright narrates an instance showing how members of both political parties were deep in land colonization schemes. After the general election of 1882, when Sir John Macdonald carried the constituency of Lennox, Cartwright purposed a contest, the expenses to be guaranteed by Allison the defeated candidate, and by himself. "To our no small surprise, while they all admitted that the corruption had been most gross, we found that there was a great reluctance to take any action. After the meeting adjourned, we sent for a very shrewd friend of ours who knew the parties, and asked what it all meant. 'Oh,' he said, 'that is very easily explained. Almost every one of these people is interested in one colonization company or another, and Sir John's friends have been pointing out to them that it was to their interest, now that he is the Minister of the Interior, to put him under an obligation to them and have him as Member for Lennox.' We prosecuted Sir John forthwith without any further reference to the committee and brought out such a scandalous state of things that his counsel, the late Mr. Dalton McCarthy, was only too glad to confess judgment and to vacate the seat if the personal charges involving disqualification were withdrawn. But my point is this: Here in one small constituency were over twenty of the leading Reformers interested in these land schemes and more or less dependent, or so they thought, on the good-will of the Minister of the Interior. Doubtless as many of Sir John's supporters were in the same situation. There were a large number of these companies floated, most of them with a large number of subscribers."— *Reminiscences,* pp. 242–243.

Thus the debate, full of acerbity, went on amid charges and counter charges. Finally, Charlton's motion to condemn the practices in question was defeated by a vote of 100 to 81.[34]

[34] *Debates, House of Commons,* etc., Session, 1891, Vol. II, p. 3507.

CHAPTER XVII

DISTRIBUTION OF RAILWAY SUBSIDIES

The circumstances of the promotion of the Caraquet Railway and the operations of its chief promoter and owner, K. F. Burns, member of the House of Commons for Gloucester, occupied discussion in Parliament on May 8, 1890. This was a railway chartered, in 1874, to run from a point near Bathurst to Caraquet in New Brunswick. This distance originally was to be about 60 miles.

Caraquet Railway Transaction

Directing his attention to this transaction, Edward Blake said that Burns represented and owned eleven-twelfths of the subsidies that the Caraquet Railway Company had received. The Dominion Government, Blake said, had given a subsidy of $224,000, of which Burns' eleven-twelfth share would be $205,000, and the Government of the Province of New Brunswick had donated a subsidy of about $180,000 of which Burns' share would be $165,000. These amounts, Blake figured, made a total from both Governments " for the corporate Burns " of $370,000.[1]

In a sort of prefatory style, doubtless to let other members know that this was not a personal attack upon Burns, nor solely applying to him, Blake quoted J. C. Rykert, then a

[1] *Debates, House of Commons, Dom. of Canada,* Session 1890, Vol. II, p. 4611. The subsidy sums as stated by Blake were exact; the amounts are so entered in the annual *Railway Statistics of the Dom. of Canada.*

member of the House of Commons, as saying in an address to his (Rykert's) constituents, " Why I should be singled out for public censure when there are dozens of members in the same House, who not only have applied for and obtained limits for themselves, but sit there daily voting money into their own pockets, I cannot understand." [2]

Blake proceeded. He told how Burns was the president, contractor, financier and altogether the general all-in-all of his own company. The capital stock of the Caraquet Railway Company had been subscribed to the full amount of $950,000, of which about $751,000 had been paid in.

Ways of Railway Contractors

" I believe," Blake went on, " that the whole cost of the enterprise, rails included, at fair values, with contractors' profits, was provided foi out of the Government subsidies and the sale in bonds in England for £100,000 sterling; and not merely was the whole cost, at fair values, with contractors' profits, so provided, but there was left an excess of a very considerable amount, which went into the pockets of the honorable member for Gloucester. So that he received eleven-twelfths of the stock, and he made a considerable fortune out of his construction account.

" It is quite possible to project a railway as disastrously as this railway has resulted, and yet make a fortune of the undertaking. . . . I believe the honorable member paid a very large proportion, probably about three-fourths, of the wages and local supplies in truck out of his store; and that he issued a sort of ticket, which passed as local currency in the country to some extent, and by this means of paying in truck he made a very considerable addition to his profits." [3]

Why, asked Blake, was the Caraquet Railway, projected

[2] *Ibid.*, p. 4611.   [3] *Ibid.*, p. 4612.

at first to cover 60 miles, represented as being 70 miles? [4]
" The honorable member for Gloucester [Burns] has a couple
of mills in the neighborhood. To one of these a branch some-
where about a mile long was built, which forms part of the
mileage, and to reach the other mill he deflected the road,
increasing its length in that way, five or six miles." The
true value of the work, including contractors' profit, Blake
said, was a great deal under $8,000 a mile, instead of $22,000
or $23,000 a mile. Blake also pointed out that in 1888 there
were five employes injured and eight killed on that railway;
perhaps it was due to bad construction.[5]

Burns made an elaborate defense, not denying that his workers got supplies from the stores of K. F. Burns and Company,
but asserting that he paid them monthly in cash. His explanations made a poor impression.

Sir Richard Cartwright attacked the subject. Saying that
Mr. Blake and William Mulock deserved thanks for exposing
the transaction, he went straightway into a denunciation of
" the thoroughly rotten system," accusing Premier Macdonald
of maintaining himself in power chiefly by the following four
methods:

"First, by the free distribution of the public domain to
certain favored parties, of which we had a recent, eminent and
notorious example; next, I was going to say of thinly-dis-
guised bribery, but I will say instead, by a system of open
bribery on the part of contractors in testimonials and otherwise; next by a system of tariff corners and subsidies; and
lastly by the method of which we had had so notable an

[4] As finally construced it was 68 miles. Blake could not be accused
of unreasonable hostility to railroad construction; his objections were
to the methods used to get the subsidies. He himself was a stockholder in various corporations; after his death, his estate was appraised,
in 1912, at nearly $300,000, more than half of which was in stocks.
These he acquired in legitimate ways.
[5] *Debates, House of Commons*, etc., 1890, Vol. II, pp. 4616–4617.

illustration just now, the method of railway subsidies among various constituencies and among various members of this House. . . ." [6]

Where Did a Certain $800,000 Go?

Dissecting Burns' explanation, Cartwright inquired that if Burns' assertion was true that he got only $600,000 of the available funds, then who pocketed the other $800,000 of the $1,400,000 that the railway was said to have cost? Cartwright was exceedingly insistent as to the destination of this $800,000; he demanded to know what became of it, but could get no real enlightenment. The English stockholders, he said, were induced to put £80,000 or £100,000 in the railway, upon the representation that there would be a profit of £1,000 a mile, but instead had met only a dead loss.[7]

Another denunciation of the transaction came from P. Mitchell, member of the House of Commons for Northumberland. He said that members of Parliament were corrupted by subsidies, local improvement appropriations and other means which formed " one of the greatest sources of bribery and corruption ever initiated in any country." He denounced it as " a cursed system, a system which has corrupted the representatives of those constituencies." [8]

A Series of Charges

Presently, there came an unfolding of another serious scandal. On May 11, 1891, J. Israel Tarte, a member of the House of Commons, formally made a series of specific charges against Thomas McGreevy, a conspicuous member of the House. McGreevy had long been a railroad promoter; he had been associated as far back as 1869 with the Hon. Hector L. Langevin and other members of Parliament in securing

[6] *Ibid.,* p. 4631.   [7] *Ibid.,* p. 4633.   [8] *Ibid.,* p. 4644.

for themselves the charter of the Levis and Kennebec Railway,[9] he had been a large railroad contractor in the Province of Quebec, and for a considerable time was chairman of the Railway Committee of the House of Commons.

Tarte's charges were as follows:

That in order to get Thomas McGreevy's influence in Parliament, the firm of Larkin, Connolly and Company, dredging contractors, took in his brother, Robert McGreevy, as a partner, giving him an interest of 30 per cent. in the firm.

That McGreevy consented to this arrangement, saying that he had first consulted Sir Hector L. Langevin, the Minister of Public Works, and secured his consent. Langevin had occupied that office for almost 20 years.

That at the same time, Thomas McGreevy was a member of the Quebec Harbor Commission, and gave his help, in an undue manner, to the firm of Larkin, Connolly and Company to secure the dredging contract.

That by manipulation and other means on Thomas McGreevy's part, the firm in question obtained the contract, for which $375,000 had been voted by the Parliament of Canada in 1882.

That a few days after Larkin, Connolly and Company had secured the contract in 1883, "the sum of $25,000 was, in fulfillment of the corrupt arrangement above stated, paid to the said Thomas McGreevy in promissory notes signed by the firm of Larkin, Connolly and Company which said notes were duly paid."

That on or about the same date, June 4, 1883, a sum of $1,000 was paid by the firm of Larkin, Connolly and Company

---

[9] *Statutes of Quebec,* 1869, pp. 217-218. The Levis and Kennebec Railway, projected for 90 miles, was voted a Government subsidy of $360,000 of which nearly the whole was paid. This railway became part of the Quebec Central Railway.

towards the "Langevin Testimonial Fund"— a fund intended as a gift to Sir Hector Langevin.

That in 1884 Thomas McGreevy received another corrupt sum of $22,000 for getting for the firm of Larkin, Connolly and Company the contract for the completion of the Graving Dock of Levis.

That to get the contract for the completion of Graving Dock at Esquimault, B. C. in 1884, the firm of Larkin, Connolly and Company gave Robert McGreevy a 20 per cent. interest in the firm; and that on the suggestion of Thomas Mc-Greevy, the firm of Larkin, Connolly and Company " approached" members of Parliament; that certain members of the firm declared that these members asked for a certain sum of money to exert their influence for the firm, and that the firm had agreed to give it to them; that McGreevy corruptly tried to get dismissed certain public officers who had incurred the ill-will of the firm, and have them replaced by others who would suit the firm's interests.

That in 1886-1887, Thomas McGreevy arranged to get $25,000 from the firm on condition that he would get for that firm at an exorbitant price, much above the lowest bids tendered, the contract for the dredging of the Wet Basin in the harbor of the City of Quebec, and that McGreevy corruptly received $27,000 as his share.

That from the year 1883 to 1890, both inclusive, Thomas McGreevy received from the firm of Larkin, Connolly and Company and from his brother Robert McGreevy, a sum of about $200,000.

That during the forementioned period Thomas McGreevy was the agent and paid representative of the firm of Larkin, Connolly and Company on the Quebec Harbor Board of Commissioners in Parliament, in connection with the Department of Public Works.

That Thomas McGreevy, on several occasions, demanded

sums of money from the firm of Larkin, Connolly and Company in the name of Sir Hector Langevin, Minister of Public Works.

That from 1882 to 1891, Thomas McGreevy had always lived when in Ottawa in the same house as the Minister of Public Works, " and that he seems to have done so in order to put in the mind of Larkin, Connolly and Company the impression that he had over said honorable Minister an absolute control, and that he was acting as his representative in his corrupt transactions with them."

Tarte further charged that certain members of the firm of Larkin, Connolly and Company " paid and caused to be paid large sums of money to the honorable Minister of Public Works out of the proceeds of the said contracts, and that entries of the said sums were made in the books of that firm." [10]

Charges Substantially Proved

A Select Committee to inquire fully into the charges was demanded by Mr. Tarte. After the committee had held 100 sittings and taken a mass of testimony, Mr. Girouard, chairman of the Select Committee, reported to the House of Commons, that the Committee had " come to the conclusion that the charges made by the honorable member for Montmorency (Mr. Tarte) were substantially — in fact amply — proved as far as the Hon. Thomas McGreevy is concerned, but as far as Sir Hector Langevin is concerned, the members of the Committee came to a division. The minority report concluded that Sir Hector Langevin knew of the conspiracy with Larkin, Connolly and Company, but the majority would not arrive at that conclusion." As to Thomas McGreevy's cor-

[10] These charges, as above given, are set forth in full in *Debates in the House of Commons, Dom. of Canada,* Session 1891, Vol. I, pp. 149-152.

rupt acts, the Select Committee's report was unanimous.[11]

Chairman Girouard reported that the total amount of the contracts awarded to Larkin, Connolly and Company was $3,-138,234; that these contracts extended over a period from 1878 to 1891; that the contractors received $735,061 in profits; and that in addition to these profits, sums totaling $170,407 were paid out in donations for political and other purposes.[12] The evidence showed that not only money but diamonds and other valuable presents were given to officials in the Public Works Department, and that large sums went to a newspaper run in Quebec by Langevin's son-in-law.

The report of the majority of the Select Committee was adopted after a long and bitter debate. Meanwhile, Langevin had, on August 11, 1891, resigned as Minister of Public Works; and, on September 29, 1891, Thomas McGreevy was expelled from the House of Commons.[13] Later he went to jail.

McGreevy Made a Scapegoat

According to Sir Richard Cartwright, "there was a general and perfectly correct opinion that Mr. McGreevy had been made a scapegoat, and that he was really far less culpable than many of the Ministers themselves." [14] Elsewhere, Sir Richard wrote that, "Mr. McGreevy was one of those men who influence the course of public affairs ten times more than any Cabinet Minister, but who are often never heard of outside a very limited circle. Mr. McGreevy was in many ways a remarkable man. He was thoroughly conversant with every irregular transaction which occurred in several great spending departments over a wide area for a long space of time, and above all, in the case of Sir Hector Langevin's, namely, the

[11] *Debates, House of Commons,* etc., Session 1891, Vol. III, p. 5778.
[12] *Ibid.,* pp. 5781–5782.
[13] *Ibid.,* p. 6286.
[14] *Reminiscences,* p. 355.

Department of Public Works. . . . Millions of corruptly gotten money, to be expended for yet more corrupt purposes, passed through his hands, and yet for all that I believe Mr. McGreevy was by far the most honest man of the lot — which was perhaps the reason he was made the scapegoat."

Then saying that McGreevy divulged only a fraction of the facts he knew, Sir Richard Cartwright went on:

" All sorts of pressure was brought to bear on him, and he may have become convinced that further disclosures would hurt some parties whom he did not wish to injure. One thing I do know, that when Mr. McGreevy was in durance nothing could exceed the solicitude for his welfare displayed by certain members of the ministry. There were few days during the time he spent in jail on which Mr. McGreevy, if so disposed, could not have held a Cabinet Council in the corridor, as far as the requisite number to form a quorum was concerned." [15]

Mr. Murphy's Opinion

The remaining question is, How was it that such facts as were brought out were divulged? Who originally informed, and why? Here we shall have to turn to an interview with Owen E. Murphy, published in the New York *Times,* and republished in the Toronto *Globe,* issue of November 23, 1891. Murphy had been an Excise Commissioner in New York City,

[15] *Ibid.,* pp. 334-335. Cartwright wrote that later, when the party to which he belonged came into power, it could, had it been so pleased, obtained and made public the whole details, but that the chief consideration which had most influence was " that the exposures which had already taken place had damaged the reputation of Canada to an enormous extent, and we dreaded the result of these further revelations." Personally, Cartwright did not, he wrote, altogether approve this policy of suppression. But his objections were not based upon the desire to let the public know to what vast extent graft and corruption had been used to acquire public property and great fortunes, but upon the partisan aim to let the Canadian public " understand how and by what means our opponents had regained power in 1878 and kept it till 1896."

and had hurriedly left there in 1877 with a shortage of $50,-
000 in his official accounts. He went to Canada, and became
a contractor associated with Robert McGreevy. In 1891 he
returned to New York City with the announcement that he
intended to make restitution to New York City for the old
shortage, and reside in that city permanently. He was interviewed by a reporter for the New York *Times*.

"His views on Canadian politics and Canadian politicians
are not flattering to us," said the Toronto *Globe* editorially.

"'We bribed them all,' he said with a smile, 'and generally
acquired nearly everything in sight. We literally owned the
Province. Public officials in Canada, so far as my experience
goes, do not have that suspicious hesitancy in accepting money
that characterizes some officials in this country. The Langevin crowd did not scruple to take all they could get.'

"In Mr. Murphy's estimation — and as a veteran Tam-
manyite his opinion is worth something — the 'Langevin
crowd is worse than the Tweed gang ever was.' He spoke
pathetically of the dissension between the McGreevys. 'The
quarrel was really one over the division of the spoils.' Had
the brothers remained on friendly terms, and had he and the
Connollys kept out of each other's hair, they 'would have
owned nearly the whole of Canada.' The reporter asked him
for an expert judgment on the moral condition of the Canadian electorate as compared with that of New York electors.
His reply was: 'Votes cost more than in New York. I
figured in one election where I myself paid out $6,500 for a
certain candidate, and the votes cost from $25 to $30 apiece.
I considered this price somewhat high, but we had to have
them.'" [16]

[16] An editorial in the Toronto *Globe*, December 1, 1891, quoted a
Quebec newspaper, *LeCorrier de St. Hyacinthe* as dividing corrupt
voters into three herds — those who demanded spot cash for their
votes; those who waived cash, but insisted on something being done
for their families, such as the payment of a store bill; and those who

Premier Sir John Macdonald was not called upon to face these disclosures and the series of further revelations now following. He died in 1891, a comparatively poor man; nobody charged that he had been personally enriched by the long-continued system of corruption, although his critics had asserted that he had been fully willing that it should be used for political campaign purposes, and that his supporters of every stripe from the railway magnate and manufacturer to the merest political henchman should be kept in line by the lavish granting of charters, subsidies, tariff benefits, contracts, offices or other largess proportionate to their power and demands. J. J. C. Abbott succeeded him as Prime Minister.

Baie Des Chaleurs Railway Disclosures

Sharply on the heels of the McGreevy disclosures, came more revelations. This scandal dealt with the means used to get subsidies for the Baie des Chaleurs Railway, in the Province of Quebec.

The Baie des Chaleurs Railway Company was chartered in 1882. In that year and succeeding years, various Acts were passed by the Dominion and the Province of Quebec governments allowing the company total cash subsidies of $1,250,000, of which $894,175 was paid on the first 70 miles constructed. Charles N. Armstrong had obtained, in 1886, the contract for constructing 100 miles of the projected 189 miles; he, in turn, subcontracted the job. A contest developed between two sets of capitalists aiming to get control of the railway, and there was danger of forfeiture of the charter for non-fulfillment of

with greater modesty refused to go to the polls unless they were paid for the day's expenses. Another Quebec newspaper, *La Justice*, was quoted by the same editorial as saying that 19 in every 20 of the leading politicians calculated upon making politics pay directly or indirectly, and that below them was a large class of "workers" who served their party so as to get Government offices or plunder in some form and who stopped at nothing to win.

conditions. Armstrong wanted to prevent forfeiture, and at the same time he sought to collect on a claim for $298,000 which he presented against the Quebec Government.

One Ernest Pacaud agreed, in 1891, to get the necessary official action favorable to Armstrong. Although his claim was for $298,000, Armstrong did not expect more than $75,000 in settlement. He readily consented to give Pacaud $100,000 if Pacaud should get $175,000 from the Quebec Government. Thereupon, Pacaud at once set matters in motion, and in 1891, the Government of Quebec by an Order-in-Council, gave an additional subsidy of $50,000 and also 800,000 acres of land convertible into cash at 35 cents an acre — $280,000 cash in all as the proceeds of the land grant.[17]

The Corruption Proved

Charges were made, in 1891, that this transaction had been accomplished by means of corruption. A Royal Commission, composed of Judges Baby, Davidson and Jette was appointed to investigate. On October 23 and 24, 1891, Ernest Pacaud, the intermediary for the corruptionists, made a full confession before the Royal Commission.[18] Pacaud confessed that he had extorted $100,000 from Armstrong to effect the settlement of Armstrong's claim against the Quebec Government.[19]

The report of Judges Baby and Davidson showed that $175,-000 in letters of credit had been given to the railway contractors in violation of the Treasury laws without the sanction of the Lieutenant-Governor, and to the detriment of

[17] Under the laws of the Province of Quebec, land subsidies were exchangeable for cash.
[18] See *Royal Commission Inquiry into the Baie des Chaleurs Railway Matter; Reports, Proceedings*, etc., 1892, pp. 361–488.
[19] Pacaud's statement of the disposition of the $100,000 "boodle fund" was full and explicit. Most of it went to politicians, and he stowed away $25,456 of it in various banks, chiefly in the National Park Bank, New York City.

public credit; the misappropriation of a sum of $175,000 from
its legislative destination; the payment made to Armstrong to
whom nothing was due by the Government or by the Company
in money; the division of the $100,000 obtained from Arm-
strong, and its employment to pay the debts of several of the
Ministers and to subsidize several members of the Legislature,
partisans of the Cabinet.   Judges Baby and Davidson reported
in both their ad interim report and their final report that it
was not proved that Premier Mercier and some of the other
Cabinet Ministers knew of the existence of the bargain between Armstrong and Pacaud, but Judges Baby and Davidson
did find that Provincial Secretary Charles Langelier " had
knowledge of the source whence came the funds out of which
Mr. Pacaud paid to him about $9,000 for his personal bene-
fit." [20]   Judge Jette, however, held that Langelier did not
know the source of the money.[21]

Such facts as were brought out in Bay des Chaleurs Railway transaction made a deep public impression.

An Entire Administration Dismissed

On the receipt of the Royal Commission's ad interim report
Lieutenant-Governor A. R. Angers, of the Province of Quebec, dismissed the Mercier administration from office, on December 16, 1891.[22]   Mercier's political opponents pushed
matters to the point of haling him to the criminal court on
charges of malfeasance in office, but the charges could not be
proved, and he was acquitted.

[20] *Royal Commission Inquiry into the Baie des Chaleurs Railway
Matter*, etc., 1892, pp. 5, 89, etc.
[21] *Ibid.*, p. 191.
[22] Mercier and his Cabinet were Liberals. " The attacks on the
Dominion Government had been largely on the score of their corrupt
practices in this very province, and now we were confronted with
evidence that the Liberal leaders in Quebec were as bad or worse than
their opponents."— Sir Richard Cartwright's *Reminiscences*, p. 309.

Quebec and Lake St. John Railway

Only a few months later, another transaction was under discussion in the Dominion House of Commons. On April 6, and May 4, 1892, James D. Edgar, a member of the House, produced charges asserting:

That during the ten years from 1882 to 1891 inclusive, the Quebec and Lake St. John Railway Company [23] received from the Dominion Government subsidies of more than $1,000,000, which subsidies were voted on the recommendation of Ministers of the Crown.

That during this whole period — 1882 to 1891 — Sir Adolphe P. Caron was, and still remained, a member of the Canadian Government — (he was at different times Dominion Minister of Militia and Postmaster-General) — and one of the Queen's Privy Councilors for Canada, and also a member of the House of Commons.

That also during this period Caron knowingly aided and participated in diverting these subsidies from the purpose for which they were granted, and that such money was used for election purposes to aid the election to the House of Commons of Caron and other supporters of the Government.

That after some of the last payments were so obtained and made, Sir Adolphe P. Caron, " in consideration thereof," corruptly aided and assisted the Quebec and Lake St. John Railway Company to obtain further and other subsidies from the Dominion Parliament.

That since October 6, 1885, the Temiscouata Railway had received about $649,200 in subsidies from the Dominion of Canada, and that Caron aided in diverting such subsidies for use in elections, and that after doing this Caron — so it was charged — had corruptly aided and assisted the Temiscouata

[23] This was a railway extending 286 miles from the City of Quebec to Chambord Junction, with various branches.

Railway Company to obtain further and other subsidies from the Dominion Parliament.[24]

These charges, put in such specific form and directly naming a high member of the Government, could not safely be ignored or lightly dismissed.

One aspect of these charges was not new. In the debate of May 28, 1886, Caron had admitted, in reply to a direct question by Edward Blake, that he was then a member of the construction company building the Quebec and Lake St. John Railway. This railway company, Caron had then explained, turned over its subsidies to the construction company, headed by James G. Ross and composed of himself and others.[25]

A heated debate followed the introduction of Edgar's charges. Sir Richard Cartwright denounced at length " the system of organized corruption," and declared that " taking the railway subsidies as a whole, they have been one of those sources of organized corruption by which the Government have held and kept their power; and I, for my part, do not wonder in the least at finding many men objecting to this investigation, knowing as I do how these same railway subsidies have been used for the corruption of members of Parliament, how they have been tolled for the private advantage of members of Parliament, how stock formerly worthless has been made valuable by means of subsidies got by political influence, how in many ways they have been used in debauching representatives and constituencies alike. . . ." [26]

[24] The Quebec and Lake St. John Railway Company received bonuses of $1,233,943.50 from the Dominion Government, $2,368,816 from the Quebec Government, and $12,000 from municipalities. The Temiscouata Railway — 113 miles from Riviere du Loup to Edmunston and Connors, N. B. — received bonuses of $645,950 from the Dominion Government, $428,250 from the Governments of Quebec and of New Brunswick and $25,000 from municipalities.

[25] *Debates, House of Commons, Dom. of Can.*, Session 1886, Vol. II, p. 1622. Ross was a conspicuous Quebec capitalist. He left a fortune of about $7,000,000.

[26] *Ibid.*, Session 1892, Vol. I, pp. 1746-1747.

Altering the Original Charges

Finally, a Royal Commission was appointed to investigate. On September 13, 1892, Mr. Edgar formally protested to the Commission that the charges he made were definite and specific and complaining that the substitute motion which had passed the House (in place of his motion which was defeated) "did not state the full charges and was designed to elude and defeat the ends of justice." This substitute motion was made by Hon. Mackenzie Bowell, a colleague of Caron in the Ministry. Edgar further protested that "my charges are not fairly stated to you."

The accusation made by Edgar that the charges brought by him had been distorted, caused a great stir, but his protests were of no avail.

James G. Scott, secretary of the Quebec and Lake St. John Railway Company, testified before the Royal Commission that Caron had been, since 1879, a shareholder in the company constructing that railway, and that other members of Parliament were shareholders. Caron, however, was not a member of the railway company. Scott further testified that in numerous applications for Government subsidies he often saw Caron who gave "loyal assistance." Still further, Scott testified that the firm of Andrews, Caron and Andrews had been for years solicitors for the Quebec and Gosford Railway.[27]

Many other witnesses, including Thomas McGreevy, were examined; McGreevy's testimony was definite, but other witnesses were mainly railway contractors and associates, and much of their testimony was more or less of a negative character.

The Royal Commission handed in the evidence with exhibits, refraining from making any comments whatever.

[27] *Sessional Paper No. 27*, 1892, pp. 98–109. This document contains the full evidence.

Sir Adolphe Caron Remains

No action adverse to Caron was taken; he remained in the Dominion Government Ministry until 1896.

The political opponents of Caron and his party regarded the substitute motion upon which the Royal Commission had to act, as a " white-washing " one. According to Sir Richard Cartwright " the evidence was overwhelming," and Caron dared not prosecute the Toronto *Globe* for publishing two whole pages of fac-similes of documents implicating him in transactions with Thomas McGreevy. Sir John Thompson (then Prime Minister) did not " dare compel Sir Adolphe Caron to resign. To have done so would have caused a split among his Quebec supporters which would have wrecked his Government at once, to say nothing of the certainty of being followed by other and even uglier revelations." [28]

Comments of the British Press

The *Pall Mall Gazette* declared that " a more sordid spectacle of corruption has never been presented to a free people. . . . Political life in the United States is not particularly pure, but we would be exceedingly surprised if the Canadian record could be beaten."

The *Speaker*, September 12, 1891, thus commented: " The undisputed facts are bad enough. The defense constantly set up when large sums are traced from a contractor or office seeker to a legislator is that the money was not for the recipient's private benefit, but for legitimate political purposes. That this is reckoned any defense at all shows the extent to which the political conscience in Canada has been blunted. . . ." Of Abbott, the successor of Macdonald as Prime Minister of Canada, the *Speaker* said that he was " the

[28] *Reminiscences*, p. 332.

man who in 1872 negotiated the great bribery scheme [the Pacific Railway transaction] by which Sir John Macdonald was driven disgraced from office. . . ."

" No honest Canadian," said the London *Standard,* September 25, 1891, " can read the testimony without feeling that corruption has saturated departmental and Parliamentary life. . . ."

The London *Despatch,* October 4, 1891, describing the system of corruption in Canada, remarked: " . . . Yes, some have been punished — the small fry who were not in a position to steal much. But the conspicuous thieves . . . where are they? Living on their stealings, some of them even blazing with decorations bestowed upon them by the Queen — quite comfortably either in Canada or the United States."

The *Saturday Review,* September 12, 1891, advanced the opinion that in the field of corruption, Canada could " modestly challenge comparison " with the United States. " Her opportunities and means are not so great as those wielded by the lobbyists and log-rollers of Washington, or the bosses and wire-pullers of New York, but the most has been made of them. . . ."

END OF VOLUME I

"His Facts are not Denied . . ."

Mr. Myers' books are recommended only to admirers
of the muck-raking school, because only they believe
that the masses are poor because of unwillingness to
imitate the vices attributed to the rich. That doctrine
is the root of much envy, hatred, and uncharitableness,
and it is noxious rather than meritorious in its
effects. This is said without disparagement of the
apparent effort of Mr. Myers to be accurate. His facts
are not denied, but his inferences from them will not
be admitted generally. All he says may be true, and
yet there are other offsetting facts which compensate
for the blemishes disclosed.

New York Times, review of *History
of Canadian Wealth*, 5 July 1914.

INDEX